Wingshooter's Guide to

Idaho

Upland Birds and Waterfowl

Wingshooter's Guide to
Idaho
Upland Birds and Waterfowl

Ken Retallic and Rocky Barker

Wilderness Adventures Press

This book was made with an easy opening, lay flat binding.

Published by Wilderness Adventures Press
P.O. Box 627
Gallatin Gateway, MT 59730
800-925-3339

10 9 8 7 6 5 4 3 2 1

Printed in the United States of America

Library of Congress Catalog Card Number: 97-060642

ISBN 1-885106-27-0

*This book is dedicated
to Ken Kohli,
an avid bird hunter whose time
in the field was cut short.*

Table of Contents

Introduction

As a boy growing up on an Illinois farm, I waited for the fall hunting season with more anticipation than Christmas.

In the 1960s, duck hunting wasn't particularly good at the eastern edge of the Mississippi Flyway, so I rarely hunted ducks. Pheasants flushed through my imagination and pushed girls, rock music, and sports into the background as the trees lost their leaves and golden tan corn stalks rustled in the wind. When the season opened in November, my Dad and Grandfather would make one ceremonial walk through our farm's fields. Then I would spend the rest of the month and on through December patrolling every cornfield within walking distance.

Sometimes I could coax our family Weimaraner to follow me through the multiflora roses along the fence lines. But usually it was just me and my Stevens bolt-action .410.

When I was able to press the rare, unwitting rooster to flush rather than run, I missed more birds than I brought down. But when feathers flew—and I successfully overcame my shock and the effects of adrenaline—I can remember few feelings more satisfying. My mother always treated me like a returning hero when I came home with a ringneck. She would send me to the basement with a big pot of boiling water to pluck the bird for dinner. Nothing ever tasted as good as the fried fowl I had taken off the land.

At year's end the season closed and I was forced to wait in suffering for the following November. I found solace in the pages of *Field and Stream* and *Outdoor Life*, reading about faraway, mystical places with names like the Seven Devils above Hells Canyon of the Snake and the River of No Return, more prosaically known as the Salmon. That sportsman's paradise, Idaho, seemed so distant and enchanting and so unlike the prairie farm country where I lived.

Even the writers had romantic names. Ted Trueblood of Boise told me of strange and alluring birds like sage grouse, sharptails, chukar partridge, and mountain quail. Clyde Ormond, a Rigby high school principal, explained the basic skills of big game hunting. Elmer Keith, Salmon's Old West outfitter and gun inventor, made me want to carry a big gun in the woods. The late Jack O'Connor, of Lewiston, nurtured my love of double-barreled shotguns.

I moved to Idaho in 1985, after detouring through Wisconsin, where I picked up a fair wingshooting eye kicking through swamps for ruffed grouse and woodcock.

I soon learned sage grouse were indeed mystical birds that explode from the desert like coveys of huge gray, black and white chickens. The blue grouse of southern Idaho were numerous, but unsophisticated. Just plain dumb, actually. They taught me a new meaning to kicking up birds—literally, in their tail feathers. Ducks and geese were everywhere. They filled the rivers and ponds of this arid land in numbers I never hoped to see in the Midwest. The pheasants, unfortunately, were ghosts, largely relegated to put-and-take hunts on a few of the state's wildlife management

areas. As elsewhere, years of clean farming practices and changes in predator population dynamics had reduced the range and numbers of the birds that first lured me
into the sport of hunting.

Even better, I found I no longer had to wait until late fall to take to the field.
Idaho's forest grouse season opens the last weekend in August, when wildflowers still
linger in the higher elevations. Dove hunters also get a short, early start before sage
grouse and sharptail seasons open in mid-September. An early goose season in the
southeast corner of the state precedes the regular waterfowl opening in October as
the first frosts are turning quaking aspen and cottonwoods to sulfur and gold.

While most hunters are chasing elk and deer, the local ducks make for fine sport
at the dozens of public hunting areas across this huge state. Then the pheasant and
partridge seasons open in late October, and extended seasons for both upland birds
and waterfowl keep weekends busy until year's end. In 1997, California quail numbers were so high that the Idaho Department of Fish and Game offered a special two-
week winter season in January.

But bird hunters don't have to sit and read by their fireplaces for long. The introduction of wild turkeys has produced one of the West's best spring hunts for thousands of hunters, who once reverted to being skiers, steelheaders, and flyfishers until
they could bring out their shotguns again in autumn.

Idaho's natural wonders tend to pound at the observer like a rock concert with
the amplifiers turned up to the highest volume. Subtlety is not a part of a landscape
that begins in the shadowy depths of rocky, narrow canyons, where rivers grind
relentlessly through bedrock, and even roll huge boulders downstream during spring
runoff. Big-shouldered mountains soar above sprawling plains to heights of 12,000
feet, their snowcapped crags sculpted by glaciers and the elements. It is this land that
grabs your attention like a gunshot blast and holds it like a circus tent evangelist.

Many resident hunters are lured to the mountains and canyons in pursuit of big
game. Most out-of-state hunters also journey here in hopes of bagging a trophy elk
in central Idaho's wilderness core and faraway backcountry forests.

Those willing to look beyond such clamorous vistas will find places where
smaller events still matter. In many of Idaho's vast expanses of public rangelands,
nature's quieter melodies still reign in virtual solitude. The desolate, wide-open sagebrush desert of Owyhee County invites man, boy, and dog to hike for miles without
seeing another human. They might kick up sage grouse, California quail, or chukars,
depending on where they choose to trek. But few dust plumes from passing vehicles
will mar the seemingly endless views of the distant horizon.

In the heavily forested mountains and swamps of northern Idaho, ruffed grouse
can be found that are as wary as any of their Midwest cousins. Last but not least is the
pastoral Idaho, where grassy irrigation ditches divide farm fields of corn, sugar beets,
onion, wheat, and, of course, potatoes. They are the homes of imported upland gamebirds, pheasants, gray partridge, and quail. These exotic newcomers to Idaho may
seem more at home on the South Dakota prairie, an Illinois cornfield, or the lush valleys of California. But like its human inhabitants who have transformed Idaho's desert

Idaho attracts waterfowl in great numbers. Western bird hunting dreams are made of days like this. (Photo: Ken Retallic)

into farms and towns, these aliens have adapted. Pheasant numbers have improved in the 1990s, and, with additional habitat protection, may once again return to a shadow of their former grace. Finally, this dry land, where water decides fecundity, is both home and rest stop to waves of waterfowl. It is hard to imagine other states that wield more productive waters and fields for duck and goose shooting.

In a nation where hunting appears to be disappearing, hunter numbers in Idaho are rising. This is no fluke; Idaho is what America was.

But it is not an island. Like most of the country, the changes man has wrought have taken their toll on the state's upland birds. Mountain quail have nearly disappeared. Sage grouse numbers have plummeted.

Ken Retallic and I, in writing this book, want to help hunters find the many wing-shooting opportunities available in Idaho. We know that hunters have traditionally been the most reliable conservationists, and by bringing more hunters to Idaho, hope that the birds and land we share with you will benefit by increased stewardship. We want this great sport to be available to our grandchildren and our grandchildren's grandchildren. Upland birds and waterfowl are the fat of the land that we all can share as long as Idaho is healthy from the tops of its craggy peaks to the depths of its deep river canyons.

Rocky Barker
Boise, Idaho
February 1997

How To Use This Guide

Idaho is a big state. Its major highways circle a wild, roadless wilderness area larger than New England. Most of its counties are bigger than some Eastern states. To get from one side of Idaho to the other requires long drives around the wilderness, sometimes over high mountain passes.

From eastern Idaho to northern Idaho, the main route is north on I-15 and west on I-90 through western Montana to get back into Idaho. From Boise, the state capital, the only major route north is U.S. 95 via State Highway 55 through McCall.

On a first trip to Idaho, it is best to dip into its broad expanses by setting your sights on specific gamebirds or waterfowl and choosing a location to hunt. Idaho has gamebird and waterfowl packages to suit all tastes. Key hunting areas are noted in the discussions of each species included in the guide. Maps showing gamebird distribution also are provided.

To further aid in planning trips to the best hunting areas, the guide details the seven administrative regions managed by the Idaho Department of Fish and Game. Information on IDGF wildlife management areas, national wildlife refuges, national forests and public range lands also is included. More than 70 percent of Idaho is public domain managed by state and federal land managers.

Details on service hubs that cater to hunters is divided up between the seven regions administered by Idaho Fish and Game. Information includes airports, accommodations, restaurants, resorts, outfitters and guides, and hunting equipment shops. In 1997, the Shoshone-Bannock Tribes of Fort Hall Indian Reservation were the only ones of the state's five Indian tribes offering a permit system to hunt on their lands. Also, 13 private landowners were licensed by the state as gamebird shooting preserves.

The state's outfitters and hunting equipment shops owners stand ready to help you have the best possible experience. Call or write for assistance in trip planning and reservations, or stop in and chat about current hunting conditions. Hundreds of phone numbers and addresses are listed.

Current hunting license fees and season dates also are listed. Fees are updated periodically. Changes in upland gamebird regulations are established and published on a two-year cycle. Waterfowl and wild turkey regulations are set annually.

IDFG phone numbers and addresses are provided for purchase of licenses, stamps and tags, or to apply for controlled hunts for wild turkey.

An equipment check list includes additional tips on trip planning.

MAJOR ROADS & RIVERS OF IDAHO

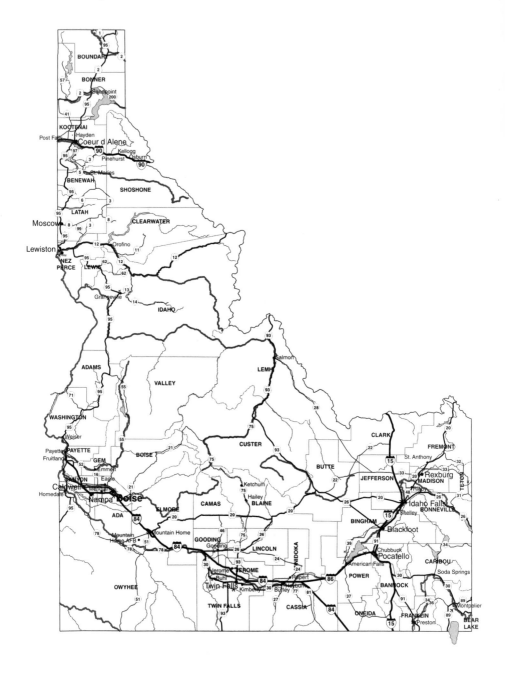

Idaho Facts

"Idaho is what America was."

Population: 1,099,056 (1993 census).

Land Area: 83,557 square miles; 13th largest state.

Water Area: 1,152 square miles.

Highest Point: 12,662 feet above sea level at summit of Mount Borah in Lost River Range in Custer County.

Lowest Point: 738 feet above sea level at Snake River in Lewiston.

Length: 479 miles in western Idaho .

Width: 305 miles in southern Idaho.

Major Mountain Ranges: Sawtooth Mountains, Owyhee Mountains, Lost River Mountains, Bitterroot Mountains, Centennial Mountains, and Salmon River Mountains.

Nickname: *Gem state,* derived from the more than 80 varieties of precious and semi-precious gemstones found within its borders.

A northern Rocky Mountains state, Idaho straddles the Continental Divide and covers two time zones, Mountain and Pacific. Its geological features are picturesque, often unique and unbridled. Its robust climate and terrain challenge wild animals and humans alike.

Idaho lies halfway between the Equator and the North Pole. Its northern border is Canada; on the south are Utah and Nevada; to the east is Wyoming and Montana; to the west is Oregon and Washington.

Weather

Idaho enjoys a semi-arid climate in the south and marine influences in the north. They combine to present a variety of weather patterns in all seasons.

Summer temperatures are moderate: nightly lows average between 45 to 60 degrees; daily highs average from 50 to 95 degrees. At higher elevations, however, late-summer nights may drop below freezing, and it can snow any time of year. Mountain storms can be intense, cold and life-threatening.

Autumn's first hard frost occurs around mid-September, but day temperatures remain moderate into late-October or early November in classic "indian summer" style. Nightly temperatures are crisp.

Generally, Idaho experiences a dry, warm weather pattern in summer and autumn. Mountain induced thunder bursts are more prevalent in summer. Winter snowfall provides most of the state's precipitation.

Winter temperatures are relatively mild at lower elevations with a range of 0 to 50 degrees, but temperatures are often extreme at higher elevations with a range of 40 to minus-20 degrees or lower.

Geography

Complex sequences of ancient forces conjured a fascinating diversity of geological features in Idaho. Ancient seas deposited layers of sediments. Tectonic upheavals created towering mountain peaks and rumpled vast plains. Fiery ash and lava flows erupted along a sweeping curve to the continent's most famous hot spot, Yellowstone National Park. Ice Age glaciers sculpted mountain crags and scoured deep lakes. Legions of rivers carved web-like arrays of steep canyons.

Idaho's 83,000 square miles contain mountains above 12,000 feet in elevation and deep canyons as low as 738 feet above sea level. More than 200 peaks are 8,000 feet or higher. Hell's Canyon on the Snake River is North America's deepest gorge at more than a mile deep. The Salmon River Canyon is the second deepest.

Idaho has 16,000 miles of rivers and streams and more than 2,000 natural lakes. Three hundred are alpine lakes. Passage to the Pacific Ocean is via the Snake River, the largest tributary of the Columbia River. The Salmon River, known as the "River of No Return" because of its difficult passage, is the nation's longest river that heads and flows within a single state.

With 40 percent of its 53 million acres covered by 10 national forests, it is the most heavily forested of the Rocky Mountains states. Its central wild heart remains pristine. Idaho's 3.4 million acres of wilderness areas and 9 million acres of roadless forest lands comprise the largest untracked expanse of land outside of Alaska. More than 70 percent of the state is public domain, administered by federal and state land managers.

Idaho's northern forests are lush and green. Central and southern Idaho's forests and sagebrush deserts are semi-arid.

Idaho Fish and Game Regions

Wildlife management areas maintained by Idaho Department of Fish and Game are key public access sites for waterfowl or upland gamebird hunting. Most offer both. All offer wildlife viewing opportunities; a number offer fishing.

In addition, the department has obtained landowner cooperation for public access to numerous hunting and fishing sites in farmlands adjacent to the state's vast expanses of federally managed range lands and national forests. The hunter's bonus from IDFG public access sites is short drives from the state's larger towns and cities. To pinpoint locations of these hunting options obtain a copy of IDFG's "Idaho Sportsmen's Access Guide" by calling or writing to IDFG Headquarters, 600 South Walnut, P.O. Box 25, Boise, ID 83707, 208-334-3700.

Many of the big game hunting units listed by region also are used in management of wild turkey hunts.

IDFG offices are open Monday through Friday, except state holidays, 8 a.m.-5 p.m. Panhandle and Clearwater regional offices are in Pacific Time Zone; eastern, central and southwestern regional offices are in Mountain Time Zone.

Region 1—Panhandle
2750 Kathleen Avenue
Coeur d'Alene, ID 83814
208-769-1414

Region 2—Clearwater
1540 Warner Avenue
Lewiston, ID 83501
208-799-5010

Region 3: Southwest
North Half: 555 Deinhard Lane
        McCall, ID 83638
        208-634-8137

South Half: 3101 South Powerline Road
        Nampa, ID 83686
        208-465-8465 (from Boise, call 887-6729)

State Headquarters: 600 South Walnut
            P.O. Box 25
            Boise, ID 83707
            208-334-3700

Idaho Fish and Game Regions

Boundary

1

Bonner

Kootenai

Benewah Shoshone

Latah

2 Clearwater

Nez
Perce

Lewis

Idaho

**Idaho Department of Fish and Game
Administrative Regions**
1. Panhandle
2. Clearwater
3. Southwest
4. Magic Valley
5. Southeast
6. Upper Snake
7. Salmon

Adams Lemhi 7

Valley

Washington

Payette

Gem Boise Custer Clark Fremont

Canyon

3 Jefferson Madison Teton 6

Ada Butte Bonneville

Elmore Camas Blaine Bingham

Gooding Lincoln Minidoka Caribou

Jerome Power Bannock

Owyhee Bear
Lake

Twin Falls Oneida

Cassia Franklin

4 5

Region 4: Magic Valley
868 East Main Street
P.O. Box 428
Jerome, ID 83338
208-324-4350

Region 5: Southeast
1345 Barton Road
Pocatello, ID 83204
208-232-4703

Region 6: Upper Snake
1515 Lincoln Road
Idaho Falls, ID 83401
208-525-7290

Region 7: Salmon
1214 Hwy 93 North
P.O. Box 1336
Salmon, ID 83467
208-756-2271

Idaho License Fees

Resident License Fees

Basic Hunting License (big game tags purchased separately) .... $ 7.50
Fishing .... $ 16.50
Combination Hunting and Fishing .... $ 21.50
Sportsman Package .... $ 78.00
Senior Resident Combination .... $ 5.50
Junior Combination (optional at age 14) .... $ 11.50
Junior Hunting (required at age 12) .... $ 5.50
Junior Fishing (required at age 14) .... $ 8.50

Resident Tags/Stamps

Turkey Tag .... $ 7.50
Controlled Hunt Fee Application .... $ 6.50
Controlled Hunt Permit Issuance Fee .... $ 1.50
WMA Permit for Pheasant .... $ 10.50
Upland Game Stamp .... $ 6.50
State Waterfowl Stamp .... $ 6.50
Steelhead .... $ 5.50

Nonresident License Fees

Basic Hunting (big game tags purchased separately) $101.50
Season Fishing .... $ 51.50
Daily Fishing (add $3 for each additional day) .... $ 7.50
3 Day Salmon/Steelhead Permit .... $ 31.50
2 Day Hunting (not valid first 5 days of pheasant season) .... $ 56.50

Nonresident Tags/Stamps

Turkey Tag .... $ 36.50
Controlled Hunt Fee Application .... $ 6.50
Controlled Hunt Permit Issuance Fee .... $ 1.50
WMA Permit for Pheasant .... $ 10.50
Upland Game Stamp .... $ 6.50
State Waterfowl Stamp .... $ 6.50

Nonresident Hunting Information

Licenses and tags are available from department offices and more than 400 vendors statewide, starting December 16 for the next season's hunts.

Licenses and tags are available for purchase by credit card.
Call 1-800-554-8685.

All licenses, permits and general season tags may be purchased at all Fish and Game offices, over the telephone via credit card, or at any of the state approved license vendors. All licenses and permits include a $.50 cents charge and permits that were previously free carry a $1.50 charge to pay for a computerized license system.

Applications for spring wild turkey controlled hunt drawings are accepted Jan. 15–Feb.15. If you plan to apply for a controlled hunt, be sure you use the rules brochure for the season in which you wish to apply, because last year's hunt numbers may not match up with this year's. All controlled hunt applications may be made by telephone at 1-800-TAG-DRAW, or on paper applications.

An Idaho upland game stamp is required for all hunters pursuing pheasant, quail and partridge. A WMA pheasant permit is an additional requirement for hunting pheasants on certain WMA's where pheasant-stocking programs exist. The $10.50 permit is required when hunting pheasants on Market Lake, Mud Lake, Sterling, Fort Boise, C.J. Strike, Montour, and part of the Lower Payette WMAs. This permit is not required for hunting pheasants in other locations.

An Idaho waterfowl stamp (in addition to the federal waterfowl stamp) is required to hunt ducks and geese. Proceeds from state waterfowl and upland stamps and limited edition artwork are used for habitat improvement.

A federal migratory bird license validation is necessary for hunting mourning dove, snipe, ducks, geese and other migratory birds managed under federal law. If you buy an Idaho waterfowl stamp, the migratory bird validation will be automatically added to your license. Response to survey questions is required.

With medical certification, physically impaired hunters may obtain a permit to hunt from a vehicle where use of a vehicle is legal, and for use of a crossbow. You may obtain the proper forms on the Fish and Game Internet home page, or contact the Fish and Game license division at **208-334-3717**.

Upland Gamebird Seasons

*These dates reflect 1997 seasons–check current
regulations before hunting.*

Wild Turkey
- Limit: 1 bird
  GMAs: 8, 8A, 10A, 11, 11A, 12, 13, 14, 15,
  16, 18, 22, 31, 32, 32A, 39 .... April 14–May 11
  GMAs: 1, 2, 3, 4, 5, 6 .... April 28–May 11

Pheasant
- Limit: 3 cocks a day
- Possession Limit: 6 birds after first day of season
  Area 1 .... October 12–December 31
  Area 2 .... October 19–December 1
  Area 3 .... October 19–December 15

Forest Grouse (Ruffed and Blue Grouse)
- Limit: 4 birds
- Possession Limit: 8 birds after first day of season
  All Areas .... September 1–December 31

Bobwhite and California Quail
- Limit: 10 birds a day
- Possession Limit: 20 birds after first day of season
  Area 2 .... September 21–December 31

Sage Grouse
- Limit: 1 bird a day
- Possession Limit: 2 birds after first day of season
  Area 1 .... Closed
  Area 2 .... September 21–September 27
  Area 3 .... September 21–October 13

Sharp-tailed Grouse
- Limit: 2 birds a day
- Possession Limit: 4 birds after first day of season
  Area 1 .... Closed
  Area 2 .... September 21–October 6

Chukar Partridge
- Limit: 8 birds a day
- Possession Limit: 16 birds after first day of season
  Area 1 .... September 21–December 31
  Areas 2 .... September 21–December 15

Gray (Hungarian) Partridge
- Limit: 8 birds a day
- Possession Limit: 16 birds after first day of season
  Area 1 .... September 21–December 31
  Area 2 .... September 21–December 15

Mourning Dove
- Limit: 10 birds a day
- Possession Limit: 20 birds after first day of season
  All Areas .... September 1–September 30

Waterfowl Seasons

*These dates reflect 1997 seasons–check current
regulations before hunting.*

Waterfowl hunting in northern and eastern Idaho peaks during October and November. South-central and southwestern Idaho hunting generally is best during late-November, December and early January.

The duck season in southwestern Idaho is split—closing in mid-October, and reopening in late October and continuing into January. Snipe and sandhill crane are included in waterfowl regulations. Steel shot is required for hunting waterfowl throughout Idaho. Bismuth shot also is approved for waterfowl hunting.

These regulations reflect 1997 rules. Always check current regulations for season dates, shooting hours, and bag limits–they often change from one year to the next.

Ducks (Including Mergansers)
- Limit: 7 a day
- Possession Limit: 14
  Area 1 .... October 5–January 5
  Area 2 .... October 5–January 5
  Area 3 .... October 5–October 13 & October 26–January 17

Common Snipe
- Limit: 8 a day
- Possession Limit: 16
  Area 1 .... October 5–January 5
  Areas 2 & 3 .... October 5–January 17

Geese (Including Brant, Canada, Emperor, White-fronted, Ross', and Snow)
- Area 1
  Limit: 4 (only 3 light geese or 2 white-fronted geese) ... September 28–January 5
- Area 2
  Limit: 3 (only 2 white-fronted geese) .... September 28–January 5
- Area 3
  Limit: 3 (only 2 dark geese) .... September 28–January 5
- Area 4
  Limit: 4 (only three light geese or 2 white-fronted) ..... September 28–January 5
- Area 5
  Limit: 4 (only three light geese or 2 white-fronted) .... October 5–January 12

Idaho's Upland Gamebirds

An Incredible Smorgasbord that Ranges from Tiny Doves to Giant Turkeys

by Ken Retallic

Upland gamebird hunters in search of variety discover superb wingshooting options in Idaho. A total of 16 gamebirds can be found in the state, a bill of fare ranging from the 4.5-ounce mourning dove to 20-pound wild turkey to, recently, the sandhill crane.

The Gem State is home to six native species of gallinaceous gamebirds—five grouse and one quail. Also residing in Idaho's mountain forests, meadows, valley grasslands, sagebrush plains, and rocky river canyons are four North American transplants—three quail and the wild turkey—plus three Eurasian imports—two partridges and the pheasant. The state also is a nesting and migratory staging area for the tiny mourning dove, common snipe, and, again, the giant sandhill crane.

The common snipe is managed under waterfowl regulations, but it is included in the upland gamebird discussion because of its similar wingshooting qualities. While the state's first sandhill crane hunt in 80 years was authorized in 1996, continued classification as a gamebird is being challenged in court.

Water is a key ingredient to locating all gamebirds in Idaho, as crystal clear streams pouring off the mountains and spring-fed tendrils meandering across its high plains provide important patches of green in sagebrush deserts and sun baked grasslands. Seventy-five percent of the semi-arid West's wildlife depends on riparian habitats for food or shelter. Wise hunters often score mixed bags by working these habitat edges—biologists call them ecotones—for species common to forest, sagebrush, or grassland niches.

Grouse, Prairie Chicken, Ptarmigan

Tetraonidae

Idaho's royal flush in grouse comprises two flatland grass species and three mountain forest species. The family *Tetraonidae* also includes prairie chicken, which do not occur in Idaho, and ptarmigan. The alpine range of the willow ptarmigan, *Lagopus lagopus*, extends south along the Continental Divide to Colorado. Sightings in Idaho are rare and there is no hunting season.

Four out of five of the grouse rank among the most exciting and toothsome of gamebirds, and except for sage grouse, populations are stable.

Many honor the sage grouse as the totem bird of south-central and eastern Idaho's sagebrush deserts. It is North America's largest grouse but relatively easy to hit and bring down. For this reason it is considered a good beginner bird for young hunters.

Eastern Idaho's grasslands harbor the West's largest population of Columbian sharp-tailed grouse, but a remnant population of this subspecies in western Idaho is off limits to hunters. The sharptail is a tougher target than its monster cousin and a favorite of wingshooters who like to work with pointing dogs. Its place on the menu is second only to the ruffed grouse.

Of the three forest grouse species, the ruffed grouse ranks as the king of game-birds. It is well established in northern Idaho, and good populations are found in the mountains of central and eastern Idaho. Hunters from the East and Midwest often are surprised at the tameness of western ruffed grouse. But as hunting pressures increase, the explosive flushes of this royal bird challenges the best of shotgunners.

Blue grouse also are high on the menu of autumn hunters. The largest of the forest grouse, blues are more common than other species in most of southern Idaho's mountains. Like the western ruffed grouse, it has a split personality. One day it's a typical "fool hen" perched immobile on a branch; another day it's a blue mountain bomber who knocks your socks off when it blasts out of a woody thicket.

But of the three forest grouse, the spruce grouse undeniably deserves the fool hen pseudonym. Also know as the Franklin's grouse, it is sparsely distributed in remote pockets of alpine conifer forests in the Payette and Salmon River drainages and north to the Canadian border. Not considered one of the more exciting species to hunt, it often presents less sport than a pen-raised pheasant, and its conifer diet makes it one of the least edible grouse.

Quail, Partridge, Pheasant
Phasianidae

Idaho's members of the family *Phasianidae* include four North American quail, two Eurasian partridges and the ring-necked pheasant of Asia; however, localized populations vary from prolific to nearly extinct.

Idaho's sole native quail species, the mountain quail (*Oreortyx pictus*), exists today in small, scattered populations in the dense mountain brush of the state's west-central river canyons. A protected species, it cannot be hunted. It is unfortunate because this, the largest of the quail species, is a gamebird unique to the West.

Hunters are asked to report sightings of any mountain quail to the nearest Idaho Department of Fish and Game office.

One of the state's three introduced quail species also is a protected gamebird. No harvest is permitted on the Gambel's quail, *Callipepla gambelii*. A desert quail from the Southwest, it is found in Idaho only near the town of Salmon in the Lemhi Valley.

A West Coast import, burgeoning populations of the California quail, *Callipepla californica*, offer renewed shooting opportunities in western Idaho. Also known as the valley quail, it is found below 3,500 feet in elevation in brushy cover near streams and other prime water sources from Twin Falls west to the Oregon border and north to the Palouse Prairie. The bobwhite quail, *Colinus virginianus*, is a distant second in shooting numbers. It was introduced into Idaho from the East in the 1880s but exists today in small, scattered populations in the Boise Valley's farmlands. About equal in size, both California quail and bobwhite are succulent delicacies.

Idaho truly offers a mixed bag of upland gamebirds. Here, a lucky hunter has taken Hungarian partridge, ring-necked pheasant, chukar partridge, and ruffed grouse in a single day. (Photo: Ron Spomer)

Hunting techniques differ for the two. California quail run before flying and flush in singles and pairs, although they often sit tighter for pointing dogs the second go-round.

Of the state's two Old World partridges, the chukar (*Alectoris chukar*), resides in a previously unexploited niche in some of the West's most physically challenging terrain. Good water years enable the tough little bird to flourish in semi-arid canyons, draws, and lava fields of the lower Snake, Bruneau, Boise, and Salmon River drainages.

Delectable trophies, chukars demand sometimes-Herculean efforts by shotgun-ners and dogs. The most exacting aspect of chukar hunting is the bird's propensity to always run before flying. First, the covey gallops uphill, then it wings it down the slope or across the canyon to freedom.

More gentlemanly in choice of habitat, the gray partridge, *Perdix perdix*, is most common in agricultural regions but are also found in grasslands abutting sagebrush throughout much of the state. Also known as Hungarian partridge, or "Huns," they get high marks as table fare, although many hunters consider them a bonus while pursuing other gamebirds.

The always-popular ring-necked pheasant, *Phasianus colchicus*, has had a checkered history in Idaho. Closest in size and taste of all gallinaceous gamebirds to the domestic chicken, its greatest hardships are the state's harsh climate and loss of protective nesting and wintering cover. Wild pheasant populations are more com-mon along the Snake River Plain from the Oregon border to central Idaho. Fewer wild birds occur in the agricultural flatlands of eastern and northern Idaho.

It is best to scout pheasant hunting territories and obtain landowners permission to hunt before the season opens. Short-ranging retrievers are the preferred bird dog.

Wild Turkey
Meleagrididae

Like elsewhere in the United States, Idaho's thriving wild turkey population is one of its best wildlife success stories.

Assigned a family of their own, the two *Meleagrididae* species—wild turkey of North America and ocellated turkey of Mexico's Yucatan Peninsula—are unique to the New World. The wild turkey was first introduced to Idaho in 1961. It currently has three of the five subspecies known to inhabit the United States.

Large, gregarious gamebirds, the most common in Idaho is the Merriam's turkey, *Meleagris gallopavo merriami*. Rio Grande turkey, *Meleagris gallopavo intermedia*, is second in number. An introductory population of Eastern turkey, *Meleagris gal-lopavo silvestris*, was recently established in north-central Idaho. The best hunting areas are in the northern panhandle, from St. Maries north to the Canadian border; north-central Idaho, from Riggins to Moscow; and southwestern Idaho, north and east of Weiser to the Hells Canyon rim.

The wild turkey is an excellent table bird and trophy gamebird. The most suc-cessful hunters of turkey are a special breed, masters of calling and decoying. Turkey hunts demand respect for both hunting ethics and safety. Idaho's high elevations also require added stamina.

Dove and Pigeon
Columbidae

One of the largest bird families, *Columbidae* are found around the world. Nine species, including the extinct passenger pigeon, have regularly occurred in the

Sean Lawson's efforts really paid off with this beautiful Idaho turkey.
(Photo: Mike Lawson)

United States. Only the mourning dove, *Zenaida macroura*, is native to Idaho, the rest of the country, and Mexico.

It is managed cooperatively under the Migratory Bird Treaty Act administered by the U.S. Fish and Wildlife Service. Opening on September 1, Idaho's season is short and sweet, as both residents and migrants soon depart for warmer climes.

The mourning dove's erratic zigs and zags and rocketing sprints make them appear to be the most aerodynamic of gamebirds, thus testing the mettle of the best of pass shooters. And, while it will decoy, it's unnecessary if hunting territories are well scouted before the season opens.

Common Snipe and American Woodcock
Scolopacidae

Of the thousands upon thousands of North American shorebirds once hunted so voraciously by old time market hunters, only the common snipe, *Gallinago gallinago*, and American woodcock, *Scolopax minor*, retain gamebird status. The woodcock's range is restricted to east of the Mississippi River. The snipe's range covers the compass from the Arctic to northern South America.

Snipe are managed cooperatively under the Migratory Bird Treaty Act administered by the U.S. Fish and Wildlife Service. Idaho offers a long season and generous bag limit, but the diminutive gamebird is lightly hunted.

Forget the practical jokes about snipe hunts. Also known as the Wilson's snipe, these delectable butterballs grace a determined hunter's table. Hunting these birds is every bit as challenging as hunting mourning doves. The necessary added equipment is a pair of hip boots.

Hunters can either "walk up" snipe or set up blinds near known feeding areas. A close-working flushing dog can't hurt, but a good retriever is more resourceful in locating downed birds.

Sandhill and Whooping Cranes
Gruidae

Idaho is home to one of the Intermountain West's largest nesting populations of sandhill cranes, *Grus canadensis*, and a major staging area for migratory cranes. The presence of the rare whooping crane, *Grus americanus*, in eastern Idaho is a product of attempts to establish a second population of the endangered species. It will probably never again reach gamebird status.

Sandhills returned to the hunting menu because of persistent complaints about crop damage in southeastern Idaho. Even if its gamebird status withstands continual court challenges, hunting opportunities will remain limited. Migratory Bird Treaty Act management restrictions set Idaho's quota at 150 birds or less.

Upland Gamebird Management

The Idaho Fish and Game Commission divides the state into seven departmental administration regions. Hunting regulations for upland gamebirds, except turkey, are set either statewide or by county. Turkey are managed by the same system of hunting units employed for big game management.

Hunting rules, bag limits, and possession limits are set for two years by the commission in even numbered years. Circumstances may require status changes for some species, so determine if there are any alterations in the rules before the start of a new season.

Idaho is home to one of the intermountain West's largest nesting populations of sandhill cranes. (Photo: Ken Retallic)

In addition to a general hunting license, a conservation stamp is required for pheasant, quail, sage grouse, and sharp-tailed grouse. No stamp is required for forest grouse. State and federal waterfowl conservation stamps are required for snipe and sand hill crane.

In recent years, Idaho biologists have banded thousands of upland gamebirds. Leg bands may be found on pheasant, quail, and chukar as well as sage, sharp-tailed, ruffed, and blue grouse. Wingshooters are encouraged to report any banded birds to the nearest Fish and Game office. This is especially important for data collection about sage grouse.

Sage Grouse Distribution

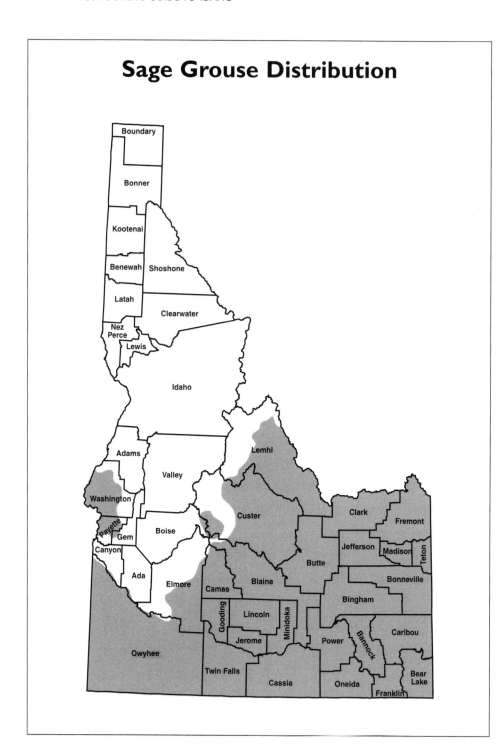

Sage Grouse

Centrocercus urophasianus

FIELD FACTS

Local Names
    Sage hen, sage chicken, sage bomber

Size
    Largest North American grouse species. Males are 28 to 30 inches in length; 36-inch wing span; 4 to 8 pounds in weight. Females are 21 to 22 inches in length; 2.5 to 3.5 pounds in weight.

Identification in Flight
    Large bird with elongated profile, long pointed tail and short blocky wings. Dark brown, buff and mottled gray in color; wing tips dark. Large black belly patch outlined by white of underwing coverts.

- Sage grouse were first reported in Idaho by Capt. William Clark of the Lewis and Clark Expedition in 1805 in the Lemhi River Valley and along the Salmon River. C. Hart Merriam reported sage grouse were abundant in 1890 in south-central Idaho. By 1914 concerns about population declines were being raised. Populations plummeted to critically low levels in mid-1990s.
- Sage grouse occur throughout sagebrush dominated lowlands and mountain valleys in southern and eastern Idaho. Largest populations occur in Butte, Clark, Blaine, Fremont, Lincoln, Gooding, Camas, Minidoka, Jefferson and Owyhee counties.
- Seasons: Two short seasons starting in late-September, both sexes; see regulations for open hunting areas and dates.

Color and Characteristics

The sage grouse has a plump oval-shaped body with a long pointed tail, feathered legs and black toes. Body plumage of both sexes is mottled gray-brown, buff and black in color, with large brownish-black patch on belly; underwing coverts are white. Cock much larger than hen and more distinctively marked. It has small yellow eye combs, black throat and black bib or band above large white ruff on breast. Yellowish air sacs on breast are used in courting display.

Sound and Flight

The almost silent rise of sage grouse often catches a first-time hunter by surprise. The low guttural clucking of cock or soft chicken-like cackle of the hen is difficult to hear.

Cocks may try to run. When flushed they are more inclined to fly longer distances than hens. Take-off is somewhat slow and ponderous, but it builds up steam quickly in straight-away flight. Females appear to dip from side to side in flight. Early season hens and young birds are often reluctant to flush or slow to follow rest of flock. Single birds, pairs, or groups of three or more rising in intervals is common at beginning of season. Birds may fly only short distance to nearest cover. Late-season birds pump and glide long distances.

Similar Game Birds

Ring-necked pheasant hen similar in size to female and young male sage grouse. Female pheasant has brown belly, more pointed tail and bare, unfeathered legs. Sharp-tailed grouse much smaller, light tan in total appearance with white under-belly and white outer-feathers on tail.

Flock or Covey Habits

Cocks disperse after spring courting season. They do not take part in incubation or care of young, and travel as singles or in loose bachelor bands through summer. Hens nest in general vicinity of leks, or traditional strutting grounds, and travel through summer as family groups with broods of up to six.

Many of Idaho's sage grouse populations are migratory and may use seasonal ranges separated by up to 50 miles. Family groups and bachelor bands collect in autumn in flocks that in prime habitat areas may number between 20 and 40. In dry years and arid areas, family groups remain more dispersed until moving onto wintering grounds, although all are within about a mile of key water sources.

Early spring congregations at leks bring together 50 to more than 100 birds. Courtship ritual begins as early as late-March in mild years and continues through April. Many strutting grounds have been in use for centuries. Stately courtship displays by males at dawn is one of nature's greatest spectacles.

Reproduction and Life Span

A sage grouse has potential life span of 5 to 7 years if it survives the first year. Chick mortality is usually 60 percent or more.

Cocks are polygamists. Dominant birds may service up to 10 hens each.

A hen's nest is a simple depression in the ground under sagebrush with good adjacent cover. Reports on clutch size range from 5 to 13 eggs, although Idaho birds appear to average about six. Incubation by hen alone takes 23 to 25 days. Chicks are precocious and, like all gamebirds, quite active shortly after birth.

Reproduction trends exhibit boom and bust cycles since the 1960s. In recent years, however, sage grouse numbers have dropped dramatically in Idaho and many

A stately, young sage grouse. (Photo: Ken Retallic)

other Western states. Some breeding populations in Idaho have experienced losses of more than 60 percent.

Major causes of the declines are poor chick production or survival due to prolonged drought and sagebrush destruction by fires, followed by cheatgrass invasion of prime habitat, which includes ouster of native bunch grasses, and continued agricultural development in some areas. Effects of pesticides and hunting on critically low populations also is being studied.

To reverse downward trend in Idaho's sage grouse populations, IDFG in 1997 initiated a comprehensive five-year management plan. The department is counting on the cooperation of hunters, private landowners, and federal and state public lands managers to achieve its goal.

"Sage grouse hold a unique place in the hunting traditions of many Idahoans," says Tom Hemker, IDFG's upland game program manager. "Besides the high value of sage grouse to hunters, it is important that this bird does not become so rare that it needs protection as an endangered species."

Feeding Habits and Patterns

Unlike most other birds, sage grouse do not have a muscular gizzard. Their thin-walled stomachs are adapted to soft foods like the leaves of sagebrush and other plants. They cannot digest hard-shelled seeds, although they feed on a variety of fruits and berries and take insects when available.

In late-spring and summer, sage grouse feed on forbs, or flowering plants, and insects in a variety of habitats. Protein from insects is especially important to young birds. Wet meadows, spring seeps and riparian zones along free-flowing or open water also are critical to brood production. Populations near agricultural areas take advantage of irrigated lands and often linger near alfalfa fields well into autumn.

Sage grouse are entirely dependent on sagebrush habitat for food in fall, winter and early spring. Sagebrush also provides critical nesting and roosting cover year-round. When large blocks of sagebrush habitat are significantly altered or reduced sage grouse populations suffer.

The birds are most active in early morning and late afternoon. They generally open and close the day by flying to water at first light and at dusk. More than forest grouse, they also will fly to feeding areas. At midday they retreat to protective cover, like brushy draws or thick undisturbed stands of sagebrush, to rest and preen and to dust or sun bathe.

Preferred Habitat and Cover

Large portions of Idaho's historical sage grouse range have been lost to agricultural development and sagebrush eradication. Much of this habitat loss occurred in key areas along the Upper Snake River Plain. The majority of the state's sage grouse habitat is now on public lands managed by the Bureau of Land Management and U.S. Forest Service in eastern, south-central and southwestern Idaho.

Of the sagebrush species, sage grouse feed more on black sage and big sage than on the smaller varieties. They like alfalfa and any hayfield at the edge of sage country is a good place to find feeding sage grouse. They also like grasshoppers and a very recent burn is worth scouting.

Desert water holes and high wet meadows in the sagebrush mesas and tables are excellent sage hen hunting places. Little trickles and seeps in the Big Desert are good morning and evening shooting areas. Sage grouse are not fond of noisy running water, but are often found in quiet bottom lands of desert rivers and creeks.

Locating Hunting Areas

Season lengths vary from year to year but are never long. Obtain a copy of the upland game regulations and scout open hunting areas in advance at times of day the birds are most active. Spring outings to learn lek locations and gain familiarity of surrounding terrain also are beneficial.

Late-summer or early fall fishing trips to desert streams offer another opportunity to scout for grouse. Good prospects are lower Silver Creek, Big Wood, Little Wood and upper Big Lost rivers in central Idaho or Camas Creek, lower Henry's Fork, Willow

A mature sage grouse in winter snow. (Photo: Ken Retallic)

Creek, upper Blackfoot, Bear and Portneuf rivers in eastern Idaho. In western Idaho, scout the Bruneau, Owyhee and Snake rivers in Owyhee County. The bonus when grouse season opens is the proverbial "cast and blast."

Preseason road trips work, too. Make them more profitable by getting out of the vehicle to look for sign or climb to higher ground to glass surrounding terrain for pockets and tendrils of green that denote water sources. In eastern Idaho's Big Desert and vast public ranges, like the Owyhee highlands, don't pass up chances to look for sign around another manmade source of water — cattle tanks and guzzlers placed on BLM lands.

Many feel the best sage grouse hunting remaining in Idaho is in Owyhee County, a desolate lonely sagebrush desert with far flung horizons.

After the season opens, some hens and their young remain relatively tame until shot over a few times. Birds may occasionally cross in front of a vehicle on remote roads or even jog along the edge. Others may be visible in nearby clearings or on alfalfa fields. For the latter it is possible to set up a pass shooting opportunity at dawn or dusk when they fly in to feed. Obtain landowner permission ahead of time when necessary.

Looking for Sign

Sage grouse droppings when feeding on sagebrush are large, dark and tarry. Droppings from other feed is lighter, somewhat greener in color and may contain pits from fruits and berries like chokecherry, Oregon grape or service berry. They do not scratch for seeds like some other gallinaceous birds, but dusting areas often contain down and feathers.

Tracks in the dust of remote roads that get little traffic are another clue sage grouse are in the vicinity. The same goes for snow, but usually the season is long over in the eastern part of the state.

Hunting Methods

Although it is North America's largest grouse, the sage grouse is relatively easy to hit and bring down. Early season hunters often get more than one chance for a shot when a flock is flushed. Rises can come from all sides, in singles, pairs and trios. For these reasons the sage grouse is considered a good beginner bird to teach young hunters to stay calm and focused.

There are many empty acres in sage grouse country. Concentrate on prime feeding areas early and late in the day. Switch to adjacent roosting or loafing locals in mid-afternoon. South-facing ridges and the edges of brushy draws near water sources are good options between feeding and watering times.

It is possible for lone hunters and small groups to walk up sage grouse, but dogs cover broader swaths plus have their noses to the ground. Easier retrieval of downed birds is greatest benefit of dogs on a sage grouse hunt. Either way plan on walking a lot. If birds aren't kicked up in an hour or two, try another location.

The ever-present winds of Big Sky country can be walk-up hunters' best friend early in the season; their worst enemy toward the end. In a stiff wind early on, walk with it at your back. Flushed birds often hover momentarily before cutting away to an escape route. If it is howling late in season, plan something else.

Chaps or heavy canvas hunting pants are recommended in sage country. Gaiters help keep debris out of low-sided hunting boots. Never wear tennis shoes. Prickly pear cactus is common in southern Idaho. Cheatgrass is a growing problem.

Hunting Dogs

Close-working flushing dogs or retrievers help hunters cover the broad expanses of sage country. Cocks usually run from slow-working dogs, but at beginning of season young sage grouse and hens hold for pointers.

Rattlesnakes may be present in some areas, especially in rocky lower elevations of state. Lava rock terrain can be tough on dogs' feet, and dryness of state's semi-arid climate needs to be recognized.

Shot and Choke Suggestions

- **Shot:** No. 6, 1 1/4 oz.
- **Chokes:** Modified and full.
- A 20-gauge will work but a 12-gauge is better for long shots.

Field Preparation and Table Fare

Juvenile sage grouse and young hens are considered excellent table fare. Opinions differ on eating quality of older sage bombers. All birds should be field dressed and cooled immediately. Some hunters prefer to let birds age a few days before skinning for a meal or the freezer. The breast is dark and rich, legs lighter and leaner in texture.

Sharp-tailed Grouse Distribution

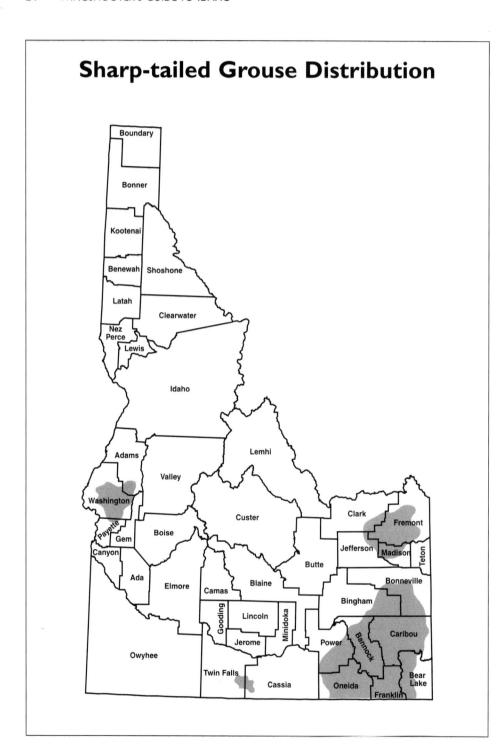

Columbian Sharp-tailed Grouse

Tympanuchus phasianellus

FIELD FACTS

Local Names
Sharptail, pintail grouse, white-bellied grouse, speckle-belly

Size
Second largest of Idaho's five native grouse. Both sexes average 16.5 to 18.5 inches in length, 20-inch wing span. Adult males average 2 pounds 1 ounce; adult females average 1 pound 13 ounces.

Identification in Flight
Both sexes appear light tan in color, white underbelly. Short pointed tail is white-edged, wings marked by light and dark bars.

- Eastern Idaho harbors West's largest population of Columbian sharp-tailed grouse. Once feared destined for Endangered Species List, its rebound has been phenomenal. A hunting harvest increase from 2,000 in 1985 to more than 10,000 per year through 1990s makes it the state's primary CRP beneficiary.
- New breeding populations southeast of Twin Falls is first success in efforts to restore historical range. IDFG transplants sharptails from Rockland and Arbon valleys to Shoshone Basin, but hunting season remains closed. Sage grouse hunters must be sure of targets in western Cassia and Twin Falls counties.
- Remnant population in Craig Mountains and Rathdrum Prairie north of Weiser also off-limits to hunters.
- Season: Split seasons starting in late-September, both sexes; see regulations for open hunting areas and dates.

Color and Characteristics

Plump bird but streamlined in appearance. Legs are feathered. Both sexes similar in coloration. Upper body color is mottled with white, buff, brown, and black feathers; conspicuous white spots on wings; breast and flanks have V-shaped brown markings on white background. Males have small yellow eye combs and pale-violet air sacs used in courtship displays.

Sound and Flight

Sharp-tailed grouse cackle nervously when flushed and throughout flight. Strong fliers, they spring high in air and cut sharply away on downwind slant. Escape flight is swift and straight as birds alternate flapping and soaring. They usually set their wings at apex of flight to glide long distances. At the start of the season, young birds, and some hens, only fly short distances until shot over a few times.

Similar Game Birds

Hen pheasants may be mistaken for sharp-tailed grouse. Female pheasant is mottled brown throughout, including belly; long pointed tail has no white on outer edges; legs are bare. Sage grouse almost double in size; both sexes have black patch on belly, white underwing coverts, brown wing tips.

Flock or Covey Habits

Annual rites of spring at leks, or traditional strutting grounds, draw in congregations of 50 to more than 100 birds. Early April mating dance of sharp-tailed grouse is more hot-blooded and musical than aristocratic posturing of sage grouse.

Cocks disperse at conclusion of mating season and do not participate in care of young. They travel through summer over broad range in loose, widely scattered flocks. Hens nest in general vicinity of leks. Family groups travel together over wide area through summer into fall.

Family and bachelor groups begin to collect in loose flocks in early autumn. Individual flocks rarely grow very large in number and remain scattered. In late fall, many populations gravitate toward roosting sites on or near breeding grounds. Riparian areas and brushy upper slopes are preferred winter haunts.

Reproduction and Life Span

Sharptails have potential life span of about 5 years. Many hens nest again if first egg clutch lost. Mortality of young is generally 50 per cent or higher. It may exceed 80 percent some years.

Hens nest on ground in dense grasses under or surrounded by shrubs. Dense grass understory is critical to reducing predation on nests and broods. Incubation of 10 to 13 eggs by hen alone takes 21 days. Young are very active shortly after hatching, and can fly in about two weeks.

Feeding Habits and Patterns

Columbian sharptails do not migrate but make seasonal rotations in dispersed flocks throughout home ranges. Early risers, they are most active near dawn and again toward dusk. Midday is reserved for loafing and plumage maintenance. They often fly to roosting, watering and feeding sites.

In spring and summer, sharptails rely on a combination of grasslands and mixed shrub communities—bitterbrush, chokecherry, and serviceberry—rich in forbs, or flowering plants, seeds, berries, and fruits. They also feed on variety of insects. In late-summer and fall, they feed in grain feeds when available in addition to eating forbs and berries.

Sharptails are ground birds through summer and autumn. When range is snow-covered they feed and rest in shrubs, but still roost on ground. Mountain brush habitats are key source of winter food and protective cover. They feed on rose hips, hawthorn, juniper berries, chokecherry, serviceberry, aspen buds, catkins, and young shoots.

Preferred Habitat and Cover

Renowned as a grasslands species, sharptails are creatures of the edge. The best places to find them are where savannas and CRP tracts meet grain stubble, sage country or aspen stands, especially if the grasslands are dotted with thickets of bitterbrush, serviceberry, and chokecherry.

They don't like heavy timber but will work fringes of aspen and willow thickets for buds and catkins as well as Oregon grape. They relish bitterbrush but are not overly fond of sagebrush. As a rule, in places where sage grouse are kicked up, sharptails are harder to find.

Sharptails are not particularly water-bound since they will fly to moisture sources. Flocks remain scattered even in dry spells.

Many species of wildlife take advantage of thick cover vegetation, but Columbian sharptails are Idaho's greatest beneficiary of the Conservation Reserve Program. Numbers grew dramatically with the federal farm program that rewards farmers for taking erodible land out of agricultural production and planting it in permanent cover. Idaho had 840,000 acres of land in CRP set-asides in 1996 when Farm Bill was revised. That total included 600,000 acres considered critical to sharptails. New guidelines may significantly reduce CRP acreages.

As good as CRP has been for Idaho wildlife, it is a temporary measure, says Tom Hemker, IDFG's upland bird manager. Increased habitat preservation is necessary to assure the future of sharp-tailed grouse and sage grouse. IDFG is working with land management agencies on long-term habitat improvement plans.

Locating Hunting Areas

In recent years, sharptail hunting has been confined to east of Interstate 15 in Upper Snake River Valley. Open area in southeast corner of state extends east and west of I-15. Both regions offer mix of public range lands and national wildlife refuges, IDFG wildlife management areas and CRP tracts.

Largest sharptail populations occur in Bigham, Bonneville, Franklin, Fremont, and Oneida counties. Smaller populations found in Cassia, Power, Bannock, Caribou, Bear Lake, Madison, Jefferson, and Clark counties.

CRP set-asides are private, but most landowners permit hunting with permission. Check with local Fish and Game offices or hunting equipment shops for who to contact and to discuss annual concentrations of birds. Preseason scouting trips similar to those employed for sage grouse save time and effort during the short season. It is also a good idea to learn locations of leks.

Looking for Sign

Chicken-like droppings light in color but difficult to locate; most concentrated in roosting sites. Feathers and down usually present at preening and dustings areas.

Hunting Methods

Sharptails fly faster and sooner then sage grouse and are tougher targets. Once shot over, sharptails in open country are more skittish, often flushing quickly and out of range.

Sharptail country may appear almost overwhelming with its broad array of habitats and wide-ranging nature of bird. A good approach is to divide it up into chunks and work each one thoroughly. Allow a reasonable amount of time but don't linger more than an hour or two. When you score, look for similar habitat nearby.

Best chance of setting up morning or evening hunts for feeding birds is on CRP tracts or in harvested grain fields. When scouting open range for feeding birds—and most other wildlife—look for movement early and late in the day. During mid-morning and early afternoon plan on walking a lot. Concentrate on edges of serviceberry or bitterbrush thickets, brushy draws and coulees, slopes of riparian areas, weedy jeep trails, and grassy ridges.

It is possible for small parties of hunters to walk up sharptails, but it is a more demanding day afield if area isn't well scouted. Locating downed birds without a dog is sometimes difficult. In high winds, reverse standard approach and work downwind; concentrate on edges of heavy cover—thickets, shrub-filled draws, weed-lined jeep trails, and fence rows.

Hunting Dogs

Wingshooters who like to hunt with pointing dogs find sharptails hold well early in the season and when birds retreat to thick cover. Close working flushing dogs and retrievers help cover more ground and locate downed birds. Hunt as close as possible to dogs during high winds and late in season.

Shot and Choke Suggestions

- **Shot:** No. 7 1/2 or 6, 1 to 1 1/4 oz.
- **Chokes:** Improved and modified.

Field Preparation and Table Fare

Meat is slightly darker but sharptails rank second only to ruffed grouse on grouse family's great menu. Field dress and cool birds in warm weather. Consider waiting day or two before skinning for meal or freezer.

Ruffed Grouse Distribution

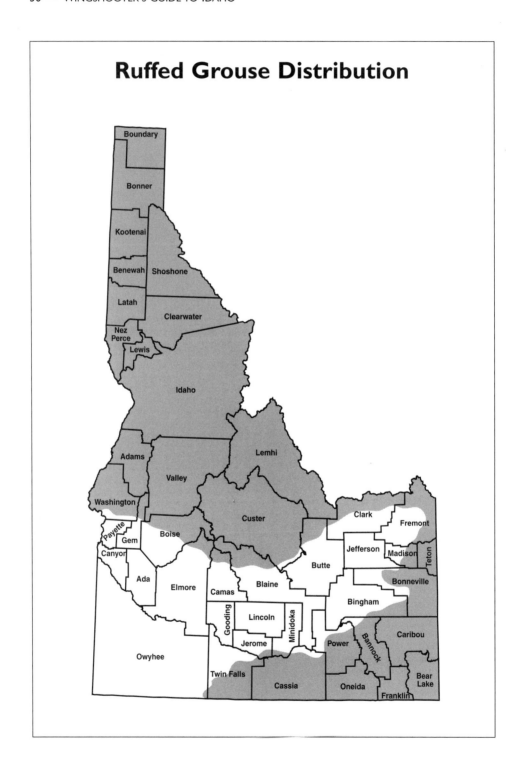

Ruffed Grouse
Bonasa umbellus

FIELD FACTS

Local Names
   Willow grouse, woods pheasant, "drummer."

Size
   Both sexes range from 16 to 19 inches in length, wing span is 24 inches; adult males range from 21 to 23 ounces in weight and females from 18 to 21 ounces.

Identification in Flight
   Medium-sized grouse with short neck, short blunt wings and widely fanned tail. Body may be mottled red/brown or gray/tan. Flared tail has black band along border. Flight speed is about 25 mph.

• Ruffed grouse are found in Idaho's mixed forests of deciduous trees and conifers, and in adjacent creek and river bottoms. All three phases are present. Darker red/brown phase, *Bonasa umbellus phaia*, is common along northern border. Lighter red/brown phase, *Bonasa umbellus affinis*, is found in northern, central and western Idaho. Gray phase, *Bonasa umbellus incana*, is found in southeast corner of state, north into Bonneville County.
• Ruffed grouse are most common in northern Idaho, where annual harvest equals 70 percent of all forest grouse taken in the state.
• Season: Begins September 1 and continues to end of year. Aggregate bag limit can include all three forest grouse in Idaho: ruffed, blue and spruce grouse.

Color and Characteristics
   Ruffled black ruff of male during courtship displays gives the species its name. Black-tipped tail also dramatically flared during courtship. Female has black-tipped tail, too, but the band is often broken in central feathers.
   Red-brown or gray/brown colorations of two phases most evident in the tail.
   Year-round, both sexes are similar. Both have black neck ruff, although less conspicuous on female, crested head, mottled brown body and thin bars on breast and flanks. Legs are feathered half-way down. By winter, ruffed grouse develop stiff fringes or pectinations on sides of toes to allow them to walk on snow.
   The hollow log drumming sound of male ruffed grouse in spring is caused by rapid beating of the air by wings. Some males perform same territorial ritual in fall.

Sound and Flight

Flushed birds burst into flight out of nowhere with an explosive roar of wings and dart and dodge through trees and shrubs to escape.

That is the typical flight pattern of jittery ruffed grouse. It is more likely to occur in northern Idaho where they are most heavily harvested. In southern Idaho, the term "kicking up birds" takes on a more literal meaning. Often, western ruffed grouse refuse to be spooked until shot over a few times. Some learn wiser ways sooner if they live near larger cities like Idaho Falls and Pocatello.

Similar Game Birds

Ruffed grouse and blue grouse territories overlap. Spruce grouse reside higher in remote areas of the mountains.

Blue grouse have black tail with gray band on border and gray/blue body feathers.

Flock or Covey Habits

Ruffed grouse are not gregarious. Family groups of 4 to 10 are often scattered. Hunters commonly encounter singles and pairs, but rarely groups larger than three or four. Keep your gun loaded in ruffed grouse country. Stay alert.

A hen and her brood stick together into September but rarely past late October. So-called "crazy flight" or autumn wandering of juveniles is classic mystery of the bird. It further spreads distribution. In winter, most ruffed grouse are solitary, although occasional flocking occurs.

Drumming by males to attract females begins in late March and continues through May. Nesting season is in late April or early May.

Reproduction and Life Span

Ruffed grouse have a potential life span of 5 to 7 years.

Clutch size ranges from 9 to 12 eggs and incubation, by the hen alone, is about two weeks. Chicks fledge and are able to fly in about two weeks. A brood sticks together about 12 weeks. Young birds are sexually mature by the next breeding season.

More than any other gamebird, ruffed grouse experience cyclical waxings and wanings of population numbers. Biologists argue whether the cycles are 10 or 20 years in length, and whether they are tied to propagation trends of aspen, a primary food source, or other factors. For hunters, the question became moot in the late-nineties as ruffed grouse numbers climbed. Hopefully, they won't need to check in again until the next century.

Feeding Habits and Patterns

Ruffed grouse are non-migratory. Individual, small home ranges are centered around perennial water sources—spring seeps, woodland ponds, marshes, wet meadows, and creek and river bottoms.

Nourishment comes from a variety of deciduous trees and shrubs, flowering plants, fruits and berries, and insects from late spring through autumn. In late fall and winter, they depend on berries and buds of deciduous shrubs and trees, like dogwood and aspen. In early spring, buds and catkins of willow and alder are welcomed.

Preferred Habitat and Cover

Ruffed grouse eat a more varied diet than their high-country relatives, the blue and spruce grouse. They also are more closely tied to a region's riparian zones. Weed and grass seeds are consumed by ruffed grouse, but succulent greens of leaves and buds of deciduous trees and forbs, or flowering plants, are preferred. In fall, orange/red squaw berries and pale-white dogwood berries and snowberries are special favorites. They also like choke cherries and service berries. But aspen communities remain the focal point of a covey's home range. They prefer new stands of aspen to old-growth thickets.

Good cover is rarely a problem in mountain forests, so the birds orient their lives around food and water sources. Like other gamebirds, their most active feeding patterns are in early morning and late afternoon toward dusk. A good drink late in the day is their most predictable habit.

Ruffed grouse are good walkers and actively cover all of their small ranges in search of food. But they do not like rain and roost in pine or fir trees most of the day in soggy weather.

Locating Hunting Areas

Escape cabin fever in spring by searching for drumming logs of displaying males. Broods of hens they attract will be in same vicinity come fall.

In fall, also do not overlook locations of drumming males trying to set up spring territory rights. Those that succeed will have broods in the same area next season.

If you find a small aspen grove with a spring seep or slow flowing stream, never give up the secret. Return before dusk in hunting season and return again the next year; good ruffed grouse territories produce year after year.

Ruffed grouse favor lower slopes of mixed forest mountain slopes down into creek and river bottoms of high plains. They feed on deciduous trees and shrubs, flowering plants, fruits and berries, but commonly roost in conifers. Look for places where the two plant communities meet near good water sources.

Idaho's best ruffed grouse populations are in the hardwood riparian zones of the lush cedar and fir forests of north Idaho. Good populations also are found in the mountains of central and eastern Idaho and the southeast corner west to the Sublett Mountains.

Most of the state's forest grouse populations are lightly harvested. IDFG biologists feel the gamebirds could sustain a higher rate of exploitation.

Hunting Methods

In early fall before frost knocks down the leaves, ruffed grouse are harder to find even though they may still be in their coveys. Water is most important to the birds at this drier time of year, and they do not stray far from prime sources. Some birds may move from higher slopes into creek and stream bottoms.

Walk selected routes early in the morning when scent conditions are better for your dogs. Let them track down birds in the bushes while you keep an eye on the trees. When you spy roosting birds, make an attempt to get them out of the trees for an honest shot. But do not let your frustrations reach the boiling point.

By mid to late fall, coveys are scattered, but hardwoods are bare and the birds are somewhat easier to spot. They also are inclined to feed higher up in aspen and shrubs in search of buds and berries. But with the increased visibility they do not stray far from protective thickets that they can dart into to escape danger.

Conifer thickets near good food sources provide shelter for the birds during late-autumn rains and winter snows. They prefer to hole up in young stands of pine or fir about 10 to 15 feet high, rather than in older, taller trees.

Explore the edges of these habitat types and small clearings as the seasons progress. Also hike along ridges of south-facing slopes, and abandoned or closed forest roads. Work each area slowly and methodically. Ruffed grouse often freeze and let fast-walking hunters pass them. They become nervous and flush when hunters pause periodically while searching good coverts.

Ruffed grouse are tough shots. Same bird sometimes can be flushed two or three times by marking its flight. It usually sits tighter the second go-round.

Hunting Dogs

Ruffed grouse are a dog hunter's best friends. Pointers and flushing dogs are equally effective in finding birds. All breeds are invaluable in retrieving downed birds.

Shot and Choke Suggestions
- **Shot:** No. 8 or 7 1/2 shot, 7/8 to 1 1/4 oz.
- **Chokes:** full or improved.

Rifles and pistols are legal to shoot forest grouse but shooters won't get much if they do not aim for the heads. If you are really hungry, it also is legal to clobber one with a stick.

Field Preparation and Table Fare

Ruffed grouse rank at the very top of the gamebird menu. Field dress and cool birds immediately.

Passing the Torch

A Son Provides a Ruffed Grouse Lesson

by Rocky Barker

Someday, these will be the good old days. Susie, our boisterous young Brittany, had run my son Dan and me up and down the fields of Tex Creek Wildlife Management Area east of Idaho Falls. She was supposed to be hunting sharp-tailed grouse since it was opening day. But the family dog—technically my daughter's birthday present less than a year before—had other ideas.

Grasshoppers and butterflies were flying everywhere, and as far as Susie was concerned, they were birds and she was pointing and chasing them with the excitement of Pete Rose chasing fly balls.

We had yelled and scolded our way through two hayfields, up and down rolling hills without seeing a single sharptail. Dan, 15, suggested we go up into the Big Hole Mountains near Ririe after forest grouse. He and I have hunted together for 13 years and he had yet to get a bird. But he had been there many times when I had and his excitement had not yet turned into frustration with our less than perfect dog. He had participated in her training and knew that, given a little more discipline and experience, she would turn into a hunter. The Big Holes are one of the many barely known mountain ranges in Idaho that rise above its arid plains and catch enough moisture to sustain thick stands of timber, at least on their north slopes. That makes these mountains perfect habitat for the ruffed, blue, and spruce grouse that live in the state.

We drove up a forest road past several clearcuts to the spot where Dan had found a covey of ruffed grouse the week before. This was his spot and he was now the guide. Susie had run most of the foolishness out of her, and the instincts bred into her were finally taking over. She trotted back and forth in front of us, her nose to the ground, as we climbed up the hill through the thick forest of Douglas fir, lodgepole pine, and wild huckleberry bushes. When she stuck her head into a bramble of bushes, we heard a bird flush. Susie locked on point, her eyes filled with fire. Even as we wanted to chase the flying bird, she stayed staunch. She knew what we didn't. There was a second bird hoping to sit us out. We finally got the message and moved in to flush the tight-sitting bird. I told my son it was his to shoot, and in a flurry of whirling wings and fluttering feathers, Dan and Susie bagged their first gamebird.

Later we shared a meal of marinated grouse, thus completing the circle of a ritual as old as human existence. I had stepped back and allowed the gun and whistle to be passed to a new generation and was rewarded with a memory for the good old days.

Blue Grouse Distribution

Boundary

Bonner

Kootenai

Benewah | Shoshone

Latah

Clearwater

Nez Perce

Lewis

Idaho

Adams

Valley

Lemhi

Washington

Payette

Gem

Boise

Custer

Clark

Fremont

Canyon

Jefferson

Madison

Teton

Ada

Elmore

Butte

Bonneville

Blaine

Camas

Bingham

Gooding

Lincoln

Minidoka

Owyhee

Jerome

Power

Bannock

Caribou

Twin Falls

Cassia

Oneida

Franklin

Bear Lake

Blue Grouse

Dendragapus obscurus

FIELD FACTS

Local Names
 Sooty grouse, dusky grouse, pine grouse, "fool hen."

Size
 Adult males range from 18.5 to 22 inches in length, have 28-inch wing span, and range from 2.5 to 3 pounds in weight. Females range from 17 to 19 inches in length and average 2 pounds in weight.

Identification in Flight
 Large-sized grouse with short neck, short blunt wings, and widely fanned tail. Body is dark gray to gray-brown, breast is gray. Black tail has broad gray band along border. Flight speed is about 25 mph.

Color and Characteristics

Both sexes have long, black tails with gray tips, blue/gray breasts and feathered legs. Males have slate-colored back and flanks, white-based neck feathers around purple air sacs, and yellow/orange eye combs. Females tend to be more brown than males and have barring on the head, neck, and back. The tail's gray band may be absent on birds in the state's northern panhandle. The Pacific Coast variation of blue grouse, extending into western Washington and Oregon, has yellow/orange air sacs.

The blue grouse, *Dendragapus obscurus*, is the largest of the forest grouse. It is found throughout the state in heavily timbered areas where Douglas fir is present.

Blue grouse follow a unique migration pattern. They spend spring and summer in valleys and on lower slopes and retreat in fall to winter on high mountain ridges. Open stands of Douglas fir are essential for food and shelter in winter.

Idaho has three color phases of the Rocky Mountain population of blue grouse. The darkest phase is *Dendragapus obscurus richardsonii*, which is limited to extreme northern Idaho. It has no gray band on its black tail. Common blue grouse, *Dendragapus obscurus pallidus*, is found throughout north-central and southern Idaho. A lighter color desert race, *Dendragapus obscurus oreinus*, more common to Utah, is found in southeast Idaho north to the Bonneville County border.

Blue grouse are the most common forest grouse in southern Idaho's mountains. They represent 70 percent of the total forest grouse harvest in the state's southern half.

Season

Begins September 1 and continues to the end of the year. Aggregate bag limit can include all three forest grouse in Idaho: ruffed, blue, and spruce grouse.

Sound and Flight

Flushed blue grouse burst into flight with an explosive roar of wings. Its basic strategy is to gain momentum by flying downhill as it darts and dodges through trees to escape. Flight speed is about 25 mph. Its second escape strategy is to jump up into a tree. Like the western ruffed grouse, the blue grouse has a split personality. One day it is a typical "fool hen" perched immobile on a branch. Another day it is a blue mountain bomber that knocks your socks off when it blasts out of a woody thicket— more often then not, after you walked past it. Tuba-like "hooting" of males is heard only in spring. But for the rest of the year, blue grouse are essentially silent.

Similar Game Birds

Blue grouse and ruffed grouse territories overlap. Blue grouse have a black tail with a gray band on the border, while the body is slate-gray or gray/brown, and the breast is gray. Ruffed grouse have a reddish-brown to gray/brown body, neck feathers are black, and its flared tail has a broad black band. Spruce grouse are usually in more remote areas of mountains. The spruce grouse has a dark gray body, black breast, dark belly with white bars, and black tail.

Flock or Covey Habits

Blue grouse descend from high mountain ridges in early spring to lower slopes and valleys. Spring through late summer they prefer sparse forest edges and openings with mix of shrubs and larger trees, and sagebrush.

Inflated air sacs and flared tail courtship displays of males are similar to sage grouse and sharptails. However, blue grouse do not gather on established courting sites and males wander randomly "hooting" in search of females. Soon after hens nest, males begin uphill migration to higher elevations.

Family groups roam through summer at lower elevations until late August, when hens begin migrating to subalpine elevations. Young birds generally linger through September on lower slopes but by October they join adults along higher ridges with open Douglas fir stands.

From October through March, few blue grouse are found below 6,000 feet. Their winter range extends to just below timber line, between 8,000 and 9,000 feet.

Reproduction and Life Span

With a potential life span of 5 to 10 years, blue grouse are among the most long lived of gamebirds. Legband returns have turned up a few older birds.

Clutch size is 7 to 10 eggs, with incubation taking two to three weeks. Chicks are active at hatching and fledge, or are able to fly, in about two weeks. They are sexually active by the next breeding season.

A female blue grouse struts her stuff. The blue grouse's nickname, "fool hen," applies here. (Photo: Ken Retallic)

Feeding Habits and Patterns

Spring through fall, blue grouse feed on forbs, or flowering plants, seeds, hardwood buds, insects, fruits, and berries. Moisture is important; they stick close to riparian areas, such as creek bottoms, mountain meadows, seeps, and springs at lower elevations.

Scattered family groups feed through late morning, and rest and loaf at midday. They return to feed and water in late afternoon, and move into roosting areas before night fall.

Even in summer, blue grouse feed a little on conifer needles. When snows fall they switch almost entirely to a conifer diet supplemented with leaf buds of deciduous trees.

Preferred Habitat and Cover

In early fall, blue grouse feed heavily on berries. They continue to forage on forbs, seeds, hardwood buds and insects, but hunters should not pass up a berry patch in their search for the elusive birds.

Choice spots in northern and central Idaho are thickets heavy with purple elderberry and pale-green huckleberry. In eastern Idaho, the birds favor locales with orange mountain ashberries, purple chokecherries, pale white snowberries, and dogwood berries. Low-growing Oregon grape in grassy swales draw blue grouse, too.

The blue grouse's early autumn, mixed-forest habitat of grassy parks, shrub thickets, and aspen growths is the same as the ruffed grouse's. Hunters may encounter either species until the blues move higher into the pines. Logging clear cuts overgrown with burgeoning deciduous trees are common places where blues and ruffs cross paths. Slash piles are prime hiding places, as well.

As blues move higher through the season, mountain springs and seeps are good spots to check before dawn brightens and, again, as twilight fades to dusk.

Locating Hunting Areas

Blue grouse typically are found higher than ruffed grouse in drier areas where sagebrush meet mountain forests in southern or central Idaho. Look for feeding blue grouse on south-facing slopes in open areas where understory of trees and shrubs is sparse. They spend the night roosting in pine or fir on north sides of ridges.

In northern Idaho, the best open places to search in denser forests may be low hardwood stands filling in around timber clearcuts from previous years.

Hunting Methods

In open mixed forests, get above feeding birds and walk ridges of south-facing slopes with conifers at your back. Concentrate on park-like flats and swales in the trees along mountain foothills, and brushy draws leading to creek bottoms. Look for other water sources. Consider returning before dusk.

Abandoned forest roads and others closed to vehicle travel during hunting season let you get further back into higher—and less traveled—stands of timber.

Keep your eyes on the trees as you hike slowly and keep dogs close in blue grouse country. They hold well for pointers and close working flushing dogs. Dogs working too far ahead may make birds run or pop up into a tree.

Good luck getting one out of a tree when you spy it early in the season. The birds become more skittish as hunter numbers increase.

If you prefer to stick closer to an open road, you can save a lot of energy by reading forest travel maps carefully. Most routes up a mountain make a lot of twists and turns to the summit. Pick a likely site and check with the local IDFG office or a hunting equipment shop to see if birds are in the area. Park on a switchback and hike the slope up or down until you are ready to return to your vehicle via the road.

Keep an eye on the weather during the late season. It can snow any time of year in the Rocky Mountains.

Hunting Dogs

Blue grouse hold well for pointing dogs, and any breed is invaluable in retrieving downed birds.

Shot and Choke Suggestions
- **Shot:** No. 8 or 7 ½ shot, ⅞ to 1¼ oz.
- **Chokes:** Full or improved.

Field Preparation and Table Fare
    A white-meat gamebird, such as ruffed and blue grouse, rank high on the menu of early autumn hunters. Its eating quality is tainted in late fall and winter when it switches to a conifer diet. Field dress and cool quickly in warm weather.

Franklin's (Spruce) Grouse Distribution

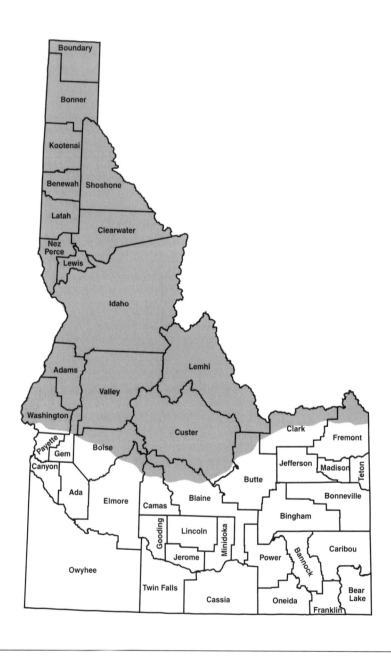

Franklin's Grouse

Dendragapus canadensis franklinii

FIELD FACTS

Local Names
Spruce grouse, black grouse, Canada grouse, "fool hen."

Size
Adult males range from 15 to 17 inches in length, have a 24-inch wing span, and range from 1.25 to 1.5 pounds in weight. Females are slightly smaller.

Identification in Flight
Medium-sized grouse with short neck, short blunt wings and widely fanned black tail. Body is dark gray, breast is black, dark belly has white bars. Flight speed is about 25 mph.

- Franklin's grouse, *Dendragapus canadensis franklinii*, is a subspecies of the spruce grouse, *Dendragapus canadensis*. It is sparsely distributed in remote pockets of Idaho's alpine conifer forests in the Payette and Salmon river drainages and north to Canada border.
- Spruce grouse are common to the north woods of Canada and Alaska. Idaho's population of Franklin's grouse is the southernmost extent of its Rocky Mountain range.
- Of the three Western forest grouse, the spruce grouse justifiably deserves its "fool hen" pseudonym. It shows little fear of humans and presents less sport than a pen-reared pheasant.
- Remote distribution and poor table quality in late season contribute to light harvest. Spruce grouse equal less than 10 percent of forest grouse taken by Idaho hunters.
- Season: Begins September 1 and continues to end of year. Aggregate bag limit can include all three forest grouse in Idaho: ruffed, blue, and spruce grouse.

Color and Characteristics
Males have a mottled dark gray body, red eye combs on the head, dark throat and breast, and white barring on lower flanks. Franklin's grouse has white spots on its upper tail coverts and lacks the rusty tip on the black tail of a common spruce grouse. The female's body may be rusty or gray and has barring similar to a blue grouse hen, but smaller.

Sound and Flight

When it can be kicked into the air, a spruce grouse flushes like other forest grouse with a roar of wings as it darts for the nearest cover. Its flight pattern is much like that of a blue grouse

Spruce grouse routinely show no indication that they fear man or beast. Birds in trees sit tight, confident they are safe. Birds on a trail or road may peck your boot toes, especially in spring when males are defending territories.

Similar Game Birds

Spruce and blue grouse territories overlap. The blue grouse's body is slate-gray or gray/brown, breast is gray, and the dark tail has a gray border. Spruce grouse have a dark gray body, black breast, dark belly with white bars, and black tail.

Flock or Covey Habits

Spruce grouse remain at higher elevations and in thicker forest stands of their home range than blue grouse. They do not migrate down mountains in spring.

Courtship display is quite different from other grouse. Males fly from tree to tree, pausing in flight to make a whirring noise by fluttering their wings.

Family groups stick together through summer into fall. Winter snows often scatter birds to treetops, where they remain inactive through most of the day.

Reproduction and Life Span

Spruce grouse have a potential life span of 5 to 7 years. Clutch size of hen is 10 to 12 eggs. Incubation takes two weeks or less. Chicks are active at hatching and fledge, or are able to fly, in about two weeks. They are sexually active by next breeding season.

Feeding Habits and Patterns

Spruce grouse continue to feed heavily on spruce and pine buds through spring. Its summer diet includes leaves of forbs or flowing plants, insects, seeds, fruits, and berries, as well as some conifer needles toward fall. Birds are almost totally dependent on evergreens for food in winter, primarily lodgepole pine.

Preferred Habitat and Cover

Spruce grouse are found in remote areas of the state's old-growth forests and wilderness areas, from the northern border south to the Salmon and Payette drainages.

Home ranges may overlap those of the blue grouse, but they are usually higher or further back in pines, spruces, and firs.

Hunting Methods

Limited sporting qualities entice few shotgunners. Still, spruce grouse often end up in the dutch ovens of big game hunters and back country hikers.

Hunting strategies are similar to those used for blue grouse.

Hunting Dogs

Spruce grouse hold for pointers and close working flushing dogs, but just as often they may hop up into trees.

Shot and Choke Suggestions

- **Shot:** No. 8 or 7½ shot, ⅞ to 1¼ oz.
- **Chokes:** Full or improved.

Field Preparation and Table Fare

Early season birds are welcome additions to standard camp fare. But, because of their conifer diet, spruce grouse are placed lower on a gamebird menu.

California Quail Distribution

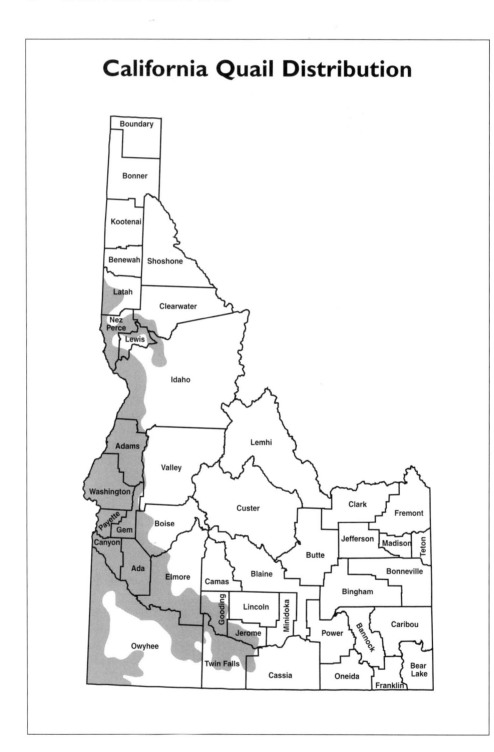

California Quail
Callipepla californica

FIELD FACTS

Local Names
Valley quail, blue quail, crested quail

Size
Average-sized quail: 9.5 to 11 inches in length; 6 to 7 ounces in weight.

Identification in Flight
Small plump bird with small wings and short tail. Black head and overall brown body evident, including brown belly patch.

- A West Coast import, burgeoning populations of California quail, *Callipepla californica*, are bright stars in western Idaho wingshooting options after a decade of drought. Also commonly called the valley quail, it is found below 3,500 feet in elevation in brushy cover near streams and other prime water sources from Twin Falls west to the Oregon border and north to the Palouse Prairie.
- California quail, the state bird of California, were introduced into Idaho in the 1930s.
- Season: Western Idaho season generally runs from the last week of September to the end of the year. In 1997, a bonus season was granted for the month of January.

Color and Characteristics
Both sexes have distinctive, forward-curving, teardrop-shaped head plumes or top knots, and small chubby bodies.

The male's black throat and face are bordered by white bands, and its head has a narrow, reddish-brown crown. Its upper breast is pearl gray above a scaled brown-and-white band that outlines a brown belly. Its brown flanks are streaked with white. The female is a more subdued brown overall, with white markings on flanks and scales on the lower breast, but lacking a black head and white markings.

Sound and Flight
Like all Western quail species, the trick is to get California quail to fly. Their small wings and short tails are designed for swift short flights to escape danger, but they prefer to run.

They are most often seen running through brushy cover, their distinctive plumes held erect. Some coveys may attempt to hide. When spooked, a covey flushes explosively—but not all at once and not all in the same direction. The flight pattern is low and often downslope. Flight speed is between 30 and 40 mph.

The California quail's call consists of three notes, with the middle note highest, "Chi–caa–go."

Similar Game Birds

The northern bobwhite has no head plume or topknot and a plump body that is uniformly brown with white scaled markings. The male's face has a white stripe through eyes and a white throat.

The Gambel's quail male differs from a California male by exhibiting a prominent black patch on a cream white belly and a reddish head. The Gambel's female has a cream white belly that identifies her from the California, which has a brown belly.

The mountain quail's tall, thin, slightly backward tilting head plume is distinctive in both sexes, which are similar in color: gray-blue head and breast and chestnut brown throat patch outlined in white; chestnut-brown flanks have stark, white bars trimmed in black.

Flock or Covey Habits

California quail are very gregarious. In late-fall and winter, flocks of 25 to 60 are common, some flocks may grow to 100 or more. They prefer to feed in open areas and post sentry birds, some occasionally in trees, to watch for danger.

They are essentially nonmigratory. Some flocks may roam in fall from home ranges in search of food, but an individual flock's territory is typically 100 acres or less, with a radius of about one-quarter mile.

Winter flocks begin to break up around April, when unpaired males aggressively compete for females. Paired mates from the previous spring reunite for the May nesting season.

The male guards the female during incubation and aids in brooding of chicks through spring and summer. In late-summer and early autumn, family groups begin to merge and congregate with other flocks.

At night, coveys roost in trees and shrubs 15 to 20 feet above the ground.

California quail are very adaptable. In urban areas they routinely visit parks and residential backyards and gardens.

Reproduction and Life Span

Quail are surprisingly long-lived, with a potential life span of 6 years in the wild. Like many gamebirds, however, chick mortality usually exceeds more than 60 percent. Less than 2 percent of a flock lives three to four years.

California quail lay clutches of 6 to 16 eggs. Incubation takes about two weeks. A hen will nest again if the first clutch is unsuccessful, and the male may care for the

California quail are among the most beautiful of Idaho's upland gamebirds. (Photo: Rob Thornsberry)

first brood while the hen produces a second clutch. Chicks fledge and are able to fly in about two weeks. They are sexually active by the next breeding season.

Feeding Habits and Patterns

California quail feed just after sunrise and again before dusk. They also visit nearby water sources during these periods. They loaf through midday in good cover within easy reach of water and feeding patches. Still, they are more active throughout the day than northern bobwhite, a bird of the East. Very wary birds, they are constantly alert to danger.

During spring, summer and fall, food is usually not a problem since quail feed on a variety of seeds and leafy plants, fruits, and berries, as well as cultivated grains, alfalfa, and other legumes. Insects are about 20 percent of its summer diet.

In more arid areas of their range, California quail tend to stay low near live water sources and brushy cover. They cannot handle snow very well and don't last long in regions where it accumulates.

Preferred Habitat and Cover

California quail are found mostly along water courses, such as river and creek bottoms, valleys, canyons, and draws with good brushy cover and adjacent open areas to feed. Scratching for seeds in weedy patches is the primary method of feeding as the season advances. They take advantage of succulent greens, fruits, and berries, as well as waste grains in cultivated areas while opportunities permit.

They are fairly comfortable with agricultural development and may be found where sagebrush country, riparian areas, or conservation reserve tracts meet wooded edges, ranches, and farms, in addition to rural backyards and estates, urban parks, and streamside greenbelts.

Locating Hunting Areas

On their native home ranges, California quail rarely experience snowfall or low temperatures. They have done best in lower-elevation areas of western Idaho where winters are mild. The state's most productive quail zones are in the lower Clearwater drainage, south along the Snake River and lower Salmon River, east along the Snake to Boise and Twin Falls, and south into the lower Owyhee and Bruneau drainages.

Long-term abundance of the state's California quail is dependent on available winter habitat. Dense shrub vegetation is important for roosting as well as for winter cover and escape cover throughout the year.

The state's decade-long drought caused serious population declines through the 1980s into the early 1990s. When it broke, quail numbers rebounded dramatically. A special bonus season was approved for the month of January 1997 to take advantage of unusually high quail numbers. The counties included in the bonus season were Ada, Adams, Boise, Canyon, Elmore, Gem, Owyhee, Payette, and Washington. Biologists reported seeing quail in unusual areas that meant typical habitat was getting crowded because of all the birds.

Nevertheless, annual numbers may fluctuate significantly.

Looking for Sign

Preseason scouting is the best method for finding birds before they become too spooky. It is also a good chance to help dogs work out their kinks.

Quail country often overlaps productive areas for pheasant or chukar and, occasionally, gray partridge. Obtain landowner permission to hunt ahead of time.

Good public access areas include federal range lands, national wildlife refuges and state wildlife management areas. Do not overlook the numerous islands of the lower Snake, Payette, and other rivers. Benches and foothills along the lower Snake's major impoundments, like Brownlee, also are prime quail country.

Hunting Methods

Because of their large size, coveys don't sit well for dogs when first encountered. The quail run from cover to cover, often for long distances before flushing. After the birds fly, singles and small groups of four or five sit well for pointing dogs. Some may freeze and require extra efforts to flush. Work the edges of good feeding and watering areas, as well as protective cover thickets.

Follow lower mountain drainages upstream. The birds may not run as far and generally fly downhill or to side hills when flushed.

The basic rule of quail hunting is that persistent hiking is just as important as shotgunning skills.

When you kick up birds and don't score, return later or another day.

Hunting Dogs

Close-working flushing dogs help kick up Western quail, but pointers work better on the second go-round when scattered birds of a flock sit tighter.

Shot and Choke Suggestions
- **Shot:** No. 7½ or 8, ⅞ to 1⅛ oz.
- **Choke:** Improved and improved/modified.

Field Preparation and Table Fare

Clean and cool birds as soon as possible in warm weather. California quail are excellent table fare.

Bobwhite Quail Distribution

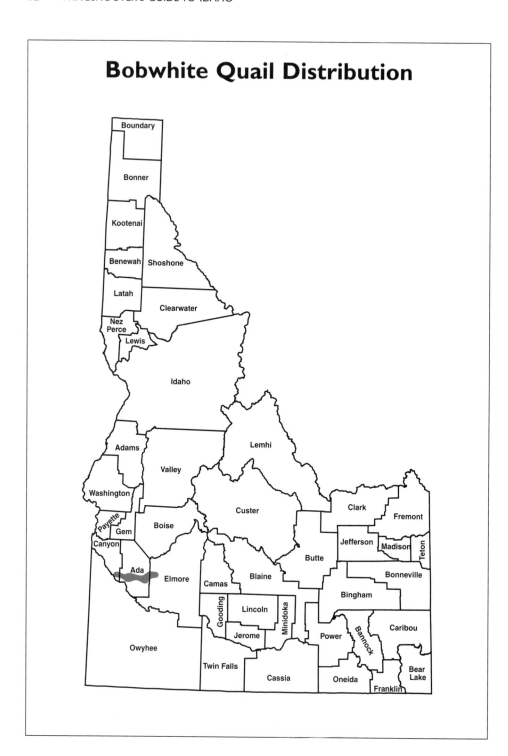

Northern Bobwhite Quail

Colinus virginianus

FIELD FACTS

Local Names
  Bobwhite

Size
  Average-size quail: 9 to 11 inches in length, 6 to 8 ounces in weight.

Identification in Flight
  Small plump bird with small wings and short tail. Body is tan to rusty-brown in appearance. Male's head has white mask and throat patch.

- The northern bobwhite quail, *Colinus virginianus*, is a distant second to California quail in shooting numbers. It was introduced into Idaho from the East in the 1880s but exists today in small, scattered populations in the Boise River Valley's farmlands. About equal in size, both California quail and bobwhite are succulent delicacies.
- Season: In western Idaho, the season runs from the last week of September to the end of year. Bag limit is included in aggregate with California quail.

Color and Characteristics

A small, chunky bird with mottled reddish brown body, scaled markings on breast and lower flanks, and short gray tail. Throat and eye stripe are white on male, buffy tan on female. Juvenile is smaller and duller in coloration.

Sound and Flight

The bobwhite's small wings and short tails are designed for swift short flights to escape danger. Coveys rarely attempt to run from danger and sit tight for pointing dogs. When flushed, a flock's rise is explosive, in unison with a whirling roar of wings as birds scatter in all directions. Flight speed is 35 to 50 mph.

Familiar rising "bob-bob-white" call is heard during spring mating season. Whistled "hoy" or "quoi-hee" covey call is heard year-round as flocks regroup.

Similar Game Birds

Both sexes of California quail have distinctive, forward curving teardrop shaped head plumes or topknots. The male's black throat and face are bordered by white bands, and the upper breast is pearl gray above a scaled brown and white band that outlines the brown belly. The female is a more subdued brown overall, with white markings on flanks and scales on the lower breast, but lacks the black head and white markings. The head plume and brown belly patch distinguishes it from the bobwhite hen.

Flock or Covey Habits

Northern bobwhites feed and roost in small flocks year-round except during nesting season. At night, a covey roosts on the ground in a tight circle with tails in and heads pointing out. This tactic helps birds conserve energy in winter and permits swift escape when endangered.

Through summer covey size is generally 12 or less. Autumn and winter congregations may number 25 to 30.

Flocks break up during spring courting season when males establish individual territories and aggressively call for mates. Both birds share incubation during the May nesting season. The male stays with its family group through summer, fall, and winter.

Reproduction and Life Span

Bobwhite quail have a potential life span of 4 to 5 years but rarely attain it. Chick mortality is high, up to 80 percent or more in some years, and the annual mortality for the entire covey can be 70 percent or higher.

Clutch size is 12 to 14 eggs and a two-week incubation is shared by both mates. A hen will renest if first clutch is lost, but rarely produces a second brood like California quail. Chicks are able to fly in about two weeks. They are sexually mature by the next breeding season.

Feeding Habits and Patterns

Bobwhites are basically vegetarians but also feed on insects and snails. Favored foods are leaves, buds, seeds, fruits, and berries, as well as cultivated crops as they become available through the seasons.

Like other gamebirds, bobwhites are most active shortly after dawn and again before dusk when they feed in open fields and weedy patches. They need to drink often and stick close to good water sources like streams, creeks, spring seeps, swamps, and cattle stock tanks.

They feed fast and often return to their loafing areas by late morning. They may hole up in cover earlier in morning on rainy days.

Preferred Habitat and Cover

Bobwhites prefer abandoned farms, fence lines, or weed-edged crop fields, overgrown pastures, weedy fields with shrub thickets, brushy creek bottoms, and edges of open woodlands. Hedgerows and shelterbelts encourage bobwhites to stick around farms.

Each covey's home range is small, about 100 acres or less, and the birds rarely wander far. Quail live in the same places year after year and usually have the same feeding areas and escape routes.

When they are not hunted, bobwhites can be quite tame and feed near houses.

Adequate winter cover and food sources are primary limiting factors of bobwhite distribution in Idaho.

Bobwhites were first introduced into the state in 1877 near Boise. Other transplants have been attempted but the only populations today are found in the general area of the Boise River Valley. They are hardy birds but vulnerable to long, cold winters, and even more vulnerable to deep snows. It is doubtful bobwhites will ever be successful gamebirds elsewhere in the state.

Locating Hunting Areas

Due to the localized nature of bobwhite populations, it is best for newcomers to make inquiries as to the bird's whereabouts at gun shops or offices of state wildlife management areas and federal wildlife refuges. The best quail country is in the Boise Valley's agriculture belt, so landowner permission to hunt is required. Make preseason scouts and obtain permission before scheduling hunts.

Hunting Methods

Few bobwhite hunters go afield without a dog. Bobwhites hold well for pointers and setters and allow hunters to approach closely before flushing wildly.

Bobwhites are a challenging shot. Focus on a single bird during the rise and let it settle into its straight away flight before shooting. Never flock shoot.

Flocks sometimes scatter widely, but single birds don't stray far after landing. But remember to keep your gun loaded and be prepared for staggered rises in case the covey was scattered when first flushed.

Dogs should work close in dense cover and should be directed to all shrub thickets, field edges, fence lines, shelter belts, grassy waterways, and weed-lined field roads. Remember to hunt the dogs, not the cover. When they start getting "birdy," move in closer. Hunt into the wind to give dogs better scenting advantages.

Bobwhites can be found without a dog, but it is harder work for decidedly fewer birds. Use the surround method by converging on good cover but remain continually aware of placement of other members in party. Another option is to crisscross fields or concentrate on edges of adjoining habitats. After birds are flushed, mark landing sites and hunt up the singles or pairs.

Hunting Dogs

The thrill of flushing a full covey of bobwhites rates it as a pointer or setter hunter's dream bird. Retrievers and flushing dogs also are effective in finding birds and kicking them out of thick brushy cover and wooded riparian areas. All breeds are very helpful in locating downed birds.

Shot and Choke Suggestions
- **Shot:** 7½ and 8 shot, ⅞ to 1⅛ oz.
- **Choke:** Improved and improved/modified.

Field Preparation and Table Fare

The bobwhite ranks at the top of the upland gamebird menu. Quail should be field dressed and cooled immediately.

Mountain Quail

Oreortyx pictus

Idaho's sole native quail species, the mountain quail, *Oreortyx pictus*, exists today in small scattered populations in the state's west-central river canyons. A protected species, it cannot be hunted. This is unfortunate because this largest of the quail species is a gamebird unique to the West. Other states that have limited hunting seasons are California, Nevada, Oregon, and Washington.

Mountain quail are birds of the high country, found at elevations of 2,000 to 10,000 feet. They favor dense mountain brush, the edges of conifer forests, and mountain meadows. More so than other quail species, they are heavily dependent on dense riparian vegetation during all phases of their lives.

Mountain quail winter at lower elevations and migrate back to the high country in spring. They are reluctant to fly and most often escape danger by running uphill. Flocks rarely number more than 20.

Dramatic declines in numbers and distribution have occurred in Idaho over the past 30 years. Remnant populations are found in the lower Little Salmon and Salmon River watersheds and in Hells Canyon of the Snake River. Sightings also are reported along the Boise River in Elmore and Owyhee counties. Its home range once extended north to the open ridges of the Clearwater River, and east along the Snake River Plain to Twin Falls and Shoshone.

Reduction of riparian habitat and loss of fruit-bearing shrubs in formerly occupied sites seem to be major causes of mountain quail declines in Idaho. Dams and impoundments on the Snake resulted in loss of important wintering areas. Other contributing factors include increased agricultural development and deterioration of riparian habitats caused by livestock grazing and possibly fire.

The state's mountain quail hunting season was closed in 1984. IDFG will continue to prohibit hunting until more information on the bird's status, distribution, and habitat requirements is obtained.

Hunters are asked to report sightings of any mountain quail to the nearest IDFG office.

Gambel's Quail

Callipepla gambelii

The Gambel's quail, *Callipepla gambelii*, is a protected gamebird in Idaho. No harvest is permitted.

Imported from the Southwest, it is found in Idaho only near the town of Salmon in the Lemhi Valley. It was first introduced in 1917 but its range never spread. A hunting season was closed in 1980 because of concerns over low populations. No other quail species occurs in the region.

The Gambel's quail is sometimes called the desert quail due to its preferred desert habitat in brush thickets close to water. It is also found in Arizona, New Mexico, California, Colorado, Hawaii, Nevada, Texas, and Utah.

The Gambel's quail is similar in appearance to the slightly smaller California quail. Both sexes exhibit forward sloping teardrop-shaped plumes. The Gambel's male differs from California male by exhibiting a prominent black patch on a cream white belly and a reddish head top. The Gambel's female has a cream-white belly which identifies her from the California, which has a brown belly. Their call is similar to the California quail's "chi–caa–go."

Chukar Partridge Distribution

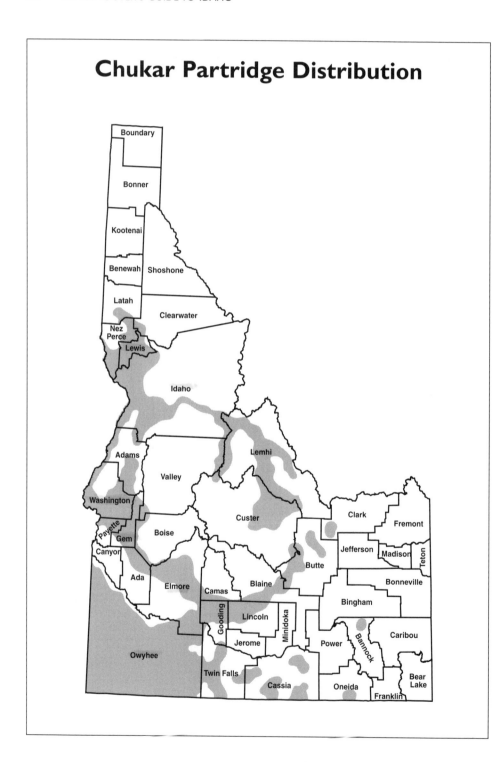

Chukar Partridge
Alectoris chukar

FIELD FACTS

Local Names
Rock partridge, red-legged partridge, "devil bird."

Size
Midway between quail and grouse in size, both sexes range from 13 to 15 inches in length; adult males average 19.6 ounces in weight and adult females average 15.7 ounces.

Identification in Flight
Small chunky quail-like bird with gray/brown body, short neck, wings and tail. Flanks have distinctive black-trimmed white bars; lower face and throat are white.

- Chukars defy Rudyard Kipling's axiom that "East is east, and West is west, and the Twain shall never meet." Imported from Asia, chukars occupy a previously empty niche in some of the most remote, untamed territory of the western United States.
- Often called "devil birds," they defy all concepts of bird hunting that most Eastern U.S. hunters might harbor. And given the gawd-awful terrain they tauntingly scurry about, chukars challenge the stamina of the toughest of Western hunters and dogs.
- Tough-as-nails hunters should remember to be merciful to their dogs. The almost mandatory need of one is acknowledged. "Watch him, though, because chukar country, like Old Texas, is great for men and horses, but hell on women and dogs," says Steve Smith, former editor of Gun Dog magazine.
- Chukars populate the arid rocky canyons of the state's southwestern and south-central rivers. They are present but less common in eastern Idaho. Hot spots are the lower Salmon River and lower Snake River drainages, and the high desert drainages of the Owyhee Mountains in the state's southwest corner.
- Idaho chukars are lightly harvested: 70,000 to 80,000 per year compared to about 200,000 forest grouse and 300,000 ducks.
- Season: Last week of September through December 31 in western Idaho. The eastern Idaho season starts at the same time but ends in mid-December.

Chukar partridge. (Photo: Blanche Johnson)

Color and Characteristics

Both sexes are identical in appearance with white cheeks and throat separated from the breast by a necklace of black that passes through their eyes. Adults are grayish brown to olive above, grading to gray on breast. Sides are buff with conspicuous black and white/tan vertical stripes. Bill, legs, and feet are red. Juvenile colors are more subdued—throat a buff-white and flanks lack vertical bars.

Sound and Flight

Approached from below, chukars prefer to run uphill. When flushed, they fly downhill or to canyon sides. Flight is strong and swift for short distances, and like western quail, flushing rise is not all at once. The downhill flight of the bird is a challenging shot for most hunters used to upward rises of other gamebirds and waterfowl.

Incessant covey chatter of chukars is a series of rapid "chuck chuck chuck" calls. Alarm call is shrill "whitoo."

Similar Game Birds

Both sexes of California quail have distinctive forward curving teardrop shaped head plumes or topknots. White bands border male's black throat and face, and head has reddish/brown crown. Female is subdued brown/tan overall. Brown belly patch of both sexes is evident.

Flock or Covey Habits

Chukars are very gregarious. Flock sizes range from a half-dozen to 60 or more. In periods of extreme dryness, flocks around a water source can grow to 300 or 400.

Brandon Loomis takes a break above the Owyhee River with Finnigan and Jenny. Chukar hunting in the Owyhees is not for the weak of heart or lung. Expect sore legs, blistered feet, and perhaps a few birds for your effort during a typical chukar hunt. (Photo: Rob Thornberry)

Pairing begins in February as males aggressively compete for mates. By the end of March, flocks begin to break up as pairs seek separate territories for late April nesting season. Males stick around hens a short while at start of incubation but soon drift off to form bachelor bands. They later return to help raise broods.

Flock sizes through summer and autumn vary with availability of water. Congregations increase in size in dry spells around open water, and birds often migrate downhill to river and creek bottoms. Winter snows also drive birds downhill or to south-facing wind-blown slopes and ridges.

An English setter points a chukar partridge for a lucky hunter.
(Photo: Ron Spomer)

Reproduction and Life Span

Chukars have a potential life span of 5 to 7 years. Chick mortality is high but, given their sparse environment, adult predation is likely not as high as for other gamebirds. Availability of water and winter cover and food are primary limiting factors. Populations flourish after series of mild, wet years.

Clutch size is 10 to 22 eggs incubated about two weeks by hen alone. She will nest again if first clutch is lost but raises only one brood per season. Chicks are active from birth. They fledge and are able to fly short distances in about two weeks. They are sexually mature by the next breeding season.

Feeding Habits and Patterns

Chukars feed mainly on seeds and leaves of weeds, but also feed on flowering buds of forbs and shrubs, fruits and berries, and bulbs and shoots. In cultivated areas, they feed on waste grains. As with all gamebirds, insects and other invertebrates are important sources of protein for chicks and adults.

Coveys and family groups roost on the ground under shrubs or in rocky outcrops at night. They fly or walk downhill in early morning to feed and water. Continuing to feed, they walk back to roosting and loafing sites by midday. Before dusk they descend downhill again to eat and drink. In sheer-walled gorges like Hells Canyon of the Snake River and the lower Salmon River, the birds don't have much room to maneuver except where there are broad river benches. Their other option is to fly to the other side—and they do, both to feed and when spooked by booming gunfire echoing off canyon walls.

Availability of water determines flock locations and sizes. In wet periods, chukars remain scattered higher in foothills and upper canyons because water is available in pools and seeps. The normal course is that in late summer and early fall dry weather drives them downhill to live water of rivers and creeks. But, when they occur, autumn rains permit the birds to scatter uphill again. Usually, several family groups continue to feed together in the vicinity of water sources.

In snow-covered areas, chukars are more willing to scratch for feed than California quail, but soon move to wind-blown slopes and ridges. They do not do well in periods of prolonged snows, nor in areas above 5,000 feet.

Preferred Habitat and Cover

Chukar country looks desolate and barren to the uneducated eye. Tough birds for a tough country, they do well in regions with cheatgrass, bunchgrass, and sagebrush. They like rocky outcroppings, cliffs, and bluffs with brushy stream bottoms and swales.

Chukars were first introduced into Idaho in Nez Perce County in 1933. Later releases succeeded in establishing the exotic gamebird in the state's remaining suitable habitat by 1957. Today, chukars occur in 25 of the state's 44 counties, primarily in its north-central, south-central, and southwestern river drainages

Unfortunately, they have done the best in areas where exotic annual plant species, such as cheatgrass and Russian thistle, have replaced native perennial grasses, forbs, and sagebrush. Throughout the West dramatic changes in vegetation have occurred due to invasions of non-native grasses and weeds that followed pioneers west and now are taking advantage of disruptions caused by wildfires and over grazing by livestock.

Natives of the Asia Minor and Himalayan foothills, chukars embraced their new home in the rugged Basin and Range region of southern Idaho, Oregon, Nevada, and

After a tough day chasing chukars, a hunter and his German shorthair enjoy a rest. Idaho's chukar hunting is physically grueling, but the rewards, as evidenced here, make the effort worthwhile. (Photo: Ron Spomer)

Utah. Steep, rocky canyons with perennial springs, seeps and streams, grasses and scattered shrubs provide prime habitat. South-facing slopes and ridges that stay relatively free of snow in winter are important, and in this mountainous terrain there are plenty of them.

Locating Hunting Areas

The arid rocky country preferred by chukars is well defined by distribution maps provided by IDFG. A bigger question is whether the annual population count justifies efforts to pursue the birds in remote desolate areas. Check with regional IDFG offices and local hunting equipment shops before going afield. Obtain specific directions.

Some locations are annual favorites: the lower Snake and Salmon canyons, the benches and foothills along Brownlee and Oxbow reservoirs upstream from Hells Canyon of the Snake, the Owyhee desert southwest of Boise, and the Bruneau and Jarbridge drainages southwest of Mountain Home and Twin Falls. The upper Salmon and lower Clearwater drainages also typically hold good populations.

Vehicle travel is limited or bordering on the impossible in many parts of these drainages. Do not go afield without good maps, a solid well-equipped vehicle, a full load of camping supplies, and extra gasoline and water. There are no convenience stores or crossroads service stations in chukar country. "Chukars are where people aren't," one friend notes.

A uniquely Idaho option is a cast-and-blast float down Hells Canyon of the Snake or through the lower Salmon gorge. The cast part is fishing for sea-running steelhead returning to their spawning waters. Outfitters in Riggins, Grangeville, Lewiston, Boise, and Weiser specialize in cast-and-blast trips through the mile-deep canyons. The general course of action is to fish in the morning and hunt in the afternoon. Some outfitters offer jet boat packages, others specialize in float boating and fly-casting. The float boats even have foot warmers in late-season.

Bass boat anglers work the coves and bays of Brownlee and Oxbow reservoirs for their own version of cast-and-blast, which can include waterfowl. Remember, though, it is illegal to shoot gamebirds or waterfowl from a moving motorized boat.

Looking for Sign

Standard chukar hunting is by sight and sound. Keep moving until you hear or kick up birds.

Hunting Methods

Rule No. 1 in hunting chukar country is to bring a dog. Rule No. 2 is be in shape, up to the physical challenge. Rule No. 3 is plan ahead. Discuss hiking routes—high, middle and low—with your hunting partners and stick to the plan when working canyon rims, slopes, and creek bottoms. Take turns hunting different levels of canyons.

Conserve energy by proceeding horizontally along sides of canyons slopes or foothill ridges, rather than hiking from top to bottom. Pointers and setters are more efficient than retrievers or slow-working flushing dogs. All breeds help in locating downed birds.

Chukars can be slow to flush. Their first choice is to run uphill. Hunters with dogs should approach from below and move birds into situations where shooting locations are more productive.

Hunters without dogs have to approach chukars from above to get them to fly— and this is where planning is important. Downslope partners get the better shots.

If birds hold after being located, allow time for partners to move into shooting positions. Flushed chukars often stay within sight or sound but, given the rugged terrain, are difficult to hunt down. It is frustrating or fun depending on your point of view—and stamina.

When looking for loafing birds in midday concentrate on low shrub thickets or rocky outcrops on steep, barren ridges.

Hunting Dogs

Because of the rugged, broad expanses they work so hard, many Western hunters sometimes overlook the value of pointers and setters; however, pointer hunters often comment on the strong scent chukars leave for dogs. They maintain their dogs provide better opportunities for hunters to get set up for a shot in tough situations.

Nevertheless, retrievers are more common in the West because they perform double duty—retrieving waterfowl and flushing upland gamebirds. Some hunters also are concerned about the presence of rattlesnakes and don't want to risk harm to valuable dogs.

Bigger problems in chukar country, and much of sage grouse environs, are cheatgrass, lava rock, and lack of water. The barbed awls of cheatgrass are as insidious as porcupine quills. Prickly pear is prevalent, too. Lava rock rips the foot pads of unprotected dog feet. Foot booties help remedy that problem. Periodic halts to check dogs for barbs and to give them a drink and rest help solve the other two. As for the snakes, they'll get out of the way or the dogs will stay far enough away.

A friend once said he preferred to go chukar hunting after a snow because it protected his dog's feet in lava flows. The next year he went hunting in dry weather and pushed his dog just as hard. Back in camp, he had to resort to wrapping the dog's feet with his own socks.

Shot and Choke Suggestions

- **Shot:** No. 6 or 7½.
- **Choke:** Improved and improved/modified.

Given the terrain, a lightweight gun like a double that shoots tight is best. Remember, shoot low.

Float boat and jetboat hunters should think twice about taking their best guns.

Field Preparation and Table Fare

Chukar rank high with a dedicated cohort of hunters as sporting trophies and excellent table fare. They are tender and juicy. Field dress and cool immediately in warm weather. Body cavities can be packed with snow in late season.

Owyhee County: Chukar Heaven and Hunter's Hell

By Rocky Barker

Idaho's crowning grace is its spacious inheritance of mountains and forests still wild and untrammeled. But secluded, arid Owyhee County makes the rest of the state's wilderness seem as tame as Central Park.

The Owyhee Mountains unfold over 11,000 square miles of dusty sagebrush desert, rumpled lava flows that gave birth to the Snake River Plain, and sculptured craggy sandstone outcroppings eroded by eons of relentless winds. The Owyhees are big, wide open, and virtually untracked by human interlopers.

Chukars love this sort of desolate isolation. They've found a home where many native gamebirds fear to tread. Their nasty fascination with galloping up and down steep, rocky terrain forces hunters and dogs in pursuit to become mountain goats to get within range.

It's a role Susie, my Brittany spaniel, takes to like Brando to Don Corleone. I, alas, perform like Jim Carrey trying to play Hamlet.

Our introduction to the Owyhees began with the Bruneau River, an idyllic desert stream meandering through a deep canyon carved into the ancient lava flows. East and west of the canyon, miles and miles of hot, brown desert present a sense of nothingness as far as the eye can see. Walk to its rim, though, and rich, green shrubbery borders an iridescent ribbon of liquid silver 300 feet below.

A faint trail led us down the sheer wall of the rocky canyon. Just below the point where the morning sun no longer filled my eyes, Susie picked up a strong scent and worked her way across the cliff to a towering rock outcropping. Before we were ready, the covey exploded down the canyon and landed by the river. It was an easy trip by air but definitely not by land. I lost the trail—fortunately not my wits—as we scrambled down the steep rock-strewn slope.

The starkly colored birds were easy to see scampering along the riverbank. Their boisterous clucking echoed through the still morning air. Such a sight would raise anyone's hopes for some quick action once back on flat land.

My optimism evaporated when we reached the bottom and tried to sneak into position. The seemingly lackadaisical chukars executed an about-face and chortled demonically as they trotted back up the cliff. I had no hope of safely matching their pace, even on a level track. But Susie was up to the challenge. She took pursuit as soon as we reached their landing point, although by that time her quarry was half way up the canyon. Not to be outdone, I labored uphill —only to be foiled again. Before we were remotely in range, the devilish birds bolted into the air near the canyon rim several hundred yards away.

A hunter and his springer spaniel struggle up a steep Idaho slope.
Chukar are the quarry. (Photo: Ron Spomer)

Susie was enjoying the brutal tag game, but I am built for comfort, not for rock climbing. Return to fight another day, I decided.

Like the Sirens of Homer's Odyssey, the chukars' song often lures me back to their rocky haunts, perhaps to my inevitable destruction. Their music and enticing ways are too much to bear and I keep returning for the lung-burning, leg-popping chase.

I don't exaggerate when I say Owyhee County is a dangerous place that requires caution and care. It got its name in 1818 when Donald Mackenzie of the Hudson's Bay Company sent three Hawaiians into the unnamed watersheds south of Fort Boise to search for beaver. The three never returned, and it was presumed that they were killed by Indians. Leaders of the fur trapping expedition named the Owyhee River after them and gave it the weird spelling based on their own mispronunciation of the word Hawaii. The name stuck.

Anyone venturing into Owyhee County should have tough tires on his outfit and at least two spares. Be prepared to spend at least one night in the boonies, and tell somebody you are going so they will worry when you don't call. Top off your tank, but don't drive a rig you think might not bring you home.

A later chukar hunt with my son Dan broke the spell of these sirens of the sidehills, but not until they had nearly broken our spirit. This time we were working a canyon on the edge of Brownlee Reservoir at the top of Hells Canyon on the Snake River. We started our walk on the bottom this time and did what we knew was necessary. We climbed to the top. Susie, now an accomplished rock hound, jumped from rock to rock like a bighorn sheep, looking back at us like a kid outside the entrance to Disneyland. No matter how many birds we might find at the top, I knew this would not be my only climb of the day so I took my time. We got to the top and hiked down the canyon on deer trails until Susie again found a scent. We approached ready for shooting but the birds were surprisingly far off, nearly 75 yards away in a mat of grass spilling over the rim down to a rocky ledge. Susie locked on point. The covey flushed out of the rocks and crossed to our right as they flew downhill. Dan and I both shot and two birds fell. Susie ran to fetch one and we crawled to the other.

So much of Idaho is up and down that chukars flourish in some of the state's most scenic country. They offer such great sport that a bird hunter would be foolish to ignore these challenging partridges. But many do since only about 10,000 of the state's 50,000 small game hunters chase chukars.

Those of us who do find a good way to keep in shape, test our mettle and learn humility.

Ring-necked Pheasant Distribution

Boundary

Bonner

Kootenai

Benewah Shoshone

Latah

Nez
Perce Clearwater

Lewis

Idaho

Adams Lemhi

Valley

Washington

Payette Custer Clark

Gem Boise Fremont

Canyon Jefferson Madison

Butte Teton

Ada Bonneville

Elmore Blaine

Camas Bingham

Gooding Lincoln Minidoka

Jerome Power Caribou

Bannock

Owyhee

Twin Falls Cassia Oneida Bear
Lake

Franklin

Ring-necked Pheasant
Phasianus colchicus

FIELD FACTS

Local Names
Ringneck, Chinese pheasant

Size
Adult males range from 30 to 36 inches in length, and average 2.9 pounds in weight. Adult females range from 21 to 25 inches in length, and average 2.1 pounds.

Color and Characteristics
Long, barred tail is distinctive in both sexes. Adult male rooster, or cock, is the most colorful of gamebirds. Its flashy colors include a bright red face patch, dark green head and throat, and broad white neck ring. Body is iridescent bronze, mottled with browns, black, and golds; lower back feathers are blue/green. Hen is a buffy mottled tan overall, much smaller and duller than cock.

The ring-necked pheasant, *Phasianus colchicus*, always will be first in hearts and minds of many wingshooters; however, the popular gamebird's western U.S. history is checkered. Cherished as the state bird of South Dakota, it had little chance to gain such status in the Gem State.

Pheasants were introduced into Idaho in 1903 near Kamiah in the Clearwater River drainage. By 1930, the Asian imports were common and well established in the state's lowland agricultural belts. Idaho's "golden age" of pheasant shooting was in the 1950s into the 1960s. But with fence to fence, road to road farming practices that evolved in the 1970s, ringneck populations crashed. The double indemnity of drought and harsh winters contributed to further declines in the late 1980s. Hunter harvests deteriorated in tandem with the loss of pheasants, from a peak of 757,200 taken in 1964 to a low of 157,700 in the late 1980s. And, as Idaho's pheasants approach the next century, drastically reduced populations appear to be barely holding their own.

Periodic mild weather patterns enable localized populations to flourish, but habitat continues to be a big problem for all Idaho upland gamebirds, especially pheasants. The need for adequate escape cover during the winter is especially important for pheasants because they live in the most intensively farmed areas of the state.

Further concern is being raised over the preponderant use of insecticides and herbicides in modern agriculture. They deprive all gamebirds of crucial foods through loss of invertebrate protein and succulent broad-leaved forbs. Chicks and juveniles, especially, need these important sources of quick-growth nourishment. While poor recruitment of young birds is one recognized affect of pesticides and herbicides, there is evidence adult birds become debilitated, too. Research is continuing on the affects of different agri-chemicals and spraying regimes on gamebird populations.

Idaho Department of Fish and Game's basic management philosophy is that ring-necked pheasants cannot survive as farmland birds alone. They deserve more.

Since the mid-eighties, the department, in cooperation with landowners and local Pheasants Forever chapters, have completed more than 3,500 habitat projects to benefit gamebirds, including pheasants. Residents and landowners who know of places where the department could cost-share restoration projects to improve pheasant habitat are encouraged to contact the nearest IDFG office.

Riparian and wetland habitats near agricultural areas also are critical to pheasant survival. They are important winter cover, along with sagebrush in different locations of the state.

Fallow farmlands permitted to return to native vegetation under the federal Conservation Reserve Program have been a boon to pheasant population renewals in some areas. One of the best was in Franklin County in the state's southeast corner, and its "best kept secret" in the 1996 hunt. Still, the ultimate goal has to be permanent conservation easements open to the public like those that so greatly benefit waterfowl hunters.

Currently, wild pheasant populations are most common along southern Idaho's Snake River Plain from the Oregon border to central Idaho. Irrigated farmlands of Lincoln and Gooding counties are most often touted as pheasant hot spots. Also well recognized are the farm belts of Canyon, Ada, Gem, and Washington counties. Fewer wild birds occur in the agricultural flatlands below 5,000 feet in eastern Idaho, and below 4,000 feet in northern Idaho, from Benewah County south to Whitebird.

In the latter areas, counties south of Pocatello and around Lewiston rate a general "OK hunting" from IDFG biologists. Prospects wax and wane with weather patterns.

Continuing the wild pheasant hunt, wingshooters should not overlook the islands of the lower Snake and Payette rivers. Both options also offer good prospects for waterfowl and, depending on the location, California quail.

Southern Idaho's federal wildlife refuges provide havens for limited numbers of pheasants. But their conservation efforts are more oriented toward waterfowl production. The Curlew National Grasslands, and the Rockland-Arbon Valley, south of Pocatello are better prospects.

Annual releases of about 5,000 game farm birds are reserved for a select number of IDFG wildlife management areas open to pheasant hunting by permit only. Eastern WMAs include Mud Lake, Market Lake, and Sterling. Western WMAs include C.J. Strike, Fort Boise, the Kennedy-Keifer segment of Payette WMA, and Montour.

Ring-necked pheasant. (Photo: Ken Retallic)

The WMA pheasant program is very costly. The Idaho Fish and Game Commission increased the WMA permit fee from $1.50 to $10 in 1997. It is still an incredible bargain—10 pheasants for $10, plus a nominal permit processing fee and an upland gamebird conservation stamp.

Hunting Tips

Only cock pheasants are open to harvest. There is no season for hens. Check current regulations for bag limits and opening dates in mid-October. The northern Idaho season extends to the end of year. In southern Idaho it ends several weeks to a month earlier depending on locations.

Since most of Idaho's pheasants are found on private lands, hunters should be aware it is illegal to trespass on any cultivated lands, including irrigated pastures. Agricultural lands do not need to be posted for "No Trespassing," so it is important to get permission from landowners even if fields are unfenced or not posted.

It is best to scout pheasant hunting territories and obtain landowners permission to hunt before the season opens.

Road hunting is not proper, nor much of an option since fence lines are mostly barren of protective vegetation for the birds. The more effective option is to find feeding fields with nearby heavy roosting cover. If you confine your hunting to areas where you know the probable feeding routes and escape paths of the birds, you will do better.

Pheasants travel from roosting cover to feeding fields in early morning and again in evening. By timing it right, you can work out from these cover areas to move in behind feeding birds. Then, as your dogs flush them, they will try to fly back to cover. You may get some pass shooting that could stoke campfire tales for generations.

Walking up birds any time of day requires stealth. It is perhaps the most important weapon in a pheasant hunter's arsenal, particularly in late-season. Avoid noise, such as slamming truck doors, commands to dogs and conversation between partners. Wear clothing that blends in with the background of hunting areas.

Work the edges between feeding fields and cover—brushy field thickets and shelter belts, weedy canals and farm roads, creek bottoms and marshes, sagebrush and weedy CRP tracts. Try to approach birds from directions they are unlikely to see you, such as the upwind sections of hedges. Walk the bottoms of irrigation ditches rather than the banks to keep a low profile until you pop up at suspected locations of birds.

Disciplined, short ranging flushing dogs or retrievers are the preferred bird dogs. Pointers are sometimes inefficient since a cock's first inclination is to run or sneak away before it flushes. Keep your dogs close, within about 25 yards, but be quiet about it. Avoid hunting with partners who have to keep shouting at their dogs to come back.

Shot and Choke Suggestions

No. 6 shot is the preferred all around load. Chokes can be improved or modified in early season, or improved, modified, or full in late season.

Table Fare

Pheasant is an excellent gamebird, with light-meat breasts and medium-dark leg meat. Draw the bird as soon as possible and hang in a cool place for at least a week. This seems to reduce stringiness and add flavor. Pick or skin the bird just prior to cooking.

WMA Pheasants: Popular Program Offers 'Chicken Delight' Outings

by Rocky Barker

On a breezy autumn day, four hunters, one dog and at least a half dozen ringnecks crossed paths in a crested wheatgrass field on the Market Lake Wildlife Management Area, north of Idaho Falls.

Since these birds were game farm birds and not wild, it might appear to some that it wasn't going to be a contest. Thank God for centuries of instinct. This day, at least, the exotic Chinese roosters performed admirably.

Some hunters derisively refer to Idaho's wildlife management area pheasant program as "chicken delight" hunts. At times, especially just after the birds are released, pen-raised pheasants can be as hard to find as barnyard roosters. But the fact is, with more and more private land tied up in hunting clubs or just closed to hunting, the only places many regular Idaho hunters get a chance to hunt pheasants are on wildlife management areas. Some, like Fort Boise WMA near Parma, have excellent habitat and hold over many wild birds year after year. Others, such as Mud Lake WMA near Terreton, no longer have much good pheasant habitat and are mostly put-and-take hunting. These conclaves of upland and waterfowl hunting are too few in a state with more than 70 percent in federal and state ownership. Unfortunately for pheasant hunters, most of the pubic land is either sagebrush desert or forest.

On this day, the pheasants had already survived the first wave of hunters and reacted with the finesse of seasoned South Dakota prairie ringnecks. They ran when my dog Susie got on their trail. They held tight as Rob Thornberry, editor of *Intermountain Hunting & Fishing*, and Dean Miller, managing editor of the *Idaho Falls Post Register*, walked with Ken and me across the field. They took us through several circuits of fields before we finally got our birds.

One ringneck thought it had outfoxed us by doubling back through our picket line and then turning at a right angle to an irrigation ditch. Susie caught its scent and trailed back with me in pursuit. The pheasant exploded from the tall grass before I could turn and fire. It made a crowing flight across the field in front of each of the hunters. Ken missed. Dean missed. Feathers flew when Rob's shotgun roared.

Susie and I walked up the ditch to a dike on another canal to block the advance of running birds. Even before our drivers started their approach, Susie locked on point. I saw what she couldn't, another red-faced rooster holding

Ken Retallic hunting pheasants with Susie, a Brittany spaniel.
(Photo: Ken Retallic)

motionless under a clump of grass. Getting in position, I sent Susie forward and the bird flushed for a quick kill. Moments later another cock climbed for the clouds ahead of Ken and he dispatched it. The next bird appeared to know the score and stayed on the ground, running over the levee and past both Susie and me. The final pheasant caught Dean off guard as it flew back over his shoulder. Rob's steady hand brought his bead down perfectly on the long shot that ended his day with a limit.

Tired and dusty, we gathered at the small parking lot at sunset to quaff some of Dean's home-brewed ale. Susie got a well-deserved drink of water.

Gray (Hungarian) Partridge Distribution

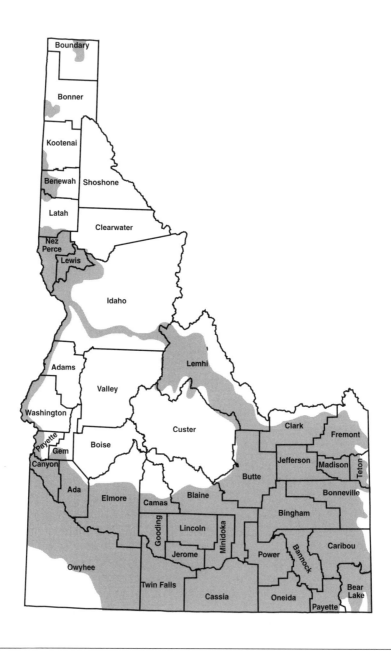

Gray Partridge
Perdix perdix

FIELD FACTS

Local Names
Hungarian partridge, Hun

Size
Adult gray partridge range from 12 to 13 inches in length and average 14 ounces in weight.

Color and Characteristics
Both sexes are similar in coloration. Adults have cinnamon colored heads, gray flanks with vertical chestnut bars, and grayish to brown backs. Brown horseshoe design on breast is more common on males, but both sexes may have it. Two central pairs of tail feathers are heavily barred, while outer feathers are rusty brown. Rufous tails are evident on gray partridges in flight.

The gray partridge, *Perdix perdix*, arrived in Idaho on its own in the early 1900s shortly after the European gamebird was released in Oregon and Washington. There is evidence it also dispersed into Idaho from Alberta, Canada.

Releases by IDFG, beginning in 1921, established gray partridge throughout the state's agricultural areas.

Gray partridge, also known as Hungarian partridge, are generally found in areas with cereal grain fields interspersed with grassy flats and woody cover. In some parts of the state, their distribution overlaps with chukars. In southern Idaho, gray partridge also are found in areas dominated by sagebrush, sometimes more than 25 miles from cultivated lands.

The state's strongest population of gray partridge is in northern Idaho. They feel right at home in the broad expanses of the Palouse Prairie's rolling wheat and seed-grass fields. Good numbers also are found in the farmlands of the lower Snake River Plain, and the grasslands and CRP fields in the state's southeast corner.

They prefer grassy areas and hay fields for nesting, but shelter belts, weedy roadsides, and ditches also are important habitat. Their diet includes cultivated grains, weed seeds, succulent greens, and insects. In winter, they roost on the ground in the open. In severe conditions they seek more protective cover. Pairing begins in January or February, but nesting does not occur until late April or early May. Broods range from 10 to 22. Family groups stick together until the next spring. Fall flocks may include two or three family groups.

Hungarian partridge in deep winter snow. (Photo: Ken Retallic)

A dwindling habitat base is the limiting factor for gray partridge populations in Idaho. The birds are losing ground to intensified agricultural practices like fall plowing, stubble and ditch burning, increased application of pesticides and herbicides, and conversion from ditch irrigation to sprinklers. Programs to enhance pheasant habitat also benefit gray partridge.

Still, IDFG biologists note that in many parts of the state gray partridge are lightly hunted and populations could accommodate heavier exploitation rates. For the most part, hunters pursuing pheasants, chukars, or sage grouse consider them a bonus.

Hunting Tips

Gray partridge share the same seasons and bag limits with chukars from the last week of September until the end of the year. They are more widely distributed across the state than their desert-loving cousins, but are most common in Idaho's agricultural valleys.

Gray partridge are tough birds and harder to bring down than chukars. They flush in unison in flocks of 10 to 15. Their rise is fast, explosive and noisy. The covey quickly builds up stream in a generally straight line until it cuts away on its escape flight. Each flock sticks together as it drops into another field. Spooked again, they continue to fly together from field to field. Eventually, they often return to their original takeoff site.

Masters of camouflage in sparse cover, Huns are difficult to approach in open ground. Work edges of grain stubble, winter wheat and alfalfa fields where they meet sagebrush or thick CRP tracts, weedy canals, brushy draws, and creek bottoms. Abandoned homesteads and old orchards surrounded by stubble or fallow fields are prime gray partridge country.

Dogs are helpful in tracking down gray partridge. Flushing dogs and retrievers work well for often widely scattered flocks, and in digging birds out of cover. A far-ranging pointer occasionally can pin down birds, but they will run from a slow-working dog. Pointers are effective in tracking down singles when flocks break up.

Suggested Chokes and Loads
- **Shot:** No. 6 or 7½.
- **Choke:** Improved and improved/modified.

Given the terrain, a lightweight gun like a double that shoots tight is best. Remember, shoot low.

Float boat and jetboat hunters should think twice about taking their best guns.

Table Fare
Gray partridge are excellent table fare—a true "bonus" to grouse, chukar, or pheasant hunting.

Dumping the Blues

Boise Foothills Huns Are the Perfect Tonic

by Rocky Barker

Moving to Boise from Idaho Falls was not easy for my family.

Both my wife, Tina, and I grew up in small towns. The biggest city we ever lived in was Idaho Falls, slightly less than 50,000 people. But even that seemed big when we first arrived. Boise, one of the fastest growing cities in the West at more than 130,000, is a sprawling metropolis complete with traffic jams, air pollution, and little of the intimacy of life in a small town. It's located, however, on the edge of the wide-open Owyhee sagebrush desert to the southwest and the imposing central Idaho wilderness to the northeast.

Hunters here tell me they used to chase pheasants just outside the city limits with the Capitol dome in clear view. But, today, subdivisions have taken away more than 30,000 acres that were farmlands less than a decade ago. Sportsmen have had to adapt and, lucky for us, much of the game has done so as well. California quail feed in my front yard and taunt my Brittany from our roof. Geese and ducks nest along the Boise River and around the many city ponds and wetlands. Best of all, gray partridge fill in the seams between rolling grasslands of the Boise foothills and the open desert. These adaptable birds, also known as Hungarian partridge, offer hunters throughout southern Idaho great sport in the ample public grasslands that lie between private farmland and sagebrush range.

I was hoping that some of that adaptability would rub off on my son David. At 17, he was having the hardest time of any of us adapting to the move. He had to leave his friends and quieter lifestyle in Idaho Falls and found the faster pace of Boise frustrating. A day of hunting, something with which he was very familiar, might help, I surmised.

We drove into the hills south of Boise no more than 10 miles from town, a place that opens into country so big that a hunter hardly knows where to start. We began at the top of a high draw and walked into the grassy canyon of a small creek. No sooner had we put our jackets on and loaded our guns than Susie, our Brittany, had flushed a covey of Huns down the draw. We called her back and headed for the birds, still tightly grouped as they landed about a quarter of a mile ahead. David had never shot a partridge and I explained how he had to pick one bird out of the flock if he hoped to be successful.

We walked into position, then sent Susie in hoping they would hold to her on point. The jittery birds didn't cooperate and took to the sky 15 yards ahead of the dog. David was ready and he put the bead of his 20-gauge on the closest

Hun and fired. It plummeted to the ground and Susie galloped into the brush in pursuit. She emerged with the partridge in her mouth.

As we walked up the drainage picking up singles, David's gait was just a little more chipper. If Boise wasn't all he hoped for, at least he could get used to hunting birds that travel in coveys.

Wild Turkey Distribution

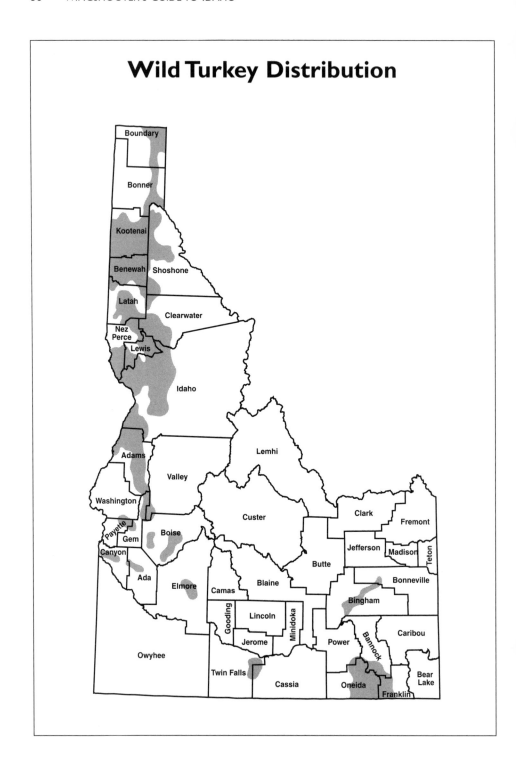

Wild Turkey

Meleagris gallopavo

FIELD FACTS

Local Names
Merriam's turkey, Rio Grande turkey, Eastern turkey, gobbler, tom

Size
Toms average 48 inches in length and weigh from 14 to 22 pounds. Hens average 34 inches in length and 9 pounds in weight.

Identification in Flight
Largest woodland gamebird in North America, the wild turkey runs first and flies as last resort. When flushed, flight is strong and direct, rising at steep angle. Birds often glide long distances.

Toms are much larger than hens. Look for male's red, white, and blue head, overall black coloration of body with iridescent bronze highlights. Long, stiff "beard" feathers on a tom's breast make it a legal gamebird. The beard is more easily seen when bird is on the ground.

- Since 1961, three turkey subspecies have been introduced to Idaho.
- A decade ago only 100 were harvested. Current spring harvest is nearly 2,000.
- Merriam's turkey, *Meleagris gallopavo merriami*, was the first subspecies released. It represents more than 90 percent of state's population. Merriam's turkey is native to mountainous woodland habitats from the Southwest to central Colorado.
- Rio Grande wild turkey, *Meleagris gallopavo intermedia*, was introduced in 1982. Rio Grande turkeys are native to riparian areas and scrub woodlands of the southern Great Plains south into northeastern Mexico. In Idaho, this subspecies has been released primarily in riparian areas adjacent to the Payette, Snake, and Weiser rivers, and tributaries of the Clearwater River.
- Eastern wild turkey, *Meleagris gallopavo silvestris*, were introduced to a few sites near Dworshak Reservoir in 1985. Eastern wild turkeys are native to deciduous forests and oak-savannah habitats common in the eastern U.S. They are 3- to 5-pounds larger than Merriam's or Rio Grande subspecies.

Color and Characteristics

Toms have series of specialized hair-like feathers, better known as the beard, extending from the breast. The beard is 3- to 10-inches long, though some gobblers have very small beards. Most toms have spurs on lower legs. A gobbler's head is devoid of hair-like feathers, and sports a bright color combination of red, white, and blue. Body feather coloration is best indicator of turkey sex; black-tipped breast feathers give the tom turkey its characteristic black, polished look. Only toms strut and gobble.

A small portion of hens have beards—regulations allow for the harvest of one bearded turkey. Hens lack spurs, and have a few scattered hair-like feathers on the head and neck. Hens are lighter in color and slimmer than toms. Breast feathers have a buff edge giving the bird its distinctive buff/brown color.

Flock or Covey Habits

Wild turkey courtship activities begin in early spring. After spending winter in common flocks, toms disperse, fight for dominance, and gobble and display to attract hens. Toms mate with as many hens as they can attract to their personal courting sites. Each tom's defended territory is about 4 to 8 acres across. Hens congregate around dominant toms.

Juvenile male turkeys, called jakes, also strut and gobble to court hens but seldom successfully mate. Some yearling hens, called jennys, mate and nest during their first nesting season.

Following mating, hens construct ground nests and lay clutches of 5 to 15 eggs. Incubation is 28 days by the hen alone. Young are able to fly and roost in trees in about four weeks.

During the incubation period a second flurry of tom activity occurs. Toms gobble and display in earnest as they attempt to fertilize unmated hens or hens that lost their first nests. This second peak of courtship activity coincides with Idaho's spring turkey hunt. Gobblers, aggressively looking for hens, readily respond to yelps of proficient callers.

Turkeys are very wary and constantly alert, on the ground and in their roosts. They have excellent hearing and eye sight. They are strong fliers but prefer to run when they sense danger. A flock of turkeys can gallop off at 20 mph if spooked.

Life Span

Average life span is 8 years. At upper end, there are records of wild turkey living 12 to 15 years.

Feeding Habitats and Patterns

Of Idaho's three subspecies, the Merriam's turkey has been the most successful. It represents more than 90 percent of the state's wild turkey population.

Merriam's turkeys are found mostly in mountainous ponderosa pine forests near good water sources. They are the tamest of the three subspecies and readily feed in agricultural areas. They occasionally interbreed with domestic turkeys.

A small Rio Grande turkey population is found primarily in lower elevation river bottoms and scrub woodlands in southern and eastern Idaho. Additional unoccupied habitat remains for continued introductions.

*The essence of spring: a camouflaged shotgun
and a turkey for the table. (Photo: Mike Lawson)*

A few sites on both sides of Dworshak Reservoir, east of Lewiston, hold the state's experimental flock of Eastern turkey. Easterns are much more wary than other subspecies and less likely to frequent human habitations. They will feed in grain stubble, but rely heavily on mast crops, such as acorns and pine seeds, for survival. Lack of available winter food may preclude their establishment in Idaho.

Wild turkeys fly off their roosts early in the morning to look for food and water. In pine country, they stick to the woods as long as the seed crop is good. If it isn't, they'll spend more time in open fields.

Midday loafing areas have a few tall trees for overhead cover and somewhat open underbrush that holds bare ground for scratching and dusting. On cool days they may sun bathe. If it is warm, they seek shade.

Feeding can start up again by early afternoon. At dusk the birds head for their roost trees. These become more dispersed in spring as winter flocks break up, and courtship and nesting begin.

Locating Hunting Areas

Wild turkey hunting in Idaho is on a roll with a string of record spring harvests.

Relatively mild winters and good production of young has allowed wild turkey numbers to expand in Idaho. The other key factor is IDFG's 15-year program to transplant turkeys into suitable but empty habitat. It moves birds to new areas when individual populations build to a point that allows capture and transplant. It also trades Idaho wildlife to other states to bring in hundreds of new birds. The Idaho Chapter of the National Wild Turkey Federation contributes funding and volunteer help to the state's turkey relocation program.

The payoff shows in hunt statistics: Harvest statewide went from 73 birds in 1985 to 1,526 in 1995, and almost 2,000 in 1996. Hunter numbers have increased dramatically during the same period to more than 7,875 in 1996.

The department's Clearwater Region continues to offer the best hunting with more than 825 turkeys taken some years, followed by the Southwest Region at approximately 385 and the Panhandle Region with about 290.

Much smaller populations along the Snake River between Idaho Falls and American Falls and along the state border south of Pocatello are regulated as controlled hunts units. Turkey hunting units are the same units used for management of big game hunting.

Idaho offers only a spring turkey hunt. It extends from mid-April to early May with a one-bird bag limit. The general hunting season is open to all hunters with a turkey stamp in units not regulated by controlled hunt permits. Hunters with controlled hunt permits can hunt only in specific units on dates designated by their permits.

Applications for about 470 controlled hunt permits are due between Jan. 15 and Feb. 15. The permits are issued in a drawing similar to a lottery.

A youth-only permit hunt is available in Unit 54, in Twin Falls and Cassia counties. In 1997, its first year, three permits were issued. The hunters, aged 12 to 14, are accompanied by IDFG mentors after taking a special hunting course.

Much of Idaho's best spring turkey range is on private lands or adjacent to it. Scout areas before the season opens and obtain permission to hunt from landowners.

General advice on the best drainages to hunt can be obtained from biologists at regional IDFG offices. The annual rules pamphlet includes a turkey distribution map.

Hunting seminars are sponsored each spring by IDFG and the National Wild Turkey Federation. Contact nearest IDFG offices for more information. An excellent free brochure that details hunting techniques and hunter safety also is available from the department. Ask for "Wild Turkey Hunting in Idaho."

Chris Lawson is all smiles after bagging a turkey. (Photo: Mike Lawson)

Looking for sign

Locating birds in the field is the key to a successful turkey hunt. Try to spend as much time as possible in planned hunting areas before the season opens to scout for birds or sign.

Wild turkey sign includes tracks and droppings. Hen tracks rarely exceed 4.5 inches. Gobblers can leave tracks up to 6 inches long. Droppings are positive evidence turkeys are in an area. Shape of droppings indicates sex of the bird. Gobblers leave J-shaped, elongated droppings. Hens leave rounded, coiled droppings.

Wild turkey are very vocal. Locate roosting sites at dawn or dusk by listening for the birds from ridge tops or along streams. Movement of feeding birds may be detected with binoculars in early morning and late afternoon.

Hunting Methods

Many hunters feel the stealth and camouflage aspects of turkey hunts are more akin to big game hunting than to upland bird hunting. Required calling skills are often compared to elk bugling.

The basic goal of the hunter is to attract a gobbler to a calling station by mimicking the sounds of an available hen. The need to wear camouflage clothing and to be well concealed can't be over emphasized. Arrive well before daybreak at your selected calling site. It should be 100 to 150 yards from a roost in a fairly open area that has a good line of sight.

Sit with your back to a wide tree. It will break up your outline and provide protection against other hunters who may mistake your calls for a turkey. Warn other hunters away from your calling site by shouting or whistling. Don't wave.

If you decide to move to a new calling site, proceed cautiously. Never wear red, white, or blue. These colors could be mistaken for a turkey's head by another hunter.

Be patient, wait for birds to come to you. Never stalk a gobbling turkey; stalking a turkey is nearly impossible. It's also dangerous, as well as unethical, since you may walk into another hunter's set-up.

Wild turkeys are tough to bring down. Call a tom to within less than 40 yards, preferably 30 to 25 yards, before shooting. Wait for it to extend its head and neck, then aim for the base of the head. Shooting for a turkey's body will only wound it because dense feathers and heavy muscles protect vital organs.

Cover a downed bird with a blanket or hunter orange wrapping when carrying it from the woods. Also cover decoys while walking to avoid confusing other hunters.

Idaho's higher elevations and vertical terrain demand more stamina of hunters than most other states.

Hunting Dogs

It is illegal to hunt turkeys with dogs in Idaho.

Shot and Choke Suggestions

A shotgun or hand-held bow are the only legal weapons for taking wild turkeys in Idaho. Lead shot cannot exceed BB size; steel shot cannot exceed T size. A 12-gauge with a full choke is recommended. Shot sizes 4, 5 or 6 are preferred because of the effective shot patterns produced.

Table Fare

Wild turkey is a delicacy as well as a trophy. Field dress a bird by opening the body cavity from just below the breast to the vent. Remove all internal organs. Don't forget the crop which may be hard to find on a fat bird. Allow blood to drain from the body cavity. Keep the bird cool and out of the sun.

Turkey Calling Basics

by Mike Lawson

Beginning turkey hunters are sometimes confused about which calls to use and when to use them. The three basic turkey calls are friction, mouth, and locator. Friction calls include box, push button, and slate or glass. The most popular mouth calls are diaphragm calls. Locator calls include owl hooters, crow calls, coyote squealers and other calls that don't make the sounds of a hen turkey. You can even use your duck or goose call as a locator call.

Box calls consist of a wooden paddle that is scraped across a wooden sound chamber. The box call is my recommendation as the best call for a beginner. It is very easy to use, and you can make all of the hen sounds as well as imitate the gobble of a tom. I rely on my box call because it carries over a long distance.

Slate calls are good for making soft calls when the gobbler starts to move in close. The slate call's sound is achieved by scraping a striker, held like a pencil, across a sheet of slate or glass. Their disadvantage is that you need both hands to use them correctly.

Push button friction calls are good because you can hold them in one hand to make all of the calls. Diaphragm calls are difficult to learn but offer the advantage of having both hands free. They are also the most versatile calls and can make all of the necessary hen sounds.

If you're really serious about turkey hunting, you'll eventually need to learn to use the diaphragm. The best way to learn is to purchase an audiotape. Keep it in your vehicle so you can practice whenever you're driving. If you start practicing around the house, I guarantee you'll make plenty of enemies.

Although you can get by with just one call, I find that some gobblers seem to like different calls. If one call doesn't work, often another will. Several years ago, I was hunting with my youngest son, Chris, in northern Idaho, and I got a gobbler to respond with a crow call, but he wouldn't answer my box call. Chris, only 13 at the time, had just learned to use a diaphragm. He couldn't wait to try his newfound skill so he gave the gobbler his best shot. The bird thundered back immediately, and Chris had his bead on him a few minutes later.

Hens yelp, cackle, cut, purr, cluck, and putt. While all these can be productive, the basic "yelp" is the sound you should use most of the time. The basic rule of thumb is to make loud excited calls to locate a gobbler and get him interested and then switch to soft yelps, purrs, and clucks as he comes in.

I believe patience, position, perseverance, and knowing when to call are as important as calling ability. In fact, some of the worst turkey calls I've ever heard were made by real hens. If I could secretly enter a live hen in a turkey-calling contest, I doubt she would win.

Wild Turkey Hunting Ethics

All ethical wild turkey hunters support a series of unwritten rules that make turkey hunting a quality experience. Following these rules will not only help maintain healthy flocks of wild turkeys in Idaho, but also add to the challenge and excitement of wild turkey hunting.

Because the spring wild turkey hunt occurs during the breeding season, it is possible you may run across a nesting hen. If this occurs, leave the area immediately and allow the hen to continue to incubate her clutch of eggs or tend her brood undisturbed.

Though legal to shoot a tom out of a roost tree, this practice is unacceptable among true sportsmen. The challenge of calling the turkey to you is the essence of the hunt. Roost shooting pales in comparison.

Depending on when and where you hunt, you may run into other turkey hunters. If you hear another hunter calling a bird, allow that hunter to continue undisturbed and leave the area.

Wild Turkey Hunting Safety Tips

Each year, other hunters in the field injure dozens of turkey hunters nationwide. Keeping these points in mind will help you have a productive and safe turkey hunt:

1. Wear hunter orange when walking to and from your calling site.
2. Never wear the colors red, white, or blue. Another hunter could mistake these colors for a turkey's head.
3. When hunting with companions, be sure of everyone's location. Remember your shooting lane.
4. Never assume you are alone in the woods.
5. Even on private land, be alert to any response to your call.
6. If you see another hunter approaching, remain still and call or whistle. Never wave, use a turkey call or stand up.
7. Never make turkey sounds to alert another hunter to your presence.
8. Be careful in using a gobbler call; other hunters may mistake you for a turkey.
9. Treat every firearm as if it were loaded.
10. Always control the muzzle of your firearm.
11. Keep your gun barrel free of debris.
12. Positively identify your target. Never shoot at movements or sounds. Never stalk a gobbling turkey. Don't ever shoot at a piece of a turkey. Observe the whole bird to determine whether it is safe and legal to shoot.
13. Don't road hunt.
14. Discuss these safety tips with your hunting companions. People in the same hunting party are often the cause of many accidents in the field.

Gobbler Fanatic: Idaho's Wild Turkeys Are Addictive

by Mike Lawson

We got up at 3:30 a.m. with turkeys on the brain. On the way to his favorite area in Missouri, Bob Lamm gave me a quick lesson in spring turkey hunting. It's been 10 years since my first hunt, but I can still remember that lesson.

It was pitch black when we got out of the truck to walk to the perfect spot. I knew the drill. I was to wait until I heard a turkey gobble, move into position and try to call the bird into shooting range. The articles I'd read made calling in a gobbler sound really difficult, so I didn't expect much. Just before dawn an owl hooted and a gobbler sounded off up the ridge. I've spent many hours hunting elk with my bow and the sound gave me the same adrenaline rush as the bugle of a bull elk.

I made my way up the ridge while the bird continued to gobble. I estimated my distance to be about 150 yards from the tom. With my back next to a large oak tree I sat and anxiously waited. The bird kept gobbling from the same spot and was actually answering my calls. I didn't have much confidence in my calling ability, so I backed off on calling as the turkey moved even closer. My heart raced when I saw his brilliant red, white and blue head bobbing above the undergrowth. It was actually happening, just like in the books.

At about 75 yards out the majestic bird stepped into the open in full strut. The big gobbler seemed to stare right through me and I didn't even dare blink. I was so transfixed that I didn't realize the turkey was closing the distance fast. In no time, he was facing me less than 20 yards away and my shotgun was still laying across my knees. As I clumsily tried to raise it, the big tom whirled, ran and flushed, creating a commotion beyond description. I watched him sail over the trees without ever firing a shot. To this day, I have never been so captivated by anything in the wild.

Since then I have killed plenty of wild turkeys. Later that year, I got my first gobbler, and I have been back to Missouri to hunt with Bob every year since. I've also killed toms throughout the West, and can now say I'm truly addicted to turkey hunting. From April 1 until mid-May, I can hardly think of anything else.

The real challenge of the sport is hunting for gobblers in spring seasons like Idaho's with a shotgun or bow. I'm thankful Idaho doesn't allow a fall season and does not allow turkey hunting with rifles. In other states that allow hunting turkeys with rifles, most of the turkeys killed during fall season are shot by deer hunters who stumble onto them.

In the spring, the toms try to attract the hens for breeding by displaying and vocalizing. The hunting is difficult because the hens go to the toms. Big gobblers do not expect to have to go find a hen. The challenge is to sound like a reluctant hen that is anxious to mate, but can't get up the courage to approach the gobbler. Calling too often or too loudly are the most common mistakes.

After you have decided on an area to hunt, you should start scouting. The best way to scout is to spend as much time as possible in likely spots before the season opens, scouting for birds or sign. But that isn't always possible for those of us who live far away from the hunting grounds. I am limited to doing my scouting after I arrive at the hunting area.

I've had my best success locating birds during the evening hours. Turkeys are very vocal and will usually start talking when it's time to roost. The hens make a yelping sound that doesn't carry over long distances but the gobble made by a tom can carry all the way across a deep canyon. Just before dusk, I like to find a good ridge or draw where I can sit and listen.

If you locate a roosting area, plan your attack for early the next morning. But don't count on bringing home Thanksgiving dinner just because you're lucky enough to get close to a roosted bird. Whatever can go wrong usually will.

The closer you can get the better. But if you get too close, you'll scare off your prize before he even gets out of his roost. I like to move within 100 yards if possible. The trick is to decide where the tom will go after he flies down from his roost. He will normally want to be out in the open so he can strut for his hens.

Turkeys have exceptional vision and hearing. They can see the slightest movement at 100 yards and can pinpoint sound at great distances. Learning to make the sounds of a reluctant hen who is intent on breeding is important, but there are other considerations that can make the difference between success and failure.

Knowing when to call is essential. You should call just enough to keep the gobbler interested and frustrated enough to investigate. Too much loud calling can convince the tom to stay where he is. Position is equally critical. Turkeys don't like to go through or fly over obstructions. A mesh fence, deep ravine, or dense brush will often hang up a tom until he loses interest and leaves.

Even after these considerations, deciding where to set up still requires a little guesswork. If the gobbler is alone, he is likely to come to you no matter where you are. If there are hens nearby, he'll probably go with them even if you are a world champion turkey caller.

If your roosted tom has hens, you'll soon know it. They will start yelping before they fly down from their roosts and continue once they are on the ground. If you hear other hens yelping, you'll need to get aggressive with your own calling to compete. There is always a chance your calling will be the first choice for the tom. The problem is the other hens won't remain stationary.

When the the tense moments are over, perhaps you, too, will carry out a big tom. (Photo: Mike Lawson)

Once the gobbler gets on the ground and starts gobbling and strutting, the hens will head straight for him.

A couple of years ago, I thought I was set up perfectly on a monster tom. But he had hens flocking to him from all over as soon as he got down out of the roost and went into his act. There were hens running up the side of his ridge and flying over to him from the other side. My only choice was to sit and enjoy the spectacle from 75 yards away.

If you're lucky enough to get a roosted gobbler interested, try not to call too much. Once the bird has heard you call, he knows exactly where you are. However, he might need to be reassured to keep his interest up. Once he starts moving your way, you should switch from yelps and cackles to some soft clucks and purrs. The turkey is doing exactly what you want him to do if he starts coming to you. There is no need to risk scaring him off by needless calling.

You'll need to get your gun up into shooting position before the turkey gets into shooting range. If you try to do that while the turkey is looking at you, he'll be gone in a flash. Remember, if he is coming to your calls, he is always looking at you. I like to wait until he steps behind a tree or other obstruction. With his head hidden, I can quickly bring my gun up so I'm ready when he

A tom turkey strutting through the forest. (Photo: Mike Lawson)

walks out. If the bird is in strut, it will sometimes turn around until its head is hidden by the fan.

Several years ago, I killed a big eastern turkey that was strutting in a field just out of range. After I was sure he wouldn't get any closer, I stood up and walked slowly toward him while he was strutting with his back to me. I walked within 35 yards before he turned around and saw me.

When cover is sparse and the turkey is not strutting, you'll have to get your gun up with the turkey looking at you. If you think the turkey can see you, lift your gun up very slowly. He might stop and start making some alarm putts but he may not start to flee until he is sure of the danger.

The mistake many hunters make is to try to body shoot a turkey. You'll just end up with a crippled bird. The shot should be centered just below the bright red waddles on the neck. When you think of the vital neck and head area, the target is very small. It is extremely important to make your shot count.

You'll need plenty of knockdown power and a very dense pattern to kill a bird that can weigh over 25 pounds. I suggest #4, #5 or #6 copper plated buffered shot. Shot sizes larger than #2 are not even legal for turkey hunting in most states. There are some excellent loads available made especially for turkey hunting.

You must also understand how your load patterns at various distances. I shoot a 12-gauge gun chambered for three-and-a-half inch shells. It patterns well up to 50 yards, but I try to limit my shots to less than 40 yards.

Be patient if you are unsuccessful at getting your bird when he flies down from the roost. Frequently a tom will get with his hens soon after coming out of the roost. He'll probably spend several hours with them before they start to disperse. I've had some of my best hunts during the late morning and early afternoon. By midmorning, hens will usually leave for their nesting areas. Even if an old gobbler has had all the hens he can handle early in the morning, he is usually ready for more action after his hens have all left.

Trying to call a gobbler in if he goes off with his hens can be futile. He will frequently answer you as if to say, "Come on, join the party!," but he's not likely to leave his harem to come to you. Your best move is to leave the area and give it a rest. When you come back later in the day, you'll have a great chance of firing the gobbler up again.

My experience has shown that Merriam's turkeys will come a long way and can cover distance quickly. During midday, I try to set up soon after I get a response from a gobbler, even if he is hundreds of yards away. If he's looking for love and companionship, it won't be long before he shows up. Hopefully, you'll be ready.

Spring turkey hunting is not for everyone. You'll like it if you enjoy walking and hunting hard, but you seldom bring home anything to show for all your hard work . Gobblers almost never play by the rules. You need to like the game more than the score.

With that said, if you want to find me during the months of April or early May, you better look in the woods.

Mike Lawson, of St. Anthony, is an outfitter and guide for flyfishers and bird hunters. He owns and operates the Henry's Fork Angler's in Island Park.

Idaho's Migratory Gamebirds

Three migratory gamebirds in Idaho are managed cooperatively under the Migratory Bird Treaty Act administered by the U.S. Fish and Wildlife Service.

A federal migratory bird license validation is required to hunt mourning doves, common snipe, and sandhill cranes. Hunters are not required to purchase federal duck stamps or Idaho waterfowl conservation stamps; however, when a hunter buys an Idaho waterfowl stamp, the migratory bird validation is automatically added to his license. Hunters are required to respond to questionnaires seeking information about migratory gamebirds.

Mourning Dove
Zenaida macroura

FIELD FACTS

Size
    12 inches in length, 18-inch wing span, and 6 ounces in weight.

Color and Characteristics
    Mourning dove's small head, slim streamlined body, and long pointed tail are distinctive. Adult bird's upper body parts are slate-gray, with a pinkish wash on its underparts, a few dark spots on wings and white trim on tail. Juvenile has more spots on wings and scale marks on breast.

Call
    Mourning doves communicate with soft "mournful" five-syllabled cous.

The mourning dove, *Zenaida macroura*, is the only gamebird that nests in all of Idaho's 44 counties. It is highly migratory, and numerous doves pass through and into the state each year.

They are very adaptable and occur in many habitats. Their food is almost entirely weed seeds or small grains in cultivated areas. A daily water source is essential, so riparian areas are especially important during nesting seasons. Generally, nesting densities decrease as distance from open water increases.

Doves nest from May to September, with the peak brood period in July. Average clutch size is two eggs and, in Idaho, a pair usually raises three broods in a season. Mortality is high, so 70 percent or more of the annual migration consists of juveniles.

Mourning doves offer excellent sport for Idaho's hunters. Present in early September, doves are among the most difficult birds to hit–bring more than one box of shells for an evening shoot. (Photo: Ken Retallic)

Opening on September 1, Idaho's season is a month long. The best shooting is early in the season as both residents and migrants depart for warmer climes on the heels of the first cold snap.

Doves will decoy, but it is unnecessary. Best option is to scout hunting territories before the season opens. Obtain landowners permission if you plan to hunt private lands.

Look for the birds around tree-lined grain stubble fields—including sunflower patches—orchards and pastures, and watering areas like rivers, creeks, lakes, marshes, and ponds. Roosting sites are usually close to water sources. Also scout state wildlife management areas and national wildlife refuges. Check with regional IDFG offices for fall count numbers.

Farmlands along the lower Snake River Plain to the Oregon border and the southeast corner of the state to the Utah border hold good dove populations in fall. The higher elevations of eastern Idaho see cold snaps earlier than other areas and the birds depart sooner. The state's lowest elevations and mildest weather occur in the lower Clearwater River drainage and southern Palouse Prairie. But even there, the best hunting is early in the season.

The main reason to scout hunting areas is to locate the doves' flyways and set up good shooting positions for opening day. Doves routinely fly the same flight patterns to feeding fields or water over and over again. If you see doves flying along fence rows or tree lines, chances are other birds follow the same paths. They are more active throughout the day during migration.

On opening day, watch for doves at a preselected shooting site along a flight path in good cover to intercept the birds. For example, set up at turning points at the corners of fence lines or shelter belts, or at openings in trees.

Even if you don't have time to make preseason scouts, take the time when hunting to work out the birds' flight patterns. Don't sit and wait in unproductive sites or roam about for random shots. Move to spots where the doves are crossing good cover.

Wear clothing that blends in with the area you are hunting and avoid quick movements.

Steel shot is not required, except on national wildlife refuges and some state wildlife management areas. Shotguns that hold more than three shells must have a plug. Check current regulations for closed areas and shooting hours.

Common Snipe

Gallinago gallinago

FIELD FACTS

Size
  10.5 inches in length, 4 to 5.5 ounces in weight.

Color and Characteristics
  Chubby robin-sized shorebird with short legs and 3-inch blunt bill. Small head has black stripes on crown, dark strip through eyes; body is boldly patterned in shades of brown, with white underparts and rusty tail.

Call
  Alarm call is a harsh "skipe." Winnowing whistle-like sound heard during skydiving courtship displays is sound of wind rushing through stiff tail feathers.

The common snipe, *Gallinago gallinago*, is a secretive, well-camouflaged bird that nests throughout Idaho. It feeds in boggy thickets, wet meadows, and shallow marshes. Numerous migrants pass through or into Idaho. A few birds winter in warmer locales near springs where the soils remain moist and invertebrates are readily available.

Adult snipe are not gregarious and usually are found only in groups of two or three. Juveniles sometimes band together in small flocks called "swifts." Within their habitats, they are often widely scattered and difficult to find. Their explosive rise and quick zigzag flight pattern make them a tough target. But they also are curious birds and may circle overhead for a closer look at an intruder. And they often return to the same feeding area in a fairly short time after being flushed.

Of the thousands upon thousands of North American shorebirds once hunted so voraciously by old time market hunters, only the common snipe and American woodcock, Scolopax minor, retain gamebird status. The woodcock does not occur in Idaho; it is strictly a bird of the East.

Idaho offers a long season and generous bag limit, but the diminutive gamebird is lightly hunted. Most of the harvest is incidental to waterfowl hunting. Also known as the Wilson's snipe or jack snipe, these delectable butterballs can grace a determined hunter's table. Their challenge to wingshooters equals the sporting qualities of mourning doves. The additional equipment needed is a pair of hip boots.

Hunters can flush snipe in open meadows, or set up blinds near known feeding areas. It is just as easy to hide at the edge of a thicket or sit with your back to a weedy

Snipe are frantic flyers and prove very difficult to hit. A hunter can get so disgusted trying to bring one down that a resting snipe, like this one on a fence post, tests all of his wingshooting ethics. (Photo: Ken Retallic)

bank. A close-working flushing dog can't hurt, but a good retriever is more resourceful in locating downed birds.

Snipe feed in early morning and at dusk. They are active throughout the day when skies are heavily overcast or during drizzling rain. Look for movement in bogs and wet meadows to spot the birds as they trot across feeding areas and probe for grubs, worms, and other invertebrates.

Other shorebirds (such as dowitchers, which are similar in appearance) generally have longer legs and different shaped bills. They also are more inclined to feed in open waters of marshes and along shore lines of ponds and lakes. Flock sizes usually are much larger.

Steel or bismuth shot is required to hunt snipe. Check current regulations for closed areas and shooting hours.

Greater Sandhill Crane

Grus canadensis

FIELD FACTS

Size
  41 inches in length, 73-inch wing span, 10 to 15 pounds in weight.

Color and Characteristics
  Very large, tall bird with long neck, prominent pointed black bill, and red crown on head. Long, almost fluffy tail feathers distinguish cranes from great blue herons. Sandhill cranes are slate-gray in winter and spring. Rusty brown coloration of most adult birds in late summer and fall is due to feathers being stained from soaking in marshes to kill parasites. Golden tan on heads and necks of juveniles is natural coloration.

Similar Birds
  The whooping crane, an endangered species, has snow-white body and wings; primary and secondary feathers of wings are black; head has red crown and black mask, bill is yellow. In flight, cranes fly with neck extended and trailing feet evident. Herons fly with head and neck curved back in S-shape, trailing feet are less evident.

Call
  Common call is persistent trumpeting, rattling croak that is easily heard a mile away. Migrating flocks flying at great heights chatter constantly in a musical bell-like tone.

Eastern Idaho is home to one of the Intermountain West's largest nesting populations of greater sandhill cranes, *Grus canadensis*, and is a major staging area for migratory cranes.

Presence of a few whooping cranes, *Grus americanus*, in eastern Idaho is due to attempts to establish a second population of the endangered species. One hybrid of the two species has been reported. A program to use sandhills as foster parents to hatch whooping crane eggs from the Texas-Northwest Territories flock was discontinued in the early 1990s. However, other strategies to establish a flock are being pursued.

Cranes lay two eggs, but usually only one "colt" survives. The strategy behind the foster parent program was to switch eggs. The sandhills raised the whooping cranes and taught them a new migration route. Prolonged drought conditions in the decade

A sandhill crane is an impressive bird. Unfortunately, Idaho's allotted limit is low, and bagging one is very difficult. (Photo: Ken Retallic)

after the mid-eighties led to heavy predation during nesting seasons. Many of the whooping cranes also were killed in collisions with fences and power lines.

In 1995, the Rocky Mountain population of sandhill cranes was estimated at 20,000. About 8,000 stage in huge migration flocks in early autumn in eastern Idaho. Most congregate at Gray's Lake National Wildlife Refuge in eastern Bonneville County. Large flocks also gather for migration in the Teton River Valley and Bear Lake areas. The majority of the population winters in southern New Mexico and Arizona.

Sandhill canes were returned to Idaho's hunting menu in 1996 because of persistent complaints about crop damage in southeastern Idaho. About 20 birds were shot. But crane hunting is controversial among many nonhunters in the state. Even if its gamebird status withstands continual court challenges, crane hunting opportunities will remain limited. Migratory Bird Treaty Act management restrictions set Idaho's quota at 150 birds or less.

Hunting rules are still being worked out, and regulations will be set annually. Most likely, hunters will be encouraged to hunt on cultivated lands. Landowner permission is required to hunt private lands.

Hunting techniques for this shyest of gamebirds is a whole new ball game for resident and out-of-state wingshooters.

Cranes have excellent eyesight and spook at first hint of danger. Escape flight requires a running start and is low as the big birds labor to gain elevation. They fly much higher between feeding and watering areas. When migrating, cranes spiral to great heights on thermals, much like pelicans, and ride the upper winds and thermals as they fly.

Reports on Idaho's first hunt in 80 years indicate that hunting was tough. The cranes were very wary and difficult to reach. In other states where cranes are legal, patient hunters find the birds can be decoyed. The other option is pass shooting from blinds near roosting areas, which are most often in open marshes or shallow streams to avoid predation.

Cranes are excellent table fare. They were very popular gamebirds for pioneer hunters.

A good retriever is just part of an enjoyable Idaho waterfowl hunt.
(Photo: Ken Retallic)

Idaho's Waterfowl

*Canada Geese and Mallards Are Primary Targets
in an Exemplary Mixed Bag*

by Ken Retallic

Idaho straddles the eastern fringe of the Pacific Flyway, one of the continent's four prolific migration routes that seasonally funnel hordes of waterfowl north and south. More than a fair share of the Pacific Flyway's autumn flights of ducks and geese pass through Idaho or come home to wintering areas. In addition to this, resident populations of waterfowl are benefiting from recent good water years.

A semi-arid state, Idaho's waterfowl congregate around its oasis-like lakes, marshes, and streams, which are fed by melting snows trickling down from its many mountain ranges. Canada geese and mallards dominate Idaho's annual waterfowl harvests. But hunters will find several species of ducks only found in the West. Combine this with "spillovers" from the central flyway, and Idaho can truly be called a waterfowler's paradise.

Approximately 35 percent of the state's waterfowlers are goose hunters. The western Canada goose represents more than 95 percent of its annual goose harvest. Snow geese total less than 2 percent, but these are rarely harvested. Geese make up about 9 percent of Idaho's yearly waterfowl harvest.

Duck hunters, who represent 65 percent of the state's waterfowlers, focus exclusively on dabbling ducks. Also called puddle ducks, they approach almost 99 percent of the duck harvest. This is typical of Intermountain hunters, who have few opportunities or lack the equipment to selectively hunt the more toothsome of the diving ducks. Also, Idaho permits only a restricted harvest of canvasbacks and redheads.

Every year, mallards make up 70 to 80 percent of the state's duck harvest. Next in line, at 5 percent each, are wigeon and green-winged teal. Other puddle ducks—pintail, gadwall, blue-winged and cinnamon teal, and shoveler—each account for only 1 to 3 percent. Coming in at less than 1 percent each are the wood duck and all the diving ducks—canvasback, redhead, lesser scaup and ring-necked duck. Rarely harvested are the ruddy duck and goldeneye, even though they commonly occur in the state. Rarest of all is the harlequin duck, a prime candidate for the Endangered Species List in the Lower Forty-eight.

Waterfowl Populations

In the mid-1990s, Idaho, like the rest of the continent, welcomed a dramatic resurgence of duck populations after more than a decade of seemingly disastrous drought years.

Ducks are thriving again, thanks to the dedicated efforts of state and federal wildlife agencies and hunter organizations like Ducks Unlimited in both the United States and Canada. Autumn duck populations in 1996 were the best since the mid-

1980s. The North American flight estimate by the U.S. Fish and Wildlife Service recorded 89.5 million ducks, which was up 16 percent from 1995. Total breeding population was estimated at 37.5 million (5 percent more than 1995 and 16 percent over the long-term average). Breeding population estimates for the ever-popular mallard dipped slightly but was still 10 percent higher than the long-term average.

Although drought could rear its ugly head again, waterfowl managers are confident the North American Waterfowl Management Plan will continue to save crucial wetlands. Idaho's foremost contribution to efforts to preserve habitat comes from the sale of its waterfowl conservation stamps and related limited-edition artwork.

In mild years, Idaho's waterfowl populations remain dispersed. This phenomenon is evident in the state's annual mid-winter waterfowl counts. In 1997, despite the previous fall's record North American flight, Idaho's midwinter waterfowl survey actually turned up fewer birds than in the previous two years.

Unusual weather in the winter of 1996–97 left many bodies of water unfrozen and created numerous temporary wetlands. This scattered the birds, according to those individuals making the counts on traditional winter wetlands. Survey members suggested some species might have been undercounted as a result.

The survey showed a total of 248,152 waterfowl in 1997, compared to 299,100 in 1996 and 284,590 in 1995. Total species counted in recent winters show:

Bird	1997	1996	1997
Mallard	140,230	159,160	149,479
Canada geese	41,433	70,257	43,855
Wigeon	3,463	9,884	10,763
Total dabblers	146,468	179,601	162,490
Total divers	32,770	34,869	53,112

The 1996 midwinter count also reflected how weather affects distribution. It showed 159,160 mallards compared to 149,479 in 1995. The vast majority crowded into the Lake Lowell-Deer Flat Refuge in southwestern Idaho where 92,238 were counted. The second largest concentration of mallards (23,528) was found in the American Falls area where there were 15,167 at the same time in 1995. In 1994, Idaho's mallard total was 171,300.

Overall, ducks showed a slight decline in the winter of 1996 from 1995. The difference was primarily in the number of redheads: 11,431 in 1996 compared to 32,829 in 1995. Total 1996 winter waterfowl numbers were higher than 1995, up from 284,590 to 299,100.

Idaho's resident geese fared better than ducks during the drought years, and populations continue to increase significantly in many regions of the state.

Large western Canada goose populations in Idaho are found near its bigger lakes and impoundments, principal rivers, wildlife management areas, and national wildlife refuges. These are the same regions that attract the largest concentrations of northern nesters from the Prairie Provinces of western Canada as well as Montana and Wyoming.

Idaho's two favorite gamebirds: Canada geese and mallards. (Photo: Ken Retallic)

The in-flow of northern geese migrants typically peaks after mid-November, which offers a second window of opportunity to hunters for relatively unwary birds. Late-season winter hunting in reasonably mild temperatures is usually very good in the southwest corner of the state. In mild years, large flocks of geese will hang around into winter, mainly in the southeastern corner of the state and on the large ice-free lakes of north central Idaho and the Panhandle.

Canada geese numbered 70,257 in the 1996 statewide winter count, far above the 1995 count of 43,855. More than half of the 1996 goose count came from the American Falls area at 38,968. Only 6,517 geese were seen in that area in 1995. One observer noted that he had never before seen American Falls Reservoir completely ice-free at that time of year, a likely explanation for the large increase in geese there. The next largest concentrations of geese were seen in the big lake country of the Panhandle. Smaller flocks were scattered along the Snake River between American Falls and the Oregon border.

Waterfowl Seasons

Idaho's waterfowl management philosophy is to permit as generous a duck harvest as possible within the bounds set by the U.S. Fish and Wildlife Service's annual fall estimate. Goose harvest allowances are more restricted due to concentration by hunters on a single subspecies, the western Canada goose.

Season lengths are as generous as conditions permit and, as much as possible, attempt to meet public demand.

Southwest Idaho has a split duck season, with a brief respite inserted to take advantage of its longer duration of good hunting conditions and sometimes later arrivals of northern migrants. Areas in the north, central, and east may have earlier starting dates and continuous seasons to take advantage of earlier freeze-up or lower waterfowl numbers after mid- to late-November.

A continuous season, sometimes with different starting or closing dates, also occurs in the area around the Fort Hall Indian Reservation, north of Pocatello, to accommodate tribal permit seasons. Idaho's other Indian reservations do not have hunting seasons for nontribal members.

Generally, Idaho's geese season starts in late September and continues into the first week of January. Duck seasons start in the first week of October and continue into the first or second week of January.

Steel shot is required to hunt waterfowl in Idaho. Bismuth shot also is approved.

A federal duck stamp and state waterfowl conservation stamp are both required to hunt waterfowl.

Public Access

About 70 percent of Idaho is federal or state forest or range lands open to the public to hunt. It also has seven national wildlife refuges and nearly 30 state wildlife management areas where waterfowl congregate, often in large numbers.

For duck hunters these public access areas offer virtually unlimited opportunities to hunt. But goose hunters face a tougher proposition, mainly because geese feed primarily in cultivated fields, and Idaho requires landowner permission to hunt.

Idaho, like most Western states, has an anti-trespass law that includes all cultivated lands, including irrigated pastures. Landowners are not required to post their lands, and a lack of signs does not necessarily indicate their lands are open to hunting. The basic rule for hunters is to ask landowners first before pursuing waterfowl or gamebirds on private lands.

Reporting Leg Bands

Thousands of leg bands are attached to ducks and geese annually to track migratory patterns and survival estimates. Hunters can assist these surveys by reporting band numbers to the U.S. Fish and Wildlife Service at its new toll-free telephone number: 1-800-327- BAND or 1-800-327-2263.

Snake River Ducks

Waterfowlers Harvest the Bounty of Secret Channels

by Rocky Barker

Heading for his favorite duck blind, I thought Marv Hoyt was going to blindfold me as we drove the backroads of Jefferson County.

Marv, an Idaho representative of the Greater Yellowstone Coalition in Idaho Falls, is as serious about his duck hunting as he is about protecting the wild country of the Greater Yellowstone Ecosystem, which includes much of eastern Idaho. He is best known as a builder of fine bamboo fly rods that are most easily obtained at auctions for a variety of conservation groups. But duck hunting usually pushes aside flyfishing and forest grouse hunting as fall matures. His two retrievers, a black Lab and a yellow Lab, are well trained and, since Marv and his son Zach hunt a lot, they get their share of practice.

The South Fork of the Snake River is Marv's sacred water. He fishes it for fat cutthroat trout in the summer and floats it for ducks in the fall. It starts at Palisades Reservoir and wanders 61 miles through a long, nearly wild canyon lined by farms and cottonwood bottoms. It is excellent waterfowl country. North of Menan, the South Fork joins the Henry's Fork to form the Snake, which flows 700 miles through southern and western Idaho and leaves the state at Lewiston. Throughout its course, waterfowlers find excellent shooting.

The day Marv took me to his secret spot was a welcomed late-season outing for this desk-weary writer. We loaded his canoe with decoys, stools, guns, and dogs and paddled into the wind up a side channel until we came to a wide spot perfect for setting out the decoys. Marv uses a mix of mallards and pintails with a couple of Canada geese thrown in for good measure.

"When the ducks see two geese sitting there it makes them let down their guard," he said.

It didn't take long to reap the wisdom of Marv's strategy. We heard the sound of whistling wings coming from behind us and four mallards—two drakes and two hens—flew over the blind. Marv chattered to them on his duck call and they circled once before cupping their wings and dropping into the decoys right in front of us. The dog, clearly holding back its excitement, looked at Marv awaiting the expected command.

"NOW!" he shouted.

We rose from the blind and the two drakes crumpled when we fired. The dog waited for Marv's command and swam for the downstream bird. The other had fallen on the other side of the channel and Marv pointed its location, with

Joe Landis (left) and Mike Bonkoski pose with a three-man limit of mallards. Trapper (left), Cody (middle), and Mollie kept the hunters from making cold retrieves in chilly water. (Photo: Joe Landis)

the command, "Mark." A few minutes later the dog brought back the drakes to complete our perfect double.

Unfortunately, my shooting didn't hold up as the day went on. More than once the retriever gave me a puzzled look after an unworthy volley; however, by the end of the morning, we loaded a mixed brace of mallards, pintails, and teal into the canoe. With the wind on our back, it was an easy paddle back to the truck.

Most duck hunters will want more than a canoe if they plan to hunt the Snake. Jet boats are perhaps the craft of choice since they give the hunter the option of moving fast up and down the river. They also can navigate shallow channels.

Idaho Fish and Game Commissioner Jeff Siddoway, of Terreton, demonstrated great skill in negotiating the often-shallow stretches of the Henry's Fork on a November goose hunt. None of us showed much shooting skills that day,

Joe Landis and Cody take a break after a morning hunt for mallards.
(Photo: Ken Retallic)

but I didn't hear anyone complain about spending a day in a blind with the Teton Mountains looming against the eastern horizon.

Whatever craft you choose, be careful. The Snake is powerful and tricky. But it offers incredible diversity for waterfowl and upland hunters alike.

Dabbling Ducks and Puddle Ducks

The dabbling ducks are surface feeders commonly seen on shallow-water marshes, sloughs, potholes, ponds, canals, and small streams. On lakes and rivers, they frequent the edges. Their name comes from a so-called dabbling method of feeding, a technique whereby the duck tips its body up and extends its head underwater to reach aquatic vegetation and invertebrates.

Puddle ducks are primarily vegetarians, but supplement their diet with insects, mollusks, and occasional small fish. Several species, particularly mallards, actively feed on agricultural plants and grains.

Many nest in uplands quite some distance from water. Good local production is dependent on expansive areas of nesting cover surrounding water sources.

Drakes are often brilliantly colored, while the plumage of hens is drab and camouflaged. Forward placement of legs on body facilitates surface swimming and walking on land. Dabblers are very agile fliers and take off almost vertically from the water.

Mallard

Anas platyrhynchos

FIELD FACTS

Local Names
  Greenhead

Size
  Large duck, 2.5 to 3 pounds, 24 to 28 inches.

Identification
  Male: brilliant green head, chestnut chest, white belly, dark rump, white tail edging; blue speculum on wings; greenish/yellow bill; orange feet. **Voice:** low raspy "rink." **Female:** drab brown with whitish tail edging; blue speculum on wings; orange bill with blackish spots or blotches; orange feet. **Voice:** loud resonant "quack." **In flight:** white tail and underwings contrast with dark chest and head of male; look for blue speculum, with white edge, and orange feet on female. Flight speed is 30 mph cruising; 50 to 65 mph chased.

Status
  Most common duck in Idaho and North America, breeds statewide; numerous fall and spring migrants; winters in large numbers throughout state as long as it finds ice-free water.

Harvest
  Most popular duck in Idaho; represents 70 to 80 percent of annual state harvest; bag limit on hens restricted.

Color

The green head and dark breast of a mallard drake makes it the best known duck species in North America; also look for yellow bill and orange feet, blue speculum, and white tail. The two curled black feathers on the tail are sometimes absent in fall.

Avoid confusion with the northern shoveler male, which has a much larger green head, broad bill, white breast, and brown flanks.

Identification of the mallard hen is critical since the bag limit is often limited to one per day. Look for a drab, dark brown body, orange bill and feet, blue speculum, and white tail.

Late fall and winter bring massive flights of northern mallards. If hunters can locate open water in November, December, and January, it's a bet mallards will be near. (Photo: Ken Retallic)

Speed and Sound

Strong, swift fliers, male mallards often fly in bachelor flocks of six or more over marshes or backwaters of rivers. They decoy well but may make passing circles before coming straight in against the wind.

The drake mallard has a call that is weak and difficult to hear. However, a hen mallard is noisy, and a hen's loud quack and muttering feeding calls are used by many waterfowlers to call in mallards to decoys. Some other species also respond.

Food and Habits

Mallards feed in grain stubble, flooded alfalfa fields, and shallow waters of marshes, ponds, and streams. Flights to feeding fields are early and late in the day, often in huge flocks at the height of migration.

When resting at midday and overnight, early season mallards prefer shallow backwaters or interiors of marshes with good cover from reeds and cattails. They are also found in irrigation canals and potholes near agricultural areas. On streams they loaf in quiet secluded backwaters, eddies, wooded side channels, and spring-fed inlets.

When marsh hunting pressure is intense and late in the season, mallards move to big water to rest through the day and fly long distances to feed.

Cody, a golden retriever, poses proudly with his catch of mallard drakes. (Photo: Joe Landis)

Migration

Migration flights are high, often in huge flocks with broad-V formations. The largest flights of northern ducks commonly come in on fronts of major storms, when the ducks are tired and hungry. Shooting can be fast and furious when good sets of decoys await their arrival.

Peak migration of northern birds generally is in mid-November. A very hardy duck, mallards winter in large numbers along the Snake River Plain in southern and southwestern Idaho, and in smaller flocks in other areas of the state as long as there is open water.

Recent winter counts have ranged from 150,000 to more than 170,000.

Sixty percent or more of the state's winter mallards crowd into the Lake Lowell-Deer Flat Refuge area west of Boise. In mild winters, the American Falls area also retains huge flocks late into the season. Refuges near Twin Falls and Mountain Home are the other key layover sites for wintering waterfowl.

Table Fare

Ranks at the top of the menu as a table duck. The mallard was the original breeding stock of the domestic duck.

Pintail

Anas acuta

FIELD FACTS

Local Names
Sprig, longneck, spiketail

Size
Large-appearing duck, 2 to 2 .5 pounds, 22 to 27 inches.

Identification
Male: chocolate-brown head, white over neck, chest and belly; bill bluish with black strip down middle; distinct, elongated black tail; green speculum on wings; feet gray. **Voice:** low mellow "whistle." **Female:** mottled drab brown; head dull brown; tail slightly pointed; bill gray with black spots; feet gray. **Voice:** low hoarse "quack." **In flight:** very elongated body and long tail, white neck and belly contrast with dark head on male; female's tail pointed, neck slender, greenish-brown speculum. Flight speed is 30 to 45 mph cruising; 65 mph chased.

Status
Fairly common summer resident in southern Idaho, rare in northern Idaho; common fall and spring migrant throughout state; rarely lingers past late-November.

Harvest
Popular duck but represents only 1 to 3 percent of annual state harvest. Bag limit is restricted.

Color

The drake pintail has a rich, chocolate-brown summer cap. Its fall eclipse plumage turns a duller brown but is still distinctive. Its white throat, breast, and belly stand out against the grayish tones of the slender, streamlined body and long pointed tail. The hen's slender neck and pointed tail are also distinctive, while its mottled brown body color is lighter than that of the female mallard. The pintail's feet are gray.

Speed and Sound

The pintail is a very swift, aerodynamic flier capable of intricate maneuvers when spooked. High graceful fliers, pintails travel in flocks of five to 30 in loose formation. They often swoop down from considerable heights just before landing on ponds.

A drake pintail is one of the more beautiful of Idaho's waterfowl.
(Photo: Ken Retallic)

The male's soft, high-pitched whistle requires special calling instrument. It will respond to careful, patient waterfowl callers.

The pintail is perhaps the most wary and cautious of the ducks, but it decoys well. Its gregarious nature will bring it into mallard decoys. Many waterfowlers mix pintail decoys with their sets as "confidence birds" to bring in mallards and other species.

Food and Habits

A shallow-water feeder, pintails are rarely seen feeding in grain stubble like mallards; however, they will take advantage of flooded alfalfa fields.

The pintail's autumn passage through Idaho is somewhat haphazard and more widely dispersed than huge spring staging flocks that occur in eastern Idaho; still, it is a very gregarious duck and often found with other species. Look for it on shallow-water marshes and ponds with good cover. When hunting pressure increases, they will move on or rest by day in large marshes and feed at night.

Migration

Fall migrants appear to pass through in stages; resident and migrant birds depart for south long before marshes freeze solid.

Table Fare

Equal to mallard as roasting duck.

Gadwall

Anas strepera

FIELD FACTS

Local Names
   Gray duck

Size
   Medium-sized duck, 1.5 to 2 pounds, 18 to 20 inches.

Identification
   Male: gray/brown appearance, white belly; black tail coverts, top and bottom; bill black with trace of orange; feet bright orangish-yellow; white speculum with black bar on wings. **Voice:** "Whistle" and "nyaak." **Female:** mottled buff and brown, white belly; bill yellow-orange with black spotting; feet bright orangish yellow; white speculum with black bar on wings. **Voice:** soft high-pitched "quack." **In flight:** white belly and dark rump, white speculum evident. Flight speed is 30 mph cruising.

Status
   Late spring migrant, common summer resident in southern Idaho, rarely seen north of Nez Perce County; among first to depart in fall; rare in winter.

Harvest
   Lightly hunted, represents only 1 to 3 percent of state harvest.

Color

White speculum says it all in identifying gadwall on the wing. The lower white band on the wing is easily seen even against the drab gray/brown body color. The male's breast is slightly darker, and its belly is white.

A gadwall hen's mottled brown coloration is more buff or tan than a mallard hen, with yellow/orange feet; it is also smaller and has a white speculum.

Speed and Sound

Gadwalls are straightforward fliers, not overly speedy, and usually fly in family groups or small flocks. One of the least wary ducks, it decoys well. It is also commonly taken in jump shot opportunities.

Drake utters rare quack-like call. The hen's quacking is softer in tone than the loud quacks of a mallard hen.

Food and Habits

Gadwall feed on aquatic vegetation in shallow marshes, edges of ponds, bays, and small streams with good nearby cover. They are rarely found in fields.

Migration

Among the least hardy of ducks, gadwalls depart for southern wintering grounds early in fall. They rarely migrate in large flocks but are often found with other puddle duck species.

Table Fare

Good table fare although not rated as high as mallard or pintail.

American Wigeon
Anas americana

FIELD FACTS

Local Names
Baldpate, "widgeon," poacher

Size
Medium-sized duck, 1.5 to 2 pounds, 18 to 20 inches.

Identification
Male: orange-brown back and flanks, white belly, black rump; head crown white or buffy, glossy green eye-mask; bill grayish blue; feet gray; wings with green speculum, white shoulder patch. **Voice:** whistle repeated in threes. **Female:** mottled brown, distinct, white belly; head grayish with dark speckles; bill and feet grayish blue. **Voice:** "Qua-awk." In flight: white belly, white wing-shoulder patch, white head crown and black rump evident. Flight speed is about 20 mph cruising.

Status
A common migrant in fall and spring; wigeon are often seen in southern Idaho in summer, but breeding status is minimal to uncertain. European wigeon is an occasional visitor.

Harvest
Popular duck, represents 5 percent of state harvest.

Color

The American wigeon drake is a handsome bird, but not quite up to the brilliant coloration of the wood duck and green-winged teal. Its head colors mimic but do not equal either. Its size is midway between the two.

The "bald pate" or white head band above a bright green eye mask sets it apart from other North American ducks. Its European cousin, an occasional visitor, has a creamy or yellowish "pate." Also look for the American wigeon's orange-tan breast darker flanks, and white belly.

The mottled brown hen has an orange/tan breast and flanks as well as a distinctive white belly.

Speed and Sound

Wigeons are wary ducks and quick to flush; however, they decoy well because of their gregarious nature. Swift fliers, they fly in small compact flocks like teal but in a

American wigeon. (Photo: Ken Retallic)

more straightforward pattern. Whistling of their wings is similar to that of goldeneyes. The drake's high-pitched whistle may be hard to hear.

Food and Habits

Wigeon are renowned "poachers" and can be seen stealing aquatic plants brought up by swans, geese, coots, and diving ducks. This tactic often places them in deeper water than most other dabbling ducks. It also puts them out where they can easily see approaching danger and are able to take flight quickly.

Wigeon feed in shallow mashes for aquatic vegetation and occasionally venture inland to graze on succulent plants and harvested crops.

Migration

Northern birds are generally among the first to migrate south from Canada. Passage through Idaho is mostly in intermittent stages. Good numbers may be found in northern Idaho during early seasons. Others may linger in southern Idaho as long as weather remains mild. Wigeon travel in small flocks and are usually found in association with other waterfowl species.

Table Fare

Good table bird, although placed a bit lower on the menu than mallard and pintail.

Green-winged Teal

Anas crecca

FIELD FACTS

Local Names
Greenwing, red-headed teal

Size
Smallest dabbling duck, about 12 ounces, up to 14 inches in length.

Identification
Male: grayish body, tan chest with dark spots, white belly; green eye patch on red head; bill and feet grayish; green speculum on wings. **Voice:** twittering whistle. **Female:** mottled brown with white belly, grayish/black bill; wings similar to male. **Voice:** high-pitched quack. In flight: small bird, flies swiftly and erratically; flies in small dense flocks that wheel and turn like shorebirds. Flight ranges from 30–40 mph.

Status
Rare summer resident in northern Idaho, more common in southern Idaho; fair number of migrants spring and fall; very hardy duck, will linger into winter as far north as Nez Perce county when conditions permit.

Harvest
This popular duck represents 5 percent of state harvest.

Color
The drake is the most multicolored of the diminutive teal, with patterns similar to that of the larger, very colorful wood duck. Its green eye mask on the red head and white belly differ it from other fast-flying teal. The equally small hen has a dark, mottled brown body and green speculum but lacks the blue shoulder coverts of blue-winged and cinnamon teal hens and drakes.

Speed and Sound
These ducks fly in small dense flocks that swiftly turn and dodge low to water or reeds. The bird's size makes its flight seem faster than it actually is, but it's still a challenging pass shot.

Greenwings decoy well to mallard decoy sets in shallow water or marshes with good cover, especially toward dusk. They often circle for another look even during firing.

Both the drake's twittering whistle and the hen's high-pitched quack are often hard to hear.

Food and Habits

Greenwings prefer to feed in shallow waters of sloughs, marshes, potholes, ponds, and small streams, but will go inland to agricultural fields.

Migration

A hardy duck, it lingers in winter in north-central and southern Idaho as long as conditions permit. They gather in much larger flocks than other teal species.

Table Fare

Delectable bird worthy of roasting whole despite small size.

Blue-winged Teal

Anas discors

FIELD FACTS

Local Names
Bluewing, summer teal, white-faced teal

Size
Small duck, less than 1 pound, 12 to 16 inches.

Identification
Male: Tan body with numerous dark spots, mottled dark brown back, white patch on flanks; dark-gray head with white crescent in front of eyes, black bill; blue shoulder patch and green speculum on wings. **Voice:** whistling "peep." **Female:** Mottled brown body with white belly; wings similar to males. **Voice:** high-pitched quack. **In flight:** Small bird, swift and erratic flier; small dense flocks dodge and weave low over water like other teal. Flight speed is 30 to 40 mph cruising; up to 50 mph chased.

Status
Growing number of summer residents in southern Idaho; late-spring and early fall migrant; local birds depart by September, northern migrants may linger slightly longer if weather remains mild.

Harvest
Lightly hunted, represents only 1 to 3 percent of state harvest.

Color
White crescent on cheeks of purple-black head and spotted cinnamon body places drake among more easily identified ducks. Hen's mottled brown body and sky blue patch on wing shoulders virtually same as cinnamon teal hen. Speculum green on both sexes of bluewings.

Speed and Sound
Bluewings are swift, erratic fliers like greenwings but fly lower in looser open flocks. In good cover, they sit tight and permit close approach, but they scatter in all directions when flushed on marsh backwaters or secluded ponds. They decoy well to mallard sets because they tend to be more active throughout the day than other ducks. Nervous whistling twitter of drakes more easily heard than faint quack of hen.

Blue-winged teal. (Photo: Ken Retallic)

Food and Habits
Prefers to feed in shallow marshes, edges of ponds, potholes and streams, but will go inland to grain fields with other species.

Migration
These are the first of the puddle ducks to migrate south. The majority are long gone by October, the start of hunting season in Idaho. If weather is exceptionally mild, northern migrants linger longer.

Table Fare
Fine eating duck.

Cinnamon Teal

Anas cyanoptera

FIELD FACTS

Local Names
  Red teal, river teal

Size
  Small duck, less than 1 pound, 15 to 17 inches.

Identification
  Male: rich cinnamon colored body and head, dark brown back; red eyes; black bill; blue shoulder patch and green speculum. **Voice:** whistling "peep." **Female:** same as blue-winged teal; identity of two cannot be separated except by skilled biologists. **In flight:** swift, erratic flier similar to other teal; generally flies only as family groups, larger flocks rare. Flight speed is more than 30 mph cruising; 50 mph chased.

Status
  Common to abundant summer resident across Idaho, breeds only in western United States; departs northern Idaho by end of summer, sometimes lingers in southern Idaho into start of fall hunting season.

Harvest
  Lightly hunted, represents only 1 to 3 percent of state harvest.

Color

The drake's bright cinnamon color makes it perhaps the most secretive of duck species. When approached it tries to fade into nearby cover of reeds and cattails. The hen's mottled brown coloration, including sky-blue wing coverts, is virtually identical to a blue-winged teal hen.

Speed and Sound

Often hard to flush, however, the cinnamon teal will dodge and weave like other teal in small family-sized flocks. Decoys relatively well when present.

Calls of both sexes mimic blue-winged teal's.

Cinnamon teal. (Photo: Ken Retallic)

Food and Habits

Shallow-water feeders that mostly stick to secluded backwaters of marshes, ponds, and sloughs with good nearby cover. Often seen in association with blue-winged teal.

Strictly a western duck, cinnamon teal are rarely found in the Midwest east of Missouri River.

Migration

Drakes depart for the south in late summer, but family groups linger longer into fall than bluewings in southern Idaho. Northern migrants may pause briefly en route south.

Table Fare

Rarely harvested, but considered a good table bird.

Shoveler

Anas clypeata

FIELD FACTS

Local Names
Spoon-bill, spoony, broad-bill, shovel-bill.

Size
Medium-sized duck, 1.25 to 1.5 pounds, 18 to 20 inches.

Identification
Male: dark brown back, cinnamon flanks and belly, white chest and tail; orange feet; green head, large black spoon-shaped bill; wing coverts sky blue with white bar on outer edge, green speculum. **Voice:** weak "took-took." **Female:** mottled drab brown, tail white; large, spoon-shaped bill; greater coverts form white bar above light-green speculum. **Voice:** silent or feeble quack. **In flight:** spoon-shaped bill and dark head of male appear large, carried low; white chest contrasts with cinnamon belly. Flight speed is 30 to 40 mph cruising; up to 50 mph chased.

Status
Growing number of summer residents in southern Idaho; late spring and early fall migrant; local birds depart by late September.

Harvest
Lightly hunted, represents 1 to 3 percent of state harvest.

Color
The male's green head may cause momentary confusion with a mallard drake, but the shoveler's head looks big because of its broad spoon-like bill. Its other main features are its cinnamon flanks and belly and white breast. The mottled brown hen also has characteristics of a large spoon-bill. The wing pattern of both sexes is similar to blue-winged teal's.

Speed and Sound
When cruising a marsh, shovelers fly rapidly in a fairly straight line low to the water or reeds. When spooked they flare wildly and dodge and weave. Flock size is rarely very large; often seen with blue-winged teal in fall. Shovelers will respond to decoys. Neither drake nor hen has an alarm call. Chattering is faint and hard to hear.

Northern shovelers. (Photo: Ken Retallic)

Food and Habits

Spoon-bill of the shoveler has comb-like teeth along edges that permit it to strain aquatic insects, larvae, and crustaceans from mud. Many hunters feel this taints its flavor, although at least 65 percent of its diet is aquatic plants, seeds, and bulbs.

Often seen in association with blue-winged teal, it favors shallow backwaters of marshes, sloughs, and ponds.

Migration

The shoveler is a bird of the south like the blue-winged teal. It is among the last to arrive in spring and the first to leave in fall. Resident birds depart by late September or the first hard frost. Northern migrants may linger slightly longer if the weather remains mild.

Table Fare

Ranks low on totem pole as a table duck but should not be wasted if shot.

The colorful wood duck drake is one of Idaho's most desirable birds. Here, two beautiful drakes explore a small pond. (Photo: Ken Retallic)

Perching Ducks

The wood duck, the single member of the perching duck family, is a woodlands species with flight characteristics and feeding habits similar to dabbling ducks. Feet have sharp claws that permit wood ducks to perch on snags and stumps and in branches of trees. Nests are made in tree cavities that may be some distance inland from ponds and streams.

Like dabblers, wood ducks spring into flight flush from the water.

Wood Duck

Aix sponsa

Field Facts

Local Names
Woody, squealer, tree duck, swamp duck

Size
Medium-sized duck, 15 to 18 inches.

Identification
Male: most brilliantly colored wild duck; dark bluish iridescence on back, white flecks on cinnamon chest, vermiculated yellow/tan sides, white belly; green crest on head, red eyes, short multi-colored bill, white throat; blue/green wing coverts and speculum. **Voice:** plaintive squeal. **Female:** drab brown body, bronze back, white belly; grayish head with crest and comet-shaped white eye rings; wings similar to males, speculum has white edging. **Voice:** variety of whistles. **In flight:** erratic flier in woods, large head held high; white belly, large, square tail evident. Flight speed is 30 to 50 mph.

Status
Common summer resident in northern Idaho; rare in southern part of the state, except around Boise in Eagle Island area; early fall migrant, often gone by mid October.

Harvest
Lightly hunted, represents less than 1 percent of state harvest.

Color

The wood duck drake is the most handsome duck in North America. Its green helmet-like crest is traced with white stripes, and white flecks dot its cinnamon/red breast. Its golden flanks are outlined in white, as well, and iridescent blue/greens glitter on its back, wing coverts, and speculum. Its rump is cinnamon and the stout tail is dark brown.

The hen appears gray overall, with white bars and flecks, but is still a striking bird. Its smaller crest mimics the drake's, and its large tear-drop eye ring is unique.

Speed and Sound

With head held high, the wood duck has the appearance of hovering, but its flight is swift and often erratic. Its stout, square tail is an excellent rudder as it dodges and darts between trees around secluded woodland ponds or along mountain streams.

Wood ducks squeal or whistle in alarm when flushed and continue to call as they dart for cover.

Its ability to spring into full flight flush from the water is the same as puddle ducks, but it is in a separate family, the perching ducks. It prefers wood duck decoys but will make passes through mallard sets.

Food and Habits

The wood duck is strictly a New World bird. Northern Idaho is on the eastern edge of its Pacific Northwest population.

It is the only northern duck that perches in trees. Like some diving ducks and mergansers, it nests in tree cavities. It also nests in wooden nest boxes turned out by the thousands by Boy Scout troops and duck clubs. But endeavors to entice wood ducks into stopping over in southern Idaho have borne little fruit. Summer birds south of Nez Perce County are rare.

The wood duck's preferred haunts are secluded woodland ponds and marshes, but it also is common along small mountain streams at lower elevations in the state's Panhandle.

It feeds on aquatic vegetation and insects as well as insects, seeds, berries, and nuts.

Migration

Northern Idaho's winters are mild, but resident wood ducks generally depart at the beginning of autumn. Most are gone by mid-October. During their route south, small flocks stop over in southern Idaho; a few wood ducks linger in the Boise area through winter.

Table Fare

The wood duck ranks at the top of the waterfowl menu. It is also a popular trophy bird, especially among flyfishers who tie their own flies.

Carved Decoys Give Waterfowlers an Edge

by Ken Retallic

There's something primeval about waterfowl hunting. Up long before daybreak, the duck hunter stumbles about in the dark to set out decoys and prepare a blind. Cattails and bulrush conspire to block passage of his boat. The muck of the marsh sucks at his boots. Ancient subconscious memories electrify his senses as whiffs of sulfur ooze from the stirred up mud.

Late in the season there are days when the boat's bow shatters skim ice into wafer-thin shards that swirl and tinkle together in its wake. His block of decoys bob placidly as the hunter sits with his dog patiently awaiting the shooting hour. Shimmering needles of ice crystals fall through the light of the brightening day. Hoarfrost rimes the reeds and cattails, decoys and boat, shotgun barrel, hunter, and dog. Great weather for ducks is always the comforting thought.

Whatever the day brings, waterfowler always pause to savor the special hush of predawn. Then, as the black of night dissolves to pearly gray and eastern clouds are brushed with broad crimson strokes, the marsh comes alive. The sound of whistling wings marks the passage of the first flight of ducks overhead. Off in the reeds, mallard hens squawk hoarsely as they splash about.

Above the bowl of darkness surrounding the marsh, more flights of ducks crisscross the sky, the white of their breasts burnished with the ruby glow of the sun. From the mud flats beyond the cattails and reeds, the high-pitched gabbling of snow geese rises to a crescendo as flocks lift off on dawn flights to the grazing fields.

The muffled boom of a distant shotgun blast is the first of many to echo through the day. Hunters keep the birds moving about the marsh until night fall.

Ducks and geese are wary by nature, and even more so after the first days of a new hunting season. To bring them into target range requires sound knowledge of their ways, and a good block of decoys.

For those who carve their own, there's an extra reward to the thrill of seeing a flock of mallards cup their wings and gracefully descend into a set of decoys. Mixed with the pride of accomplishment is confidence in their creations; many hours at the workbench pay off in the hunting blind.

"We outshoot the plastic (decoy) guys ten to one," declares Ted Kellogg, an Ashton, Idaho, carver.

"The real test of carved decoys is along about two-thirds into the season. The birds still come into them up to the last week."

Kellogg's hunting partners and fellow carvers, Joe Landis and Mike Bon-koski of Idaho Falls, agree. All three feel the key advantage of hand-carved decoys over mass-produced dekes is that they draw the ducks in closer and hold them longer over a spread.

"Forty yards. That would be a long shot. Most of the birds we shoot are well within 30 yards," Bonkoski said.

Each decoy is a product of a carver's knowledge, imagination and skill. All contribute to the individuality of the decoys and the more authentic appear-ance of their art of deception.

"The different head positions, shapes of the body, and different paints and species mix, all look more natural," Bonkoski said.

Wood and cork decoys also outperform plastic ones, Kellogg said.

"They sit heavier in the water like a boat and ride better...a plastic decoy rides high, slips around—it's less natural."

Kellogg likes to carve low-riding, low-headed decoys with wide bodies in the classical style developed on eastern waters in the market hunting days of the 1800s. Bonkoski and Landis favor decoys painted with greater detail than the traditional solid, drab colors of the old-time models. But, while the feather-ing of the bodies is fairly well articulated, they concentrate most of their detail work on well-carved heads attached to cork or hollow-wood bodies.

The three also like to set out a spread with a good mix of bird species and a few confidence decoys, such as tip-ups simulating ducks feeding underwater or coots and other waterbirds easily spooked. Teal and pintails will be mixed in with larger blocks of mallards and a few floating geese decoys. On shore, they'll stake out a flock of geese silhouettes and a few more full-bodied decoys.

Kellogg has more fun with this concept than most carvers.

"I like making shorebirds—yellowlegs and curlews—and for awhile I was using great blue herons. I make stick decoys—two-dimensional profiles of the birds."

"These can have as much time into them as birds carved in the round," Landis pointed out. "It can take even more time with the painting."

"How many guys do you know who have a merganser in their decoys," Kellogg laughed. To top off his spread, he may toss a few crows and gulls on top of the blind.

All three learned their craft in the East. Landis hunted the tidewaters of coastal Virginia and Kellogg prowled the bays of Long Island Sound and lakes of upstate New York. Bonkoski grew up hunting for ducks on the prairie pot-holes of southern Minnesota but developed his affinity for geese on the flooded rice fields of California.

They were drawn together by their mutual interests in carving and have hunted together for more than a decade in the Upper Snake River Valley. Landis

Carved decoys, like these canvasbacks and a cinnamon teal, are beautiful art and effective decoys. There's only one problem: after you get a decoy that looks like these, who would want to toss it out into a muddy pond? (Photo: Ken Retallic)

and Bonkoski are former Snake River Woodcarvers club officers, and have taught numerous classes in decoy carving.

"I've been carving for a long time, but these two guys have taught me a lot," Kellogg said.

Passing on tricks of the trade is a time-honored part of the craft's traditions.

An original North American folk art, the ancestry of decoy making dates back to prehistoric times. The sloped head of a canvasback duck is easily recognized in the woven bundle of reeds tied together more than 3,000 years ago by a Southwestern Indian. Tucked away in a cave and brought to light again by an archaeologist, its charm is as captivating as contemporary wooden sculptures.

Simplistic turn-of-the-century models of diving ducks that once bobbed on the waves of Chesapeake Bay are treasured today as antiques. They adorn fireplace mantles throughout the country. A whole cottage industry has evolved to churn out imitations. Taking their lessons from the ancient masters, a new school of carvers has elevated the craft to the realms of fine art. Intricately carved and painted sculptures, complete in every biological detail, are now prized collector items along with those crude mementos from the past.

In addition to their working decoys, Landis and Bonkoski carve highly detailed decorative decoys. Both have collected ribbons at national competitions. Kellogg also wiles away his winter hours carving fish on contract for Bass Pro Shop.

But their true interest in the craft is in matching wits with waterfowl in the field. While they are convinced carved decoys give them an edge, it doesn't hurt to speak the language.

"All of us can call," Kellogg said. Success in the blind is "50 percent decoys and how well you can shoot. The other 50 percent is calling" in the birds.

A mark of a good waterfowler also is his ability to identify the species and sex of an incoming duck, Bonkoski added. "We're real careful about not shooting hens. We save our limit for mallards (drakes)."

Landis noted that they are heartened by the rebound in duck populations. "During the reduced (bag) limit seasons, we made our own limit. We agreed to shoot only three."

And they make a point of taking turns shooting, especially at single birds coming into the decoys.

"That's where we have our own gentlemen's club, if you will," Landis said.

Total involvement in the sport is their ultimate satisfaction.

"When you reload your own shotgun shells or tie your own (fishing) flies, it all adds to the joy of what you're doing," Landis said.

"It's the whole thing," Bonkoski said. "We like the outdoors, the birds and the water."

"Yeah," Kellogg said. "Even the ice on the willows."

Diving Ducks and Bay Ducks

Diving ducks are commonly found on lakes and ponds and back bays of river dams. In marshes and sloughs they favor deep channels or large holes in open water.

Also listed as pochards or bay ducks, divers commonly dive from the surface to swim underwater to feed on aquatic vegetation and invertebrates. Several species are chiefly vegetarians; others take in slightly higher quantities of insects, mollusks, and occasional small fish. Most nest in marshes, while several species nest in tree cavities.

Plumage of drakes is generally brighter and more strikingly marked than drab plumage of hens. Legs set far back on body and wide apart to facilitate diving. This placement makes walking awkward. Heavy bodies require a running start on water for takeoff.

Canvasback

Aythya valisineria

FIELD FACTS

Local Names
Can

Size
Large duck, up to 3 pounds, 18 to 21 inches.

Identification
Male: Burnished red head, sloping forehead, grayish white body, black chest and rump; elongated black bill, red eyes, gray feet. **Voice:** croak or growl. **Female:** mottled gray-brown, belly white; head, neck and rump brown; sloping forehead. **Voice:** quack. **In flight:** feet outstretched beyond tail; elongated neck and body; white belly contrasts with black chest and rump. Flight speed is 40 to 50 mph cruising; 70 miles per hour chased.

Status
Common summer resident in southern Idaho where water conditions permit; uncommon spring and fall migrant; winters in small numbers when conditions permit.

Harvest
Popular duck but represents less than 1 percent of annual state harvest. In Idaho, and nationally, the canvasback is making a hard, slow comeback from overharvesting in the past and the loss of breeding habitat that continues today. Harvest is strictly regulated but many hunters allow it free passage.

Color

The drake's large size and long, dull red sloping head are the best clues to its identity. The black breast and rump contrast with its plump gray body.

Mottled tan hen has a distinctive long sloping head, plump body, and pointed tail.

Speed and Sound

Among the supposedly slow takeoff diving ducks, the canvasback is quickest to get off the water. Its flight is amazingly fast, low, and direct over a pond. Both sexes are basically silent in autumn.

They decoy well to large sets, but are also one of the most wary and cautious of ducks.

Possibly the most stately duck on Earth, the drake canvasback rates high as a trophy. Most hunters, if lucky enough to bag one, take the bird to a taxidermist. (Photo: Ken Retallic)

Food and Habits

Like many other wintering coastal birds, the canvasback nests in the interior of the continent. Idaho is at the southern fringe of its breeding range. Summer populations in southern Idaho are often very localized and dependent on annual water conditions. It feeds primarily on submerged aquatic vegetation, some insects, and invertebrates.

A diving duck, the canvasback rarely lingers near shorelines in fall and winter during daylight hours. They sometimes comes closer to shore during rainy, windy weather.

Migration

The canvasback is one of few birds that migrates east and west. It may show up anywhere in autumn. When migrating, it flies in fast-moving V-shaped flocks.

Small numbers linger in southern Idaho through winter when conditions permit.

Table Fare

Considered one of the best eating ducks by many waterfowlers.

Redhead

Aythya americana

FIELD FACTS

Local Names
Pochard, red-headed duck

Size
Medium-sized duck, 2 to 2.5 pounds, 20 to 22 inches.

Identification
Male: rounded rusty red head; back and sides grayish, chest and rump black, belly white; yellow eyes, gray bill with white band toward tip; gray feet. **Voice:** deep "meow" or "purr." **Female:** mottled gray/brown with dusky white belly; pale area at base of bill and around dark brown eyes; light gray bill and feet. **Voice:** loud squawk or quack. **In flight:** rapid wing beat; white belly contrasts with black rump and red head. Flock usually flies low in a well-formed V. Flight speed is 42 mph cruising; 55 mph chased.

Status
Localized summer resident in southeastern Idaho; common late spring and late fall migrant; common winter resident in southern Idaho, uncommon in northern Idaho.

Harvest
A popular duck but represents less than 1 percent of annual harvest in Idaho. Bag limit is restricted.

Color

The round dome-like shape of the drake's rusty head identifies a redhead from a canvasback. Its body color is also a darker gray above the white belly, and the breast is more solid black. The mottled gray/brown hen has a white belly and dome-shaped head.

Speed and Sound

Fast fliers, redheads fly in tight flocks or staggered lines over marshes. When alarmed they twist and turn erratically and call nervously. They decoy well to diving duck sets.

Both sexes are noisier than canvasbacks.

A red-headed duck. (Photo: Ken Retallic)

Food and Habits

During migration redheads tend to feed at night. They rest during the day in large flocks, called rafts, in the middle of deep water in bays and lakes. They are excellent divers and feed heavily on submerged aquatic vegetation. At dawn or dusk they may move in closer to shore to feed in shallower waters.

Redheads are often found in association with other diving ducks, particularly canvasbacks. Like the canvasback, they have experienced a severe population decline due to habitat loss.

Migration

Migrating redheads fly high in V-shaped flocks. They are known for dropping straight down onto ponds from great heights.

Migrating redheads generally pass through Idaho between mid-October and late November. Many stay for the winter, however. Recent winter counts have ranged from 11,000 to more than 30,000.

Table Fare

The redhead is equal to the canvasback at the top of the waterfowl menu.

Lesser Scaup

Aythya affinis

FIELD FACTS

Local Names
   Bluebill, broadbill

Size
   Medium-sized duck, 1.75 to 2 pounds, 15 to 18 inches.

Identification
   Male: Purple-black head; gray vermiculated back with white sides and belly; chest and rump black; yellow eyes; light blue bill; gray feet; speculum white. **Voice:** "purr." **Female:** Dull brown with distinct white belly; prominent white patch at base of bill; eyes yellow; light blue bill; gray feet. **Voice:** "purr" or silent. **In flight:** Rapid wing beat. Dark head and chest contrast with white belly; white band on wings. Flight speed is up to 50 mph.

Status
   Locally common summer resident in southern Idaho; common migrant spring and fall; often linger into winter in small numbers in southern Idaho when conditions permit.

Harvest
   Represents less than 1 percent of annual state harvest.

Color

The dark purple head and slightly smaller size of the lesser scaup drake distinguishes it from the greater scaup drake, whose head has a greenish sheen. Greater scaup also show more white on their wings but are rare in Idaho. The mottled brown lesser scaup hen has a white band between the eyes and bill, which distinguishes it from a goldeneye hen.

Speed and Sound

Bluebills flush in unison and fly in swift, compact flocks low over water with a rocking, weaving flight pattern. When traveling between feeding ponds and resting areas, lesser scaup cruise in scattered U-shaped flocks that are often in pass-shooting range. They also decoy well. The high-pitched whistling of flying scaups' wings announce a flock's approach and swift passage.

Lesser scaup or "bluebills" can be found during fall in Idaho. (Photo: Ken Retallic)

Food and Habits

Bluebills are strong swimmers and excellent divers. They like ponds and marshes with some depth to them. There they dive for aquatic vegetation, insects, and crustaceans. They also feed in rivers and streams. Their diet is higher in invertebrate protein than most other diving ducks. They also take fish. Scaup are restless and often active through the day, particularly on streams. Late fall and winter flocks may be found in association with goldeneyes.

Migration

Migrating flocks of scaup can be quite large and commonly collect in large "rafts" on larger lakes. They are late fall migrants and pause to rest and feed for extended periods en route south. Between staging areas they fly high, but in feeding areas they stay fairly low. Late afternoon flights from deep water resting sites to feeding ponds and marshes offer both decoying and pass-shooting options.

Small flocks of scaup overwinter in mild years in southern Idaho.

Table Fare

Lesser scaup are good eating, although they are more popular in the Midwest and Great Lakes area.

Ring-necked Duck

Aythya collaris

FIELD FACTS

Local Names
  Ringbill, blackjack

Size
  Medium-sized duck, 1.75 to 2 pounds, 15 to 18 inches.

Identification
  Male: black back, chest and rump with white crescent on side; belly white; head blackish purple; yellow/orange eyes; bill gray with white bands at base and forward tip; gray feet. **Voice:** "purr." **Female:** blackish brown back and brown head, neck and sides; white belly; whitish eye ring and face-patch; brown eyes. **Voice:** Occasional "purr." **In flight:** dark head, neck, back and rump contrast with white belly; white band in front of wings. Wing beat fast, flight formation open. Flight speed is up to 45 mph.

Status
  A common spring, summer and fall resident in southern Idaho. The tufted duck, the Siberian version of the ring-necked duck, was reported at Hagerman in winter 1996.

Harvest
  Represents less than 1 percent of annual state harvest.

Color
  Ring-necked ducks are often confused with lesser scaups, but both sexes of the ring-necked duck lack white band on wings common to scaup. A ring-necked drake has a white bar on the flanks in front of the wings. Both sexes share a gray/blue speculum, and the hen's key feature is a white band around the base of its bill. The drake has a minor crest on the head.
  The bird's name comes from its reddish/brown band at base of the drake's neck, but it is difficult to see, even in hand. Both sexes have a white bar near the tip of its gray/blue bill.

Speed and Sound

Ring-necked ducks are very wary and easily flushed; however, they decoy well with little circling.

When cruising, they fly in small open flocks in a swift, straight line, but twist and turn when spooked. Since they favor small tree-ringed ponds, they get off the water quicker then most diving ducks.

Ringneck's soft calls are difficult to hear.

Food and Habits

A bird of the North Woods, ring-necked ducks tend to inhabit small wooded lakes and ponds more frequently than other diving ducks. They migrate in small flocks or in association with scaup.

The ringneck's diet is more concentrated on submerged aquatic vegetation than the scaup's, but it also feeds on invertebrates.

Migration

Ring-necked ducks follow favored routes south and often show up at key locations each year. Progress south, starting in mid-October, is leisurely, and a few flocks linger into early winter in southern Idaho.

Table Fare

The ring-necked duck rates high marks on the waterfowl menu.

The awkward-looking ruddy duck is present in huntable numbers in Idaho.
(Photo: Ken Retallic)

Other Ducks in Idaho

Stiff-Tailed Ducks

Stiff-tailed ducks have small stubby bodies. Their necks are short and their stiff tail is held erect as they swim. They dive for most of their food, and dive rather than fly when they sense danger.

Ruddy Duck

Oxyura jamaicensis

FIELD FACTS

Local Names
Ruddy, spiketail

Size
Small duck, 1 to 1.5 pounds, 13 to 15 inches.

Identification
Male: reddish brown body, stiff black tail; black crown on head, white cheek patch, sky blue bill; no speculum on brown wings. **Voice:** low "cluck." **Female:** barred brown body, dark back; dark crown on head, black bar on grayish cheek patch. **Voice:** weak cluck. **In flight:** small, stubby-necked duck; has difficulty getting off water, flies low. Prefers to dive to escape danger.

Status
Growing number of summer residents in southern Idaho; late-spring and early fall migrant; local birds depart by September, northern migrants may linger slightly longer if weather remains mild.

Harvest
Rarely harvested, although some consider it a fair table bird.

Sea Ducks

Several species of sea ducks, which share characteristics and flight habits with diving ducks, occur in Idaho as migrants. A few stopover as summer or winter residents in small numbers. Goldeneyes are sometimes listed with diving ducks but their diet of mollusks, aquatic insects, and small fish is 80 percent higher.

None are actively hunted, but it is illegal to leave birds to waste if shot.

Harlequin Duck (*Histrionicus histrionicus*)

The rarest duck in the Lower Forty-eight, the harlequin is listed as a species of concern in Idaho. An early fall migrant, it is doubtful hunters will encounter it during waterfowl season. But IDFG requests reports on all sightings to nearest regional office.

A small duck, the harlequin would be easily overlooked except for its beautiful colors. Its name comes from the clown-like white face "paint" on the drake's blue head. Breast and back are also blue with white bars and bands. Flanks are cinnamon/red.

Harlequin inhabit mountain forests in summer, where they feed in rapid streams for aquatic insects and invertebrates. They are easily disturbed. Hikers are asked to observe them from a distance. They generally migrate to the coast before the start of waterfowl season.

Common Goldeneye (*Bucephala clangula*)

Common migrant fall and spring; nests in northern Idaho; winters in scattered flocks in southern Idaho.

Goldeneyes frequent Idaho's larger waters. However, hunters rarely shoot them— they are easy to kill but taste like fish and smell like hell. (Photo: Ken Retallic)

Barrow's Goldeneye (*Bucephala islandica*)
Uncommon migrant fall and spring; nests in northern Idaho; rare in winter.

Bufflehead (*Bucephala albeola*)
Common spring migrant, rarer in fall; nests in northern Idaho, rare in winter.

Oldsquaw (*Clangula hyemalis*)
Occasional winter visitor in southern Idaho.

Surf Scoter (*Melanitta perspicillata*)
Rare winter visitor in southern Idaho.

Duck-like Birds

American Coot (*Fulica americana*)
Very common spring, summer and fall; some linger through winter.

The American coot, a slate-gray duck-like bird, has a heavy white bill similar to a chicken or grouse. Feet have large lobes on toes but are not webbed like ducks. Often dive rather than fly when spooked.

Considered poor table fare; yet, it is illegal to waste if shot.

Common Merganser (*Mergus merganser*)
Common migrant; nests throughout state.

Mergansers, sometimes called fish ducks, have long slim bills with serrated edges. Bodies are more elongated and streamlined than diving ducks. Webbed feet are far back on body. Often dive rather than fly when spooked.

Considered poor table fare because of fish diet. Illegal to waste if shot.

Hooded Merganser (*Lophodytes cucullatus*)
Common to uncommon migrant; nests in northern Idaho.

Red-breasted Merganser (*Mergus serrator*)
Uncommon to rare migrant; does not nest in Idaho.

The lowly coot is a temptation for those hunters with an itchy trigger finger. Just remember, if you shoot one, you eat one. It's not only the law to utilize birds that you shoot, it's also a matter of ethics. (Photo: Ken Retallic)

Canada Goose

Branta canadensis

FIELD FACTS

Local Names

Honker, western Canada goose, Canadas

Size

The western Canada goose, Branta canadensis moffitti, is the most common migrant and only nesting subspecies in Idaho. It is at the upper end in size of the 5 to 12 recognized races: 35 inches in length, 69-inch wing span, and average weight of 10 pounds.

The common Canada goose, *Branta canadensis canadensis*, migrates through Idaho in small numbers. It is slightly larger: 39 inches in length, 76-inch wing span, and average weight of 13 pounds.

The much smaller races—lesser Canada goose, dusky Canada goose, Aleutian Canada goose, cackling Canada goose, and Richardson's goose—that nest in the high Arctic rarely migrate through Idaho. They range in size from 7 pounds to less than 3 pounds. The giant Canada goose, *Branta canadensis maxima*, is the fabled "honker." It reaches 45 inches in length and 20 pounds in weight. Few in number, it is rarely found outside the northern Midwest.

Bird Identification

Both sexes are alike in size and color. The head and neck of both are jet black with a white cheek and throat patch and dark brown back and sides. The western Canada goose's chest is a darker brown than that of the grayish brown of the common Canada goose. Tail is black, while undertail coverts and the rump are white. Bill and feet are black. Coloration of immature birds is the same as adults. **In flight:** Black head and neck with white chinstrap are evident. Also look for large dark wings, white undertail coverts, and white U-shaped rump band, black tail and black feet. **Flight speed:** The Canada goose cruises at 20 to 45 mph but can gain speeds of 60 mph when chased.

Status

The western Canada goose nests throughout Idaho and large numbers migrate into and through the state. Common Canada geese pass through state in small numbers. The black brant, *Branta bernicula*, is an occasional visitor but rarely more than two or three birds at a time.

> **Harvest**
>   The Canada goose represents more than 95 percent of the goose harvest in Idaho. Resident geese numbers were unaffected by recent drought years, and populations continue to increase significantly in most regions of the state. Large western Canada goose populations in Idaho are found near its bigger lakes and impoundments, principal rivers, wildlife management areas and national wildlife refuges. Northern migrants typically arrive after mid-November and offer a second window of opportunity to hunters for relatively unwary birds. Late-season hunting in relatively mild temperatures often is good in the southwest corner of the state. In mild years, large flocks also linger into winter in the southeastern corner of state and on large ice-free lakes of north-central Idaho and the Panhandle.

Color

The Canada goose's "tuxedo" coloration—black head and neck, white chinstrap—is recognized worldwide. Colors are the same for both sexes as well as immature birds.

The Canada goose is much larger than the black brant, which has a very dark, small stocky body. White-fronted geese have a white band between the bill and eyes, but no white chinstrap; the brown breast has dark bars, while its feet and bill are yellow/orange. The blue goose, which very rarely occurs in Idaho, has a white head and upper neck, slate blue body, and pink bill and feet.

Speed and Sound

When flushed or flying to their feeding fields, Canada geese lift off the water with almost the same ease as dabbling ducks. They rise at a shallow angle in a direct line until they reach flight altitude and level off. Their large size and steady unhurried wing beat makes their flight appear deceptively slow. Family groups flying over marshes do not always form a classic V-formation of larger flocks. On clear days, flights to feeding fields are usually high. Birds fly lower on blustery, overcast days and when raining or snowing.

The deep musical "honk-a-honk" of the Canada goose is universally considered a true call of the wild and a harbinger of changing seasons.

Food and Habits

The Canada goose primarily feeds on land, where it grazes on young forbs and grasses or gleans waste grains from cultivated fields. It also feeds in wetlands and on mudflats. During migration it prefers succulent regrowth in harvested or chisel-plowed fields over standing grain crops. Winter wheat and alfalfa fields are favored feeding choices. It also feeds on harvested and unharvested grains, beans, peas, and potato plants.

Large flocks and family groups may fly long distances from resting sites to feed in uplands after daybreak and again in late afternoon. During a full moon, birds may feed at night, which often delays morning feeding flights.

Canada geese provide some of the finest wingshooting in Idaho.
(Photo: Ken Retallic)

Both feeding and resting flocks are very wary and adults take turns acting as sentry birds. In flight they have excellent eye sight and flare at bright colors or movement of hunters in blinds.

During hunting season, wild geese quickly learn to rest at sanctuaries and crowd into protected zones of national wildlife refuges and state wildlife management areas. When marshes freeze over, they will move in large flocks to quiet areas of major rivers, such as the Snake, Clearwater, and Coeur d'Alene, or ice-free impoundments, such as American Falls Reservoir, and large lakes, such as Coeur d'Alene and Pend Oreille.

Migrating Canada geese linger in colder, higher elevation areas of state, such as eastern Idaho, as long as conditions permit. When snow covers feeding fields, they depart.

Hunting Tips

Decoy blocks should contain sentry birds, however, too many in a set is counter-productive. Large blocks of 50 to 100 decoys work best in field shooting options. Silhouettes work as well as full-body decoys, or the two can be mixed. Always leave an appropriate area for decoyed flocks to land.

Smaller blocks of decoys work off the points of islands or in side channels of streams. On lakes look for places to hunt off land points and in inlets and coves. In most cases a boat or canoe is required. Do not wade large, powerful rivers like the Snake.

These four Canada geese are dwarfed by trumpeter swans. Trumpeters are a protected species—don't confuse them with snow geese. (Photo:Ken Retallic)

Pass shooting options are best along flight routes between resting and feeding areas in blustery, overcast weather and during rain or snow. So-called "firing lines" are found at several national wildlife refuges and wildlife management areas where hunters line up for the proverbial dawn patrol flights of geese lifting off for their feeding fields.

Scout ahead of time to locate feeding and loafing areas, and check with local hunting equipment shops on status of migration before setting out.

Landowner permission is required to hunt private lands—so remember not to dig pit blinds without permission and fill them in when done. A permit is required to hunt Fort Hall Indian Reservation, west of Blackfoot and north of Pocatello. Home development is increasing on some lakes, so check ahead to be sure a favorite hunting spot doesn't have new houses on it. Avoid hunting too close to developed lake areas.

Migration

With the Continental Divide defining long sections of its eastern border, Idaho straddles the eastern fringe of the Pacific Flyway. Early fall arrivals of northern nesters are usually heaviest in the northern Panhandle. Late arrivals peak after mid-November in southern regions of the state.

U.S. Highway 95 is the approximate dividing line in Idaho between the two recognized populations of western Canada geese in the Pacific Flyway. Generally, the Rocky Mountain population is found east and Pacific population west of U.S. 95. Much mixing of the two occurs in south-central Idaho. The Rocky Mountain population is highly migratory and most of its birds migrate spring and fall between wintering and nesting areas. The Pacific population is essentially nonmigratory and most birds winter on or near nesting areas. Flocks of non-breeding one- to two-year-old birds, and some of the more northern nesters, make summer molt migrations.

Most of Idaho's autumn migration of Canada geese comes from the western Canadian prairies, Montana, and Wyoming. Some migrants stop over shortly en route to more southern wintering grounds. Others spend much time in southern Idaho and provide the bulk of the state's harvest.

Table Fare

The Canada goose ranks at the top of the waterfowl menu, with its lean and dark meat.

Late Season Geese

Master Hunter Never Gives 'em a Second Chance

by Rocky Barker

A skein of Canada geese broke through the curtain of sunrise fog to the south along the Boise River. Cacophonous calls trumpeted their swift approach.

Chuck Lobdell, a U.S. Fish and Wildlife Service biologist, immediately stood up in the blind and began waving a black cloth flag attached to a wood cross like a kite. Its wings flapped loudly as he frantically swung the stick back and forth.

Like magic, the flock turned and headed straight for the decoys staked out in front of our camouflaged hide. Chuck sat down and called in the Canadas, creating a commotion that seemed to bring the plastic decoys to life.

My son, Dan, and I hunkered down in the corn-stalk blind on the edge of Chuck's snow-covered grain field. Our white medical coveralls helped to blend us into the December landscape.

Nine geese came in over our right shoulders, locked their wings into a glide, and tipped them up and down as they maneuvered to settle into the decoys. Their extended webbed feet were allowed no chance to touch ground.

Chuck signaled and all three of us leaped up, cheeks firmly pressed to the stocks of our shotguns jammed into our shoulders. Dan fired first and a goose crumpled and fell like a stone. Chuck's 10-gauge boomed and a second bird tumbled down right on top of us. Dan dodged to his right at the last second. The big-bodied gander careened off his coat and thumped onto the stubble at my feet.

But too many birds flared and flew away for Chuck's liking. These were wary, heavily-hunted Canadas on the edge of Boise, and Chuck has special techniques for hunting them. First, he only hunts them about once a week during most of the season so they don't shy away from his fields on Eagle Island along the Boise River. Next, he changes his decoy pattern and placement each time, again to keep the birds none the wiser. Finally, he makes sure that few flocks are educated by wounded birds and escapees.

In his blinds, hunters placed on the left shoot at the geese on the left side of the flock, and hunters placed on the right aim at the geese on the right side. This maximizes the opportunity to drop an entire flock, limit out quickly, and minimize the number of birds that may learn his tricks.

This particular hunt occurred on one of Chuck's personal hunting grounds. Even though not every hunter can afford to buy such a strategic farm or get landowners' permission to hunt along Idaho rivers such as the Boise, Payette, Weiser, and Snake, there are many public access areas near lakes and other waterways where late season goose hunting can be as good, or better, than most waterfowl regions nationwide.

Lesser Snow Goose

Chen caerulescens

FIELD FACTS

Local Names

Snows, white geese, light geese

Size

Medium-sized goose, 27 to 31 inches long, 60-inch wing span, 4 to 6.5 pounds.

Identification

Both sexes are alike in color and size. Snow-white head, neck and body; black wing tips very distinct in flight, difficult to see on ground or water; pink bill and feet. Immature snow geese have dusky gray body, dark wing tips; black bill and feet.

Hunters should be aware that large flocks of tundra swans and smaller collections of the rare trumpeter swan routinely occur in Idaho. They are not legal gamebirds. Swans are much larger than geese, with all-white bodies and no black wing tips. Bills and feet are black. The tundra swan has a small yellow patch at base of bill. Trumpeter swan bill has thin salmon orange rim at back of mouth.

In flight: Snow-white body and distinct black wing tips of snow geese are evident. Body of immature birds are dusky gray, wing tips dark.

Flight speed: cruise at 30 to 45 mph, approach 50 mph when chased.

Status

Snow geese spend limited time in Idaho during spring and fall migrations, although in mild winters they may linger until the end of the season in southern regions of state.

Harvest

Snow geese represent less than 2 percent of goose harvest in Idaho.

- Spring migrants follow frost thaw north. They may linger in huge flocks in southern Idaho until conditions permit next stage in flight to high Arctic nesting grounds. Autumn flocks are much smaller, migration patterns more sporadic. They generally depart the state before feeding fields become snow covered.

Color

Snow geese and the tiny Ross' geese are the only wild geese with all-white bodies. Black wing tips of both are prominent, and easily seen in flight; bills and feet are pink.

The Ross' goose, *Chen rossii*, is a miniature version of the snow goose occasionally seen in association with flocks of snows, less often with Canada geese. Among the rarest of geese, it is about the size of a mallard duck. It also has a rarely seen blue phase like the lesser snow goose.

Once considered a separate species, the blue goose is a second color phase of the snow goose. The most distinctively colored North American goose, its white head and dark body set it apart instantly.

The blue goose is commonly found in the Central Flyway but rarely seen in Idaho or elsewhere in the Pacific Flyway. It has a white head and upper neck, slate-blue gray body, dark wing tips, pink bill and feet. Immature bird has light-gray head, dull blue/gray body, dark wing tips, black bill and feet. Its primary nesting grounds are in the Hudson Bay region, where mixed pairs of the two color phases are common.

Black wing tips distinguish snow geese from much larger trumpeter and tundra swans, which have all-white bodies and wings, black bills and feet. Similar-sized American white pelican has black wing tips and secondary primaries, but has long bright-orange bill and feet.

Speed and Sound

Snow geese fly in huge flocks that form and reform into fluttering V-shaped formations, long waving lines and broad undulating U-shaped curves. They are strong fliers with more rapid wing beats than Canada geese and appear faster because of smaller size. Snow geese need no running start to take off, and spring easily into the air from land and water.

Snow geese are very vocal. On the water and in the air, flocks constantly chatter in high-pitched shill cries that sounds much like a kennel of yelping dogs.

Food and Habits

Snow geese graze inland and on mud flats on basically the same plants and crops as Canada geese; however they grub for succulent new growth more aggressively than other geese. Flooded alfalfa fields are a favorite layover. Other field landings are in the open parts of fields, far from borders like shelter belts or weedy canal banks.

Early risers, they usually lift off for their feeding fields as soon as dawn brightens the horizon. Snow geese are very restless and may move back and forth between feeding areas until midday when they return to a convenient sanctuary to rest.

This restless nature of the bird also is apparent on water. Elements of huge flocks continually rise and land in other sections of massed bands, or they wheel around marsh or lake before settling down again.

Late-afternoon flights to feeding fields are more erratic and harder to predict than Canada geese. Snows also commonly feed at night during the full moon.

Snow geese offer a brief window of opportunity during fall in Idaho. When they do arrive, as evidenced here, they arrive en masse. (Photo: Ken Retallic)

Snow geese are very wary and easily spooked. Flocks flush wildly in unison like many dabbling ducks. They have excellent eye sight and easily detect bright colors or movements of hunters in blinds, although they typically approach landing areas lower than Canada geese.

Hunting Tips

Snow geese decoy very well but incidental harvest in Idaho doesn't warrant expense of large sets of full-body decoys common to Central Flyway and southern California. Still, silhouettes are easy to produce and two or three dozen are handy to have when opportunities arise. Some enterprising hunters use disposable baby diapers as impromptu decoys. Best bet is to place decoys in the same place snows were seen feeding previously.

A large flock of snow geese may circle a decoy set several times before deciding to come in or, more often than not, set down off to the side. In any decoy spread, allow room for new birds to land close to your shooting zone.

Aggressive, louder versions of standard Canada goose calls are effective in getting snows to respond. Pit blinds are not necessary. Lay down flat in the decoy spread with camouflage netting or swatches of grain draped over you to break up your outline. Another good option is to nestle into or against an isolated rock pile often found in dry land wheat fields.

Snow geese are easily identified in the air by their dark wing patches.
(Photo: Ken Retallic)

Lone snow geese are easiest to call into Canada goose decoy sets. Family groups also may be induced into separating from a passing flock. Occasionally, loners even look over mallard decoys.

Afternoon flight patterns to feeding or resting areas may be very low, particularly over broad marshes on overcast or blustery days. Because of this, snow goose shooting hours end at 1 p.m. in some Midwestern states. There is no suspension of waterfowl shooting hours in Idaho.

Fremont and Teton counties, north and east of Idaho Falls, are closed to the taking of light geese to protect against accidental shooting of swans.

Migration

Snow geese migrating through western and southwestern Idaho are en route to central California. Look for them in the Coeur d'Alene system, lower Clearwater River area, and lower Snake River Plain from Thousand Springs west to Deer Flat National Wildlife Refuge. They rarely occur in the northern Panhandle.

Migrants passing through the eastern corner of the state winter in southern New Mexico and Arizona. Layovers commonly occur at American Falls Reservoir, Blackfoot Reservoir, and the Bear Lake area.

Table Fare

Snow geese are less lean than Canada geese and are placed lower on the menu by many hunters; however, young birds are excellent table fare.

White-fronted Goose

Anser albifrons

FIELD FACTS

Local Names

Speckled belly, tiger breast, laughing goose

Size

Medium-sized goose, 27 to 30 inches long, 60-inch wing span, 4.5 to 7 pounds.

Identification

Both sexes alike in color, female smaller than male. Grayish brown body, white rump and tail, yellow-orange bill and feet. Black bars on breast and white on front of face distinguish adult from immature bird. In flight: Yellow-orange feet and black-barred breast of adult evident in flight. Flight speed: white-fronted geese can reach speeds of 45 to 50 mph.

Status

Considered an occasional migrant through Idaho; however, due to their secretive nature and early season migration, many white-fronted geese may be overlooked.

Harvest

Autumn numbers appear to be increasing, but very few white-fronted geese are harvested in Idaho.

Color

The white band between the bill and eyes of this goose is the source of its name. The head and neck are dark brown, not jet black, and it has no white chin strap like the Canada goose. The male's grayish brown breast has dark bars, and the feet and bill are yellow/orange. Immature birds do not have bars on the breast or white on the face, while bills and feet are dull yellow.

Both the white-fronted and Canada goose are much larger than the black brant, which has a very dark, small stocky body. Blue goose, which very rarely occurs in Idaho, has a white head and upper neck; slate-blue/gray body, and pink bill and feet.

Speed and Sound

White-fronted geese are agile swift fliers. Flight speed appears slower than it actually is due to large size of body and its slow steady wing beat in flight. When flushed the white-fronted labors harder to get off the water and needs more of a running start than other wild geese.

They often migrate in huge flocks in a V-formation similar to Canada geese and, at a distance, may be mistaken for their more common brethren. Flock formations over marshes and en route to inland fields are generally more dispersed and spread out in wavy lines.

The white-fronted are very vocal. Musical "wah-wah-wah" call is often described as a loud laughing sound. Some hear its call as "kah-lah-aluck."

Food and Habits

White-fronted geese are found during migration in wetlands, grassy fields, and grain fields. Small flocks and family groups migrating separately routinely mix with Canadas and snows. They are commonly seen feeding on fringes of other geese flocks.

White-fronted geese awake before dawn and are among the first on inland feeding fields. They rarely linger and return to resting spots by early morning. More secretive than Canadas or snows, white-fronted geese prefer shallow marshes with good stands of reeds and cattails for cover.

Migration

White-fronted geese are among the first to depart the Arctic's prolific nesting grounds. Usually en route south by September, they often migrate at night and pause to rest and feed by day.

Southwestern Idaho is on the northern fringe of their smaller inland wintering grounds, and a few flocks may linger until driven out by ice. The majority of migrants passing through Idaho winter in California's Central Valley. Some white-fronted geese in the Pacific flyway winter in the southwest states and northern Mexico.

They are strictly a Western bird, and only rare stragglers are found east of the Mississippi.

Table Fare

White-fronted geese rank at the top of the waterfowl menu.

Waterfowl Hunting Ethics

Courtesy to fellow hunters and ethical behavior are fundamental ingredients to successful, pleasant waterfowl hunts.

1. Do not leave good manners at home.

2. Do not crowd fellow waterfowlers. Crowding is not safe and it is disrespectful.

3. Hunting on public land is first-come, first-served. If someone is in your favorite spot, move to another location.

4. If ducks are flying into a neighbor's decoys, it is discourteous to expand your shooting range to get in on the action

5. Resist temptation to flock shoot. Always target individual birds.

6. Do not shoot at waterfowl outside reasonable range. "Sky busting'" is the most common shortcoming of undisciplined bird hunters. Besides infuriating fellow hunters, shooting at high-flying birds increases the loss of wounded waterfowl.

7. Always make your best effort to retrieve wounded birds.

8. Do not trespass. Request landowner permission to hunt on private lands.

9. Do not litter. That includes picking up spent shells from a blind.

Keep an Eye Out for Trumpeters

Transplanted trumpeter swans might show up just about anywhere in southern Idaho due to trapping and transplanting efforts in Fremont County.

There is no hunting season for swans in Idaho. Also, Fremont and Teton counties are closed to the taking of light geese—snow geese and Ross' geese—to further protect both trumpeter and tundra swans.

Waterfowl hunters should have no trouble distinguishing the huge white swans from snow geese or any other huntable species. Trumpeter swans are even larger than the more common tundra swans and, like the tundra species, are nearly pure white with white wingtips. Young swans, called cygnets, are gray in color but do not have dark wing tips. Snow geese are much smaller and have black wingtips.

The majestic trumpeter swan has become relatively rare in the Intermountain West since the late 19th century. Most of the remnant population lived in or near Yellowstone National Park until trapping and transplanting began in

Resting Canada geese and trumpeter swan. (Photo: Ken Retallic)

1988 to disperse growing numbers of wintering birds. Biologists and conservationists worried trumpeters might be vulnerable as a species if disaster struck
their small habitat areas. Also, the bird's numbers were beginning to outgrow
smaller wintering grounds.

Under the direction of the U.S. Fish and Wildlife Service and with the cooperation of Idaho Fish and Game, trumpeters have been trapped in the Island
Park area and freed in other parts of Idaho and in Oregon, Wyoming, and Utah.
Nearly 2,000 swans have been moved and have been observed in recent years
in all western states, western Canada and in Mexico.

Biologists are tracking the success of this dispersal and ask for help from
wildlife observers. Transplanted trumpeter swans have been neck-banded
and some marked with pink dye. Most neck-bands are green but some are red,
yellow, or white. A few have wing tags. Each band carries a unique letter/num-
ber code in which the orientation of the digits is critical. Anyone seeing a band
should record its color and numbers carefully, along with time and location of
the sighting.

The band numbers can be reported to the U.S. Fish and Wildlife Service,
1246 Yellowstone, A-4, Pocatello, Idaho 83021, 208-237-6616.

Region 1–Panhandle

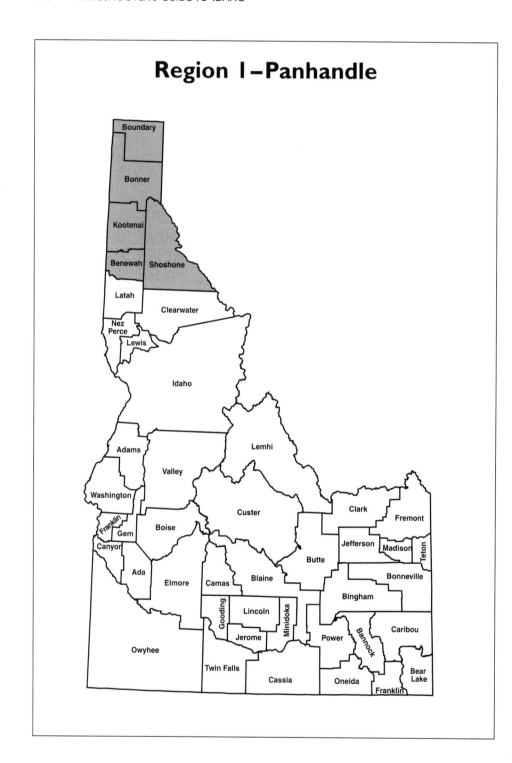

Region 1–Panhandle

This region is in the northern extension of the state below the Canadian border. It consists of Boundary, Bonner, Kootenai, Benewah, and Shoshone counties. Big game hunt units include 1, 2, 3, 4, 4a, 5, 6, 7 and 9. Regional office is located in Coeur d'Alene. Hunters, anglers, and outdoor enthusiasts will find dense forests and the greatest concentration of lakes in the western states. The Panhandle Region leads the state in ruffed grouse and wild turkey harvests. Elevations range from 2,100 at Priest River to 8,643 at Needle Peak.

Wildlife Management Areas
- McArthur Lake—1,200 acres, waterfowl and upland gamebirds; 17 miles north of Sandpoint via U.S. 95 (3.5 miles south of Naples).
- Coeur d'Alene—2 acres (public acess to lake), waterfowl; 3 miles south of Harrison on State Highway 97 at Thompson Lake Outlet (10 miles east of Coeur d'Alene).
- St. Maries—6,200 acres, upland gamebirds; 7 miles south of St. Maries on State Highway 3.
- Snow Peak—12,055 acres, upland gamebirds; 16 miles south of Avery via St. Joe River Road (Forest Road 50).

Blue & Ruffed (Forest) Grouse Distribution Region 1–Panhandle

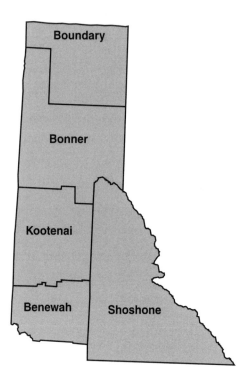

Gray (Hungarian) Partridge Distribution
Region 1–Panhandle

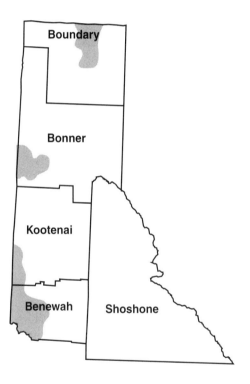

Pheasant Distribution
Region 1 – Panhandle

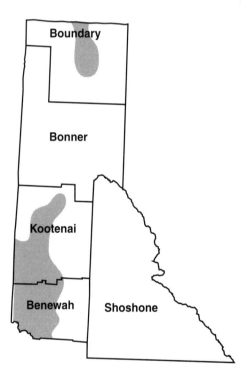

Franklin's (Spruce) Grouse Distribution Region 1–Panhandle

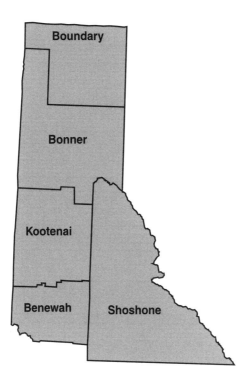

Wild Turkey Distribution
Region 1–Panhandle

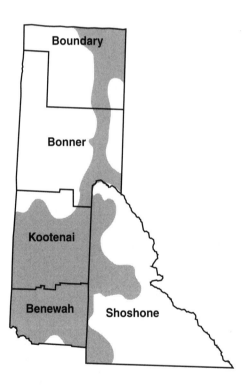

Boundary and Bonner Counties

Population–34,954	Two County Area–2,041,000 acres
October Temperature–47°	Annual Precipitation–17.4
Acres in CRP–3,022	

Located in the northern edge of the state, wedged between Washington, British Columbia and Montana, Boundary and Bonner counties included grain and hops farms and many miles of forested mountain terrain with big lakes and rivers. There is excellent ruffed grouse and turkey hunting in the forests,upland birds on the farms and good early season waterfowl hunting.

UPLAND BIRDS
Blue & Ruffed (Forest) Grouse, Gray (Hungarian) Partridge, Pheasant, Spruce Grouse, Turkey

WATERFOWL
Ducks & Geese

Bonners Ferry
Population–2,000 • Elevation–1,775

Bonners Ferry is a small town located in very northern Idaho. It offers cozy lodging and adequate eateries for the visiting hunter. Forest grouse, turkey, pheasant, Hun and waterfowl hunts can be combined with big game ventures in the fall. The surrounding forests support dense populations of whitetail and mule deer, plus elk and black bear.

ACCOMMODATIONS
Kootenai River Inn, Kootenai River Plaza / Allows pets / 208-267-8511 / Fax 208-267-8511

Sunnyside Motel, P.O. Box 29 / Allows pets / 208-267-3611

Town and Country Motel and RV Park, Rt 4 Box 4661 / Allows Pets / 208-267-7918

Bonners Ferry Resort, Rt 4, Box 4700 / No pets / 208-267-2422

CAMPGROUNDS
Blue Lake Camp & RV Park / 20 full hook-up sites, showers, laundry, tent sites available / 208-267-2029

Twin Rivers Canyon Resort / 26 full hook-up sites, showers, restrooms, tent sites available / 208-267-5932

RESTAURANTS
China Kitchen, Hwy 95 South Main / 208-267-5412
Family Restaurant, Hwy 95 South Main / 208-267-7323
R Place, Hwy 95 South Main / 208-267-7347

SPORTING GOODS
Hobby Shop, 6791 Denver / 208-267-7811

VETERINARIANS
Bonners Ferry Veterinary Clinic, 24-hour emergency service / 208-267-7502

HOSPITALS
Boundary County Hospital, 551 Kaniksu Street / 208-765-400 or 800-826-2390

AIRPORTS
Coeur d'Alene Airport, 11401 Airport Drive / Closest commercial airline service /
208-772-7838

AUTO RENTAL
Bonners Ferry Nissan, Chrysler, Plymouth, Dodge, 6471 Bonner / 208-267-3181
Riverside Chevrolet Oldsmobile Pontiac, 302 West Bonner / 208-267-3100

AUTO SERVICE
Riverside Chevrolet Oldsmobile, 6471 Bonner Street / 208-267-3181

FOR MORE INFORMATION
Bonners Ferry Chamber of Commerce
P.O. Box 375
208 East Riverside
208-267-5922

SANDPOINT
Population–4,800 • Elevation–2,100

A popular, growing little resort town that rests on the edge of Lake Pend Oreille, Sandpoint offers quick access to some of the best waterfowl hunting in Idaho and it offers turkeys and mountain grouse in the surrounding forests. But, ducks and geese, lots of them, are the true advantage to staying in this town. Hunters can literally look out the hotel window and see flights of mallards and Canada geese heading to and from the mud flats of Lake Pend Oreille.

ACCOMMODATIONS
Best Spa Motel, 521 North 3rd Avenue / Allows pets / 208-263-3532
Bottle Bay Resort and Marina, 1360 Bottle Bay Road, 7 miles south of Sandpoint off Hwy 95 / Allows pets / 208-263-5916
Leucocyte Inn, 106 Bridge Street / Allows pets / 208-263-3717
Monarch West Lodge, P.O. Box 3171, 1 mile north of Sandpoint Mall / Allows pets / 208-263-1222
Sandpoint Quality Inn, P.O. Box 187 / Allows Pets / 208-263-2111

CAMPGROUNDS
KOA Sandpoint / 20 full hook-ups, 64 rustic sites, ice, grocery, laundry, phone, tent sites available / 208-263-4482
Pines Mobile Home & RV Park / 18 full hook-ups, tent sites available / 208-262-0621

RESTAURANTS
The Past Time Cafe, 209 North 1st Avenue / Open 24 hours 208-263-201

SPORTING GOODS
Past Time Sport Center, 207 North 1st Avenue / Sporting goods and flyfishing supplies / 208-263-4409
Outdoor Experience, 314 North 1st Avenue / Sporting goods and flyfishing supplies / 208-263-6028
Sports Cellar, 402 Sherman Avenue / 800-676-8450

VETERINARIANS
Bonner Animal Hospital, 511 Poplar / 208-263-7551 / Emergency number: 208-263-7551
Pend Oreille Veterinary Service, Kootenai Cutoff Road / 208-263-2145

HOSPITALS
Bonners General Hospital, 520 North 3rd Avenue / 208-263-1441 / Emergency number: 208-265-473

AIRPORT

Coeur d'Alene Airport, 11401 Airport Drive / Closest commercial airline service / 208-772-7838

AUTO RENTAL

Evergreen Ford Mercury Nissan, 3215 Hwy 95 North / 208-263-3127
Taylor Parker Motor Co, 300 Cedar Street / 208-263-2138

FOR MORE INFORMATION

Greater Sandpoint Chamber
P.O. Box 928
Sandpoint, ID 83864
208-263-2161 / Fax 208-265-5289

Kootenai, Benewah and Shoshone Counties

Population–91,664	Three County Area–3,021,000 acres
October Temperature–48°	Annual Precipitation–25.4"
Acres in CRP–17,871	

The Silver Valley and the St. Joe River Valley are forest and lake regions with only a small portion of farmland. Ruffed grouse and turkey hunting is excellent in the Panhandle National Forest and waterfowl hunting is good on the rivers and lakes.

UPLAND BIRDS
Pheasant, Gray Partridge, Forest Grouse, Turkeys

WATERFOWL
Ducks & Geese

Coeur d'Alene
Population–4,800 • Elevation–2,100

A popular summer haven for water sports enthusiasts, Coeur d' Alene is an excellent location for the fall bird hunter. Forest grouse and turkey make up most of the take here, but there are a few pheasants and Hungarian partridge hanging around. Ducks and geese abound. The city itself offers excellent lodging, great restaurants and plenty of sporting goods if needed. In north Idaho, you will be hard-pressed to find a prettier setting or a more comfortable town to reside in.

ACCOMMODATIONS
Bennett Bay Inn, East 5144, 3 miles east on old I-90 / Pets allowed / 800-368-8609
Coeur d'Alene Bed and Breakfast, 906 Foster Avenue / Pets allowed / 208-667-7527 / Fax 208-667-7527
Comfort Inn, 280 West Appleway / Pets allowed / 208-765-5500 800-228-5150
Holiday Inn, 414 West Appleway / Pets allowed / 208-765-3200 / Fax 208-664-1962
Coeur d'Alene Resort On the Lake / Allows Pets / 208-765-400 or 800-826-2390

CAMPGROUNDS
Cedar Motel & RV Park / 41 full hook-ups, showers, tent sites available / 208-664-2278
Alpine Country Store and RV Park / 25 full hook-ups, tent sites available / 208-772-4305

RESTAURANTS
Jimmy D's Restaurant, 320 Sherman Avenue / 208-664-9774
Iron Horse, 664 Sherman Avenue / 208-667-7314
Dennys Restaurant, 2300 North 4th / 208-664-3712 / Open 24 hours
Wally's Wolf Lodge Inn Steak House, East I 90 Exit 22 / 205-664-6665
Cedars Floating Restaurant, Blackwell Island / 208-664-2922

SPORTING GOODS STORES
Fins and Feathers, 1816 1/2 Sherman Avenue / 208-667-9304
Black Sheep Sporting Goods and Toys, 2424 North 24th / 208-667-7831
Cast and Blast, 9521 North Government Way Hayden Lake / 208-772-3748

VETERINARIANS
Alpine Animal Hospital, 655 Best / 208-664-2168 / After hours call 208-667-1961
Hayden Lake Animal Hospital , 8761 North Government Way, Hayden Lake /
 208-772-3288 / 24 hours-208-723-3288
Animal Medical Center, 1902 Sherman Avenue / 24 hours 208-67-3418

HOSPITALS
Kootenai Medical Center, 2003 Lincoln Way / Emergency / 208-666-2000 /
 Switchboard 208-666-3000
North Idaho Immediate Care Center, 1701 Lincoln Way / Open 7 days a week
 7AM–11PM / 208-667-9110

AIRPORTS
Coeur d'Alene Airport, 11401 Airport Drive / 208-772-7838
Spokane International Airport / Major carriers: Northwest, United, Delta,
 Southwest, Horizon, & Alaska / 509-455-6455

AUTO RENTAL
Thrifty, 101 Best Avenue / 208-765-277
Dollar Rent a Car, Hwy 95 & Dalton Avenue / 208-664-0682

AUTO SERVICE
Bowlers Automotive, 1148 North 4th Street / 208-664-9319
Jerry's Automotive, 1280 Last Chance Road / 208-664-3081

FOR MORE INFORMATION
Coeur d'Alene Convention and Visitors Bureau
P.O. Box 908
4199 West River Bend Avenue
Coeur d'Alene, ID 83854
208-773-4080

St. Maries

Population–2,794 • Elevation–2,150

The St. Maries Mission is the main draw to this town, but it does offer some acco-modations for the travelling bird hunter. There are good numbers of turkey and mountain grouse in the nearby forests. Ducks and geese are abundant, too. Bird hunts here could be combined with a hunt for elk or whitetail deer. There are some big bucks and bulls in the area.

ACCOMMODATIONS

Benewah Resort, Rt 1 Box 50C, 7 miles West on Hwy 5 / Allows pets / 208-245-3288

Knoll Hus Bed and Breakfast, P.O. Box 572, Mission Point, 7 miles north of St. Maries on Hwy 3 / No pets / 208-245-4137

The Pines Motel, 1117 Main / No pets / 208-245-2545

AIRPORT

Coeur d'Alene Airport, 11401 Airport Drive / 208-772-7838

Spokane International Airport / Major carriers: Northwest, United, Delta, Southwest, Horizon, & Alaska / 509-455-6455

FOR MORE INFORMATION

St. Maries Chamber of Commerce
P.O. Box 162, 906 Main
St. Maries, ID 83861
208-245-3563

Spokane
Population–185,000 • Elevation–1,893

Located in far eastern Washington, Spokane is a good place for a traveling bird hunter, especially from western Washington or British Columbia, to lay over on the way to Idaho. You can pick a place to stay from numerous motels and hotels, and there are a number of great restaurants. Spokane is also a good place to pick up sporting goods before heading to Idaho.

ACCOMMODATIONS
Cavanaugh's River Inn, 700 North Division / Allows pets / 509-326-5577 or 800-THE-Inns
Comfort Inn North, North Division / Allows pets / 509-467-7111 or 800-221-2222
Spokane Red Lion, North Sullivan / Allows pets / 509-924-9000
The Ramada Inn, Spokane Area Airport / Allows pets / 509-272-6232 or 800-272-6232
Nendel's Valu Inn, 1420 West 2nd / Allows pets / 509-838-2026 or 800-246-6835

CAMPGROUNDS
KOA Spokane / 196 sites, 82 full hook-ups, sewage disposal, laundry, phone, grocery, ice, tables, grills, swimming pool / Open March through November 1 / 509-924-4722
Ponderosa Hill RV Park / 168 full hook-up sites, tent sites available, laundry, pool / 800-494-7275

RESTAURANTS
Denny's, North 4903 Division / 509-489-8060
    North 6 Pines Road / 509-926-2408
    East 5815 Sprague / 509-535-8371
    West 1412 2nd / 509-747-8992 / All open 24 hours
The Calgary Steakhouse, East 3040 Sprague / 509-535-7502
Clinkerdagger, West 621 Mallon (located in the Flour Mill) / 509-328-5965
Ankeny's, 515 West Sprague Avenue / Open 11:30AM–1:30PM and 5:30–10PM; Friday to 11PM; Saturday 5:30–11PM; Sunday 9:30AM–1:30PM / 509-838-2711
Chapter Eleven, 9304 North Division (Jct of US 2 (Division Street) and I-90 exit 281, then 7 miles north to Jct of US 2 and 395 / Open 11:30AM–10PM; Friday to 11PM; Saturday 4–11PM; Sunday 4–10PM / 509-467-7011
The Old Spaghetti Factory, 152 South Monroe (downtown) / Open 5 9:30PM; Friday & Saturday to 11PM; Sunday 4–9PM / 509-624-8916
Sea Galley, 1221 North Howard Street (downtown) / Open 11AM–10PM; Friday & Saturday to 11PM; Sunday Noon–10PM / 509-327-3361

SPORTING GOODS
Outdoor Sportsman, 1602 north Division and Mission / Sporting goods and flyfishing supplies / 509-328-9900
REI (Recreational Equipment Inc,) North 1125 Monroe / Sporting goods sales and rentals / 509-328-9900

VETERINARIANS
South Care, East 2718 57th / 509-448-4480
Pioneer Veterinary Services, 5311 South Hwy 27 / 509-928-2597
Garland Animal Clinic, West 623 Garfield / 509-326-3151

HOSPITALS
Holy Family Hospital, 2633 North Lingerwood / Switchboard 509-482-0111 / Emergency 509-482-2460
Valley Hospital and Medical Center, 12606 East Mission / Switchboard 509-924-6650 / Emergency 509-922-9466

AIRPORT
Spokane International Airport / Major carriers: Northwest, United, Delta, Southwest, Horizon, & Alaska / 509-455-6455

AUTO RENTAL
Avis, Spokane International Airport / 509-747-8081
Budget, 8325 East Sprague Avenue / 509-922-4466
　　　　430 West 1st Avenue / 509-624-2255
　　　　Airport / 800-527-07700
Hertz, Spokane International Airport / 509-747-3101

AUTO SERVICE
Barry's Downtown Automotive Specialists, East 430 Sprague / 209-467-5493
Bob's Chevron Auto Center, Corner of Frances & Wall / 509-467-5493
Mechanic's Pride, West 1002 3rd / 509-747-5371
　　　　10101 North Newport Hwy / 509-467-6034
　　　　South 3103 Grand / 509-624-9839

FOR MORE INFORMATION
Spokane Area Chamber of Commerce
1020 West Riverside
Spokane, WA 99201
509-624-1393 or 800-248-3230

Guides and Outfitters
Region 1–Panhandle

ACTION HUNTS
120 East Lake Street #207, Sandpoint, ID 83864
Phone 208-265-4789 / Fax 208-263-1056
Bird Hunting – Forest Grouse
Accommodations–Backcountry lodge
Other Services–Big game hunting

HIDDEN CREEK RANCH
7600 East Blue Lake Road, Harrison, ID 83833
Phone 208-689-3209 / Fax 208-689-9115 / Toll-free 1-800-446-3833
Contact–John Muir, Iris Behr
Email–hiddencreek@hiddencreek.com
Web Site–http://www.nidlink.com/~hiddencreek
Bird Hunting–Forest Grouse
Accommodations–Guest Ranch
Other Services–Big game hunting, flyfishing, horse pack trips, trail rides, back-
    packing, mountain biking

RIVER ODYSSEYS WEST, INC.
P.O. Box 579, Coeur d'Alene, ID 83816
Phone 208-765-0841 / Fax 208-667-6506 / Toll-free 1-800-451-6034
Contact–Peter Grubb
Email–rowinc@aol.com
Web Site–http://www.rowinc.com
Bird Hunting–Forest Grouse
Accommodations–Lodge
Other Services–Flyfishing, rafting, drift boating, horse pack trips, backpacking

ST. JOE HUNTING/FISHING CAMP, INC.
Willard Judge
HC 01, Box 109A, St. Maries, ID 83861
Phone 208-245-4002 / Fax 208-245-4002
Contact–Willard Judge
Bird Hunting–Forest Grouse
Accommodations–Backcountry lodge
Other Services–Big game hunting, backcountry lake fishing, river/stream fishing,
    horse pack trips, trail rides

Region 2–Clearwater

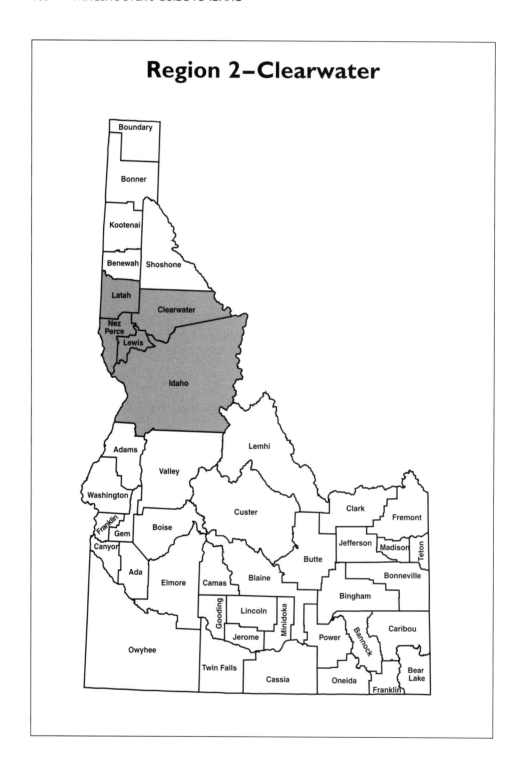

Region 2–Clearwater

The Clearwater Region is the state's second most northern area and consists of Latah, Clearwater, Nez Perce, Lewis, and Idaho counties. Big game hunting units include 8, 8a, 10, 10a, 11, 11a, 12, 13, 14, 15, 16, 16a, 17, 18, 19 and 20. Its regional office is located in Lewiston. Some of North America's largest wilderness and primitive areas are found here, accessible only by foot or horseback, and challenging even to the most experienced hunters. Chukar, turkey, and forest grouse abound. Elevations range from 753 at Lewiston to 9,393 at He Devil Peak above Hells Canyon of the Snake, deepest river gorge on the continent.

Wildlife Management Areas
- Craig Mountain—22,960 acres in three units, upland bird hunting; approximately 25 miles south of Lewiston via Waha Lake Road.
- Red River—IDFG education center for anadromous fisheries; forest grouse in national forest; east of Grangeville and south of Elk City via State Highway 14.

Blue & Ruffed (Forest) Grouse Distribution Region 2–Clearwater

Chukar Distribution
Region 2–Clearwater

Gray (Hungarian) Partridge Distribution Region 2–Clearwater

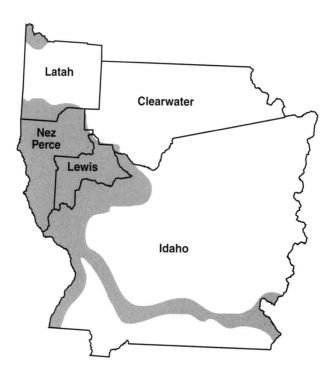

Pheasant Distribution
Region 2–Clearwater

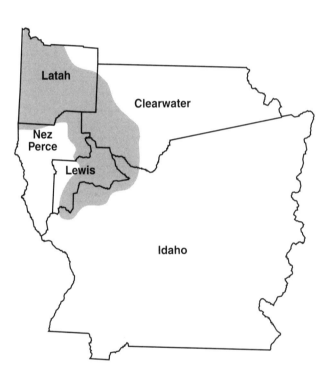

Quail Distribution
Region 2–Clearwater

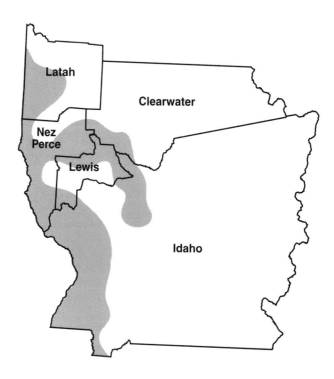

Spruce Grouse Distribution
Region 2–Clearwater

Wild Turkey Distribution
Region 2–Clearwater

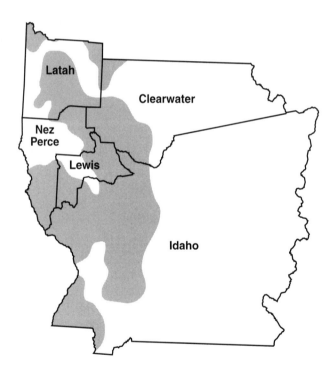

Latah County

Population–30,617
October Temperature–49°
Acres in CRP–35,517

County Area–698,000 acres
Annual Precipitation–24"

Latah County is the home of the University of Idaho and lies in the center of the great Palouse grasslands that today is mostly wheat country. It also has a part of the Clearwater National Forest so it offers a wide variety of upland hunting opportunities.

UPLAND BIRDS
Blue & Ruffed (Forest) Grouse, Gray (Hungarian) Partridge, Pheasant, California Quail, Spruce Grouse, Turkey

WATERFOWL
Ducks and Geese

Nez Perce and Lewis Counties

Two-County Population–37,270
October Temperature–49°
Lands in CRP–11,712

Two-County Area–853,000
Annual Precipitation–14"

Nez Perce and Lewis counties range from mountainous terrain along the Snake River to substantial plains with rolling farms. Pheasants, gray partridge and chukar hunting is excellent.

UPLAND BIRDS
Blue & Ruffed (Forest) Grouse, Chukar, Gray (Hungarian) Partridge, Pheasant, California Quail, Spruce Grouse, Turkey

WATERFOWL
Ducks & Geese

Lewiston

Population – 30,000 • Elevation – 750

Lewiston stakes claim to the jet boat capital of the world and it is with a jet boat, or a quality raft, that wingshooters can access Hell's Canyon of the Snake River. The canyon offers some of the best chukar hunting in the world, but you'll have to work hard to get them — that shouldn't surprise seasoned chukar hunters. Lewiston also offers excellent pheasant and forest grouse hunting, and there are many good restaurants and lodging sites.

ACCOMMODATIONS

Churchill Inns, 1021 Main Street / Allows pets / 208-743-4501
Pony Soldier Motor Inn, 716 Main Street / Allows pets / 208-743-9526 / Fax 208-746-6212
Ramada Inn, 21st Street / Allows pets / 208-799-1000, 800-232-6730 / Fax 208-746-8321
Sacajawea Motor Inn / Allows pets / 208-746-1393, 800-333-1393 / Fax 208-743-3620
Super 8 Motel, North-South Hwy off Hwy 95 South / Allows pets / 208-743-8808, 800-800-8000 / Fax 208-743-8808

CAMPGROUNDS

Hell's Gate State Park / 64 full hook-ups, sewage disposal, public phone, store, tent sites available / 208-799-5015

RESTAURANTS

Rusty's Ranch Cafe, 2418 North and South Highway / 208-746-5054
Jonathan's, 301 D Street / 208-746-3438
Meriwether's/ M.J. Barleyhoppers 621 21st Street / 208-799 1000
Waffles n' More, 1421 Main Street / 208-743-5189

SPORTING GOODS

Lolo Sporting Goods, 1026 Main Street / 208-743 1031
Dave's Husky Sport Shop, 158 Thain Road / 208-743-6445
Rae Brothers Sporting Goods, 247 East Main / 208-983-2877
Gart Bros., 625 21st Avenue / 208-746-8040
Folletts Mountain Sports, 1019 21st / 208-743-4200

VETERINARIANS

Orchards Pet Hospital , 207 Thain Road / 24-hour service / 208-743-5432
Lewiston Veterinary Clinic, 421 22nd Street North / 24 hour service / 208-743-6553
Southway Animal Clinic, 705 16th Avenue / 208-743-0280 / Emergency service available

HOSPITALS
St. Josephs, 416 6th Street / 208-743-2511

AIRPORTS
Lewiston Nez Perce County Airport, 406 Burnell / 208-746-7962
Spokane International Airport / Major carriers: Northwest, United, Delta, Southwest, Horizon, & Alaska / 509-455-6455

AUTO RENTALS
Budget Rent a Car, Lewiston Nez Perce Airport / 208-746-0488
Enterprise Rent A Car, 625 21st Street / 208-746-2878

AUTO SERVICE
Auto Village, 21st St & 16th Avenue / 208-746-2391
Dale Marshalls Auto Service & Repair / 208-746-4335

FOR MORE INFORMATION
Lewiston Chamber of Commerce
2207 East Main
Lewiston, ID 83501
208-743-3531 / Fax 208-743-2176

Clearwater & Idaho Counties

Two-County Population–22,288
October Temperature–49°
Acres in CRP–15,015

Two County Area–7,068,000
Annual Precipitation–21"

Much of western Idaho County is in large grain farms on the Camas Prairie, which has good upland bird hunting. The Salmon and Clearwater river canyons offer good chukar hunting and California quail can be found in healthy numbers in the brushy river bottoms near cultivated land. Turkey hunting is excellent and in the wild areas good forest grouse hunting can be found.

UPLAND BIRDS
Blue & Ruffed (Forest) Grouse, Chukar, Gray (Hungarian) Partridge, Pheasant, California Quail, Spruce Grouse, Turkey

WATERFOWL
Ducks and Geese

Orofino
Population – 3,800 • Elevation – 1,027

Orofino is one of the finer places in the West to live if you are a sincere outdoorsman. Steelhead in the Clearwater River, smallmouth bass in Dworshack Reservoir, chukar and mountain grouse in the hills, pheasants in the agricultural lands and deer, elk and bear in the mountains -- Orifino has it all. That statement applies to the ammenities availabe to bird hunters in this town as well. You can find nice rooms, good restaurants and all the gear you need for a hunt.

ACCOMMODATIONS
Helgeson Place Hotel, P.O. Box 463 / Pets allowed / 208-476-5729
Konkolville Motel, 2000 Konkolville Road / Pets allowed / 208-476-5584
Vacation Land Motel & RV, 14115 Hwy 12 / Pets allowed / 208-476-4012
White Pine Motel, P.O. Box 1849 / 208-476-7093 / Fax 208-476-3099
Riverside Motel, 10560 Hwy 12 / Pets allowed / 208-476-5711

CAMPGROUNDS
Hidden Village / 14 full hook-ups, tent sites available, sewage disposal, laundry / 208-476-3416

RESTAURANTS
Konkols, 2000 Konkolville Road / Open 6AM / 208-476-4312

Ponderosa Restaurant, 220 Michigan Avenue / 208-476-4818
Fiesta In Jalisco, 246 Johnson Avenue / 208-476-7506

SPORTING GOODS
West's Sporting Goods, 106 Michigan Avenue / 208-476-5314
Riverside Sport Shop, 11320 Hwy 12 / 208-476-5418
Clearwater Trading Co. , P.O. Box 2289 / 208-476-4440

VETERINARIANS
Burnam Veterinary Hospital, 2234 Michigan Avenue / 208-476-3349
Clearwater Animal Hospital, 10720 Hwy 12 / 208-4776-5757
Orofino Animal Hospital, 807 Michigan Avenue / 208-476-5995

HOSPITALS
Clearwater Valley Hospital, 301 Cedar / 208-476-4555

AIRPORTS
Orofino Aviation Inc / 208-476-4714
Lewiston Nez Perce County Airport, 406 Burnell / 208-746-7962
Spokane International Airport / Major carriers: Northwest, United, Delta,
    Southwest, Horizon, & Alaska / 509-455-6455

AUTO RENTAL
Hansen Garage In, 218 1st / 208-476-5536

AUTO SERVICE
Clearwater Lube & Service, 330 Main / 208-476-0709
Jim's Automotive Service Center, 10640 Hwy 12 / 208-476-3130

FOR MORE INFORMATION
Orofino Chamber of Commerce
P.O. Box 2221
Orofino, ID 83544
208-476-4335

Riggins

Population – 500 • Elevation – 1800

Located on the banks of the Salmon River, Riggins rests in classic chukar and mountain grouse country and it offers excellent shooting on both of those birds...if you aren't afraid to climb. Riggins itself, offers ample services for the bird hunter and it is an ideal place to stay, whether you plan to hunt the Salmon River breaks or you want to strike out into Hell's Canyon.

ACCOMMODATIONS

Bruce Motel, P.O. Box 208 / Allows pets / 208-628-3005

Half Way Inn, HC 75, Box 3760, New Meadows, Little Salmon River between milepost 182 & 183 / Allows pets / 208-628-3259

Riggins Motel / Allows pets / 208-628-3001 or 800-669-6739 / Fax 208-628-3524

River View Motel, P.O. Box 453 / Allows pets / 208-628-3041 / Fax 208-628-3908

The Lodge at Riggins Hot Springs, P.O. Box 1247, Located on Salmon River / 208-628-3785 / Fax 208-628-3785

CAMPGROUNDS

Riverside Gardens RV Park / 8 full hook-ups, sewage disposal, phone, tent sites available / 208-628-3777

RESTAURANTS

This Old House, 1449 Hwy 95 South / 208-628-3338

Glenns Deli, 303 South Main / Open 6AM–3PM / 208-628-3997

Summervilles Bar & Grill, Hwy 95 / Open 5AM–9PM / 208-628-3311

SPORTING GOODS

Hook Line & Sinker, Main Street / 208-628-3818

FOR MORE INFORMATION

Salmon River-Riggins Area Chamber of Commerce
P.O. Box 289
Riggins, ID 83549
208-628-3778

Grangeville

Population – 3,666 • Elevation – 3,390

Grangeville is located just off Highway 95 south of Lewiston and Orofino. For bird hunters traveling north from Boise, Grangeville is an excellent layover site. From town, hunters can take Highway 95 to Lewiston or head north on Highway 12 to Orofino. Either route takes a hunter past prime forest grouse, pheasant, Hungarian partridge and waterfowl areas.

ACCOMMODATIONS
Downtowner Inn, 113 East North Street / 208-983-1110
Elkhorn Lodge, 820 Southwest 1st Street / 208-983-1500
Junction Lodge, HCV #67 Box 98 / 208-842-2459
Monty's Motel , West 700 Main Street / 208-983-2500
Whitebird Motel, Hwy 95, Whitebird

CAMPGROUNDS
Mt. View Mobile Home and RV Park / 20 full hook-up sites, tent sites available /
208-983-2328

RESTAURANTS
Camas Cafe, 123 West Main / 208-983-9843
The Shanghai Restaurant, 124 West Main / 208-983-0485
Crossroads Cafe & Lounge, 622 West Main / 208-983-0675

VETERINARIANS
Grangeville Veterinary Clinic, 835 East Main / 208-983-0080 / After hours
208-983-1312

HOSPITALS
Syringa General Hospital, 607 West Main / 208-983-1700

AIRPORT
Grangeville Air Service / 208-983-0490
Lewiston (72 miles) for closest commercial airline service

AUTO RENTAL
See Lewiston

AUTO SERVICE
Hafer's Auto Repair / 208-983-2499
Thompson's Auto Repair, 907 North College / 208-983-2240

FOR MORE INFORMATION
Grangeville Chamber of Commerce
Box 212, 201 East Main
Grangeville, ID 83530
208-983-0460

Guides and Outfitters
Region 2–Clearwater

BARKER RIVER TRIPS
2124 Grelle, Lewiston, ID 83501
Phone 208-743-7459 / Toll-free 1-800-353-7459
Contact–John Barker
Email–jbarker@portal.lcsc.educ
Bird Hunting–Chukar
Accommodations–Lewiston
Other Services–Big game hunting, steelhead fishing, rafting, drift boating

BOULDER CREEK OUTFITTERS
P.O. Box 119, Peck, ID 83545
Phone 208-486-6232
Contact–Tim Craig
Bird Hunting–Forest Grouse
Accommodations–Guest Ranch
Other Services–Big game hunting, backcountry lake fishing, horse pack trips, trail rides

FLYING B RANCH
Rt. 2, Box 12C, Kamiah, ID 83536
Phone 208-935-0755 / Fax 208-935-0705 or 983-1516
Contact–Robert Burlingame
Bird Hunting–Chukar, Forest Grouse
Accommodations–Guest Ranch
Other Services–Big game hunting, backcountry lake fishing, river/stream fishing, rafting, drift boating, horse pack trips, trail rides
Special–Clay course, Hungarian partridge hunting.

IDAHO AFLOAT
P.O. Box 542, Grangeville, ID 83530
Phone 208-983-2414 / Fax 208-983-9259 / Toll-free 1-800-700-2414
Email–idafloat@camasnet.net
Web Site–http://www.idafloat.com
Bird Hunting–Chukar
Accommodations–Grangeville, Whitebird, Riggins
Other Services–Steelhead fishing, rafting, drift boating
Special–Combination horseback and lodge trips

INTERMOUNTAIN EXCURSIONS
1120 Bryden Avenue, Lewiston, ID 83501
Phone 208-746-0249 / Fax 208-746-4620
Bird Hunting–Chukar
Accommodations–Backcountry lodge
Other Services–Steelhead fishing, jet boating, charter boat fishing

SHATTUCK CREEK RANCH/OUTFITTERS
Box 165, Elk River, ID 83827
Phone 208-826-3405 / Fax 208-826-3284
Contact–Andre Molsee
Bird Hunting–Forest Grouse
Accommodations–Guest Ranch
Other Services–Big game hunting, backcountry lake fishing, river/stream fishing, charter boat fishing, horse pack trips, trail rides

SHEPP RANCH
P.O. Box 5446, Boise, ID 83705
Phone 208-343-7729
Contact–Virginia Hopfenbeck
Web Site–http://www.ioga.org/shepp/
Bird Hunting–Chukar
Accommodations–Guest Ranch located on Salmon River, southeast of Grangeville
Other Services–Big game hunting, steelhead fishing, jet boating, rafting, trail rides
Special–Charter air services

Region 3–Southwest

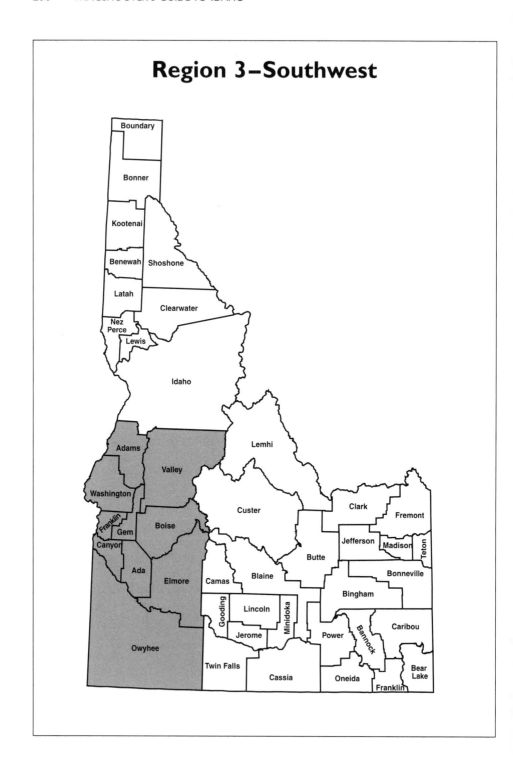

Region 3–Southwest

Located in the southwestern corner of the state, this region consists of Adams, Valley, Washington, Payette, Gem, Boise, Canyon, Ada, Owyhee, and Elmore counties. Big game hunting units include 19a, 20a, 22, 23, 24, 25, 26, 31, 32, 32a, 33, 34, 35, 38, 39, 40, 41 and 42. Regional offices are located in Nampa and McCall, with Fish and Game Headquarters in Boise. Diverse in terrain, the Southwest Region offers a wide range of outdoor sports and activities. Upland gamebird, turkey, and waterfowl hunting continue to grow in popularity with record harvests. Elevations range from 1,688 at Hells Canyon dam to 10,582 at Elk Peak.

Wildlife Management Areas

- Cecil D. Andrus—24,000 acres, wild turkey, upland gamebirds; 10 miles west of Cambridge via State Highway 71; some gates are locked to control access but keys are available at headquarters near Mile Marker 9 on highway.
- Payette River/Birding Islands—765 acres in three units, waterfowl, upland gamebirds; permit required for pheasant; 3 to 4 miles northeast of New Plymouth via U.S. 30 (approximately 20 miles west of Emmett).
- Montour Cooperative Wildlife Area—1,225 acres, waterfowl, upland gamebirds; permit required for pheasant; 13 miles east of Emmett via State Highway 52.
- Fort Boise—1,490 acres, waterfowl, upland gamebirds; permit required for pheasant; 5 miles northeast of Parma via U.S. 95 (west of Boise).
- Boise River—20,000 acres, upland gamebirds; 10 miles northeast of Boise via State Highway 21.
- C.J. Strike Reservoir—8,300 acres, waterfowl, upland gamebirds; permit required for pheasant; 4 miles west of Bruneau via State Highway (south of Mountain Home).

Blue & Ruffed (Forest) Grouse Distribution
Region 3–Southwest

Chukar Distribution
Region 3–Southwest

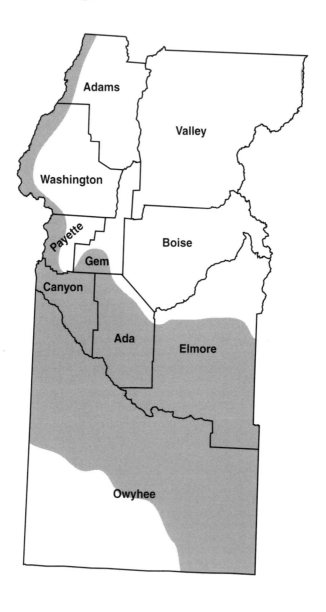

Gray (Hungarian) Partridge Distribution
Region 3–Southwest

Adams

Valley

Washington

Payette

Boise

Gem

Canyon

Ada

Elmore

Owyhee

Pheasant Distribution
Region 3–Southwest

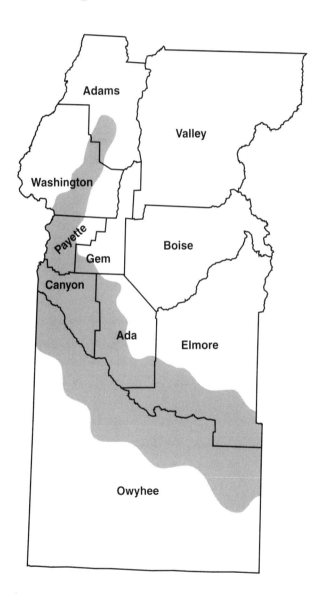

Quail Distribution
Region 3–Southwest

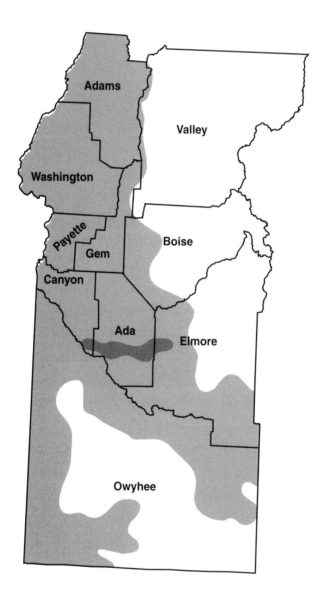

Sage Grouse Distribution
Region 3–Southwest

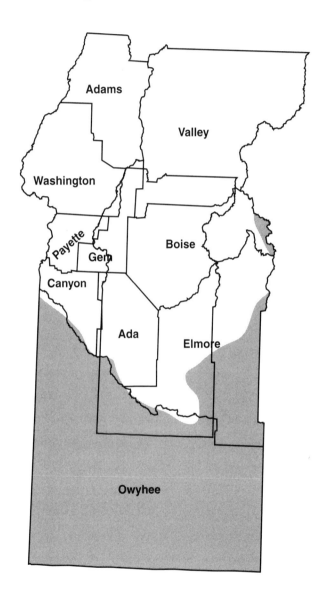

Sharp-tailed Grouse Distribution
Region 3–Southwest

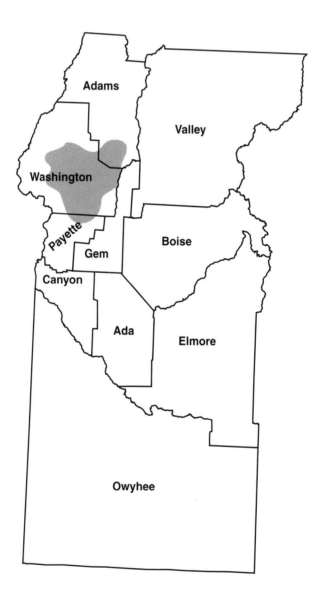

Spruce Grouse Distribution
Region 3–Southwest

Wild Turkey Distribution
Region 3–Southwest

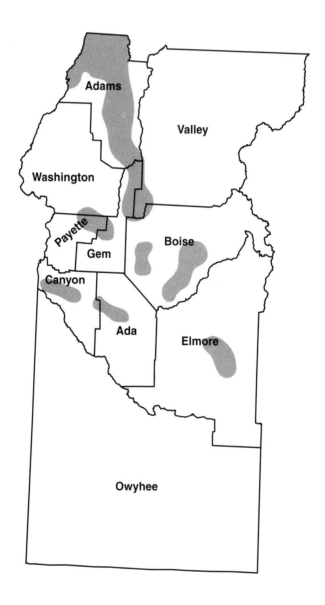

Adams and Valley Counties

Two-County Population–9,363 October Temperature–48° Acres in CRP–2,696	Two County Area–3,276,000 acres Annual Precipitation–21"

Adams County has some of the best chukar hunting in the state along Hells Canyon and Brownlee Reservoir, but access is difficult. Valley County includes a mix of farmland, much of it in hay, but most land is forested. The Payette National Forest covers much of both counties.

UPLAND BIRDS
Pheasants, Gray (Hungarian) Partridge, Chukar, Sharp-tailed Grouse, Sage Grouse, Blue & Ruffed (Forest) Grouse, California Quail, Turkey

WATERFOWL
Ducks and Geese

McCall
Population–2,488 • Elevation–5,021

McCall is a pleasant little resort town nestled at the south end of Payette Lake, just north of Cascade Reservoir. With that plentiful water, waterfowl visit the area in masses during fall. For the visiting hunter, comfortable lodging, good meals and adequate sporting good supplies are available.

ACCOMMODATIONS
Best Western McCall, P.O. Box 4297 / Pets allowed / 208-634-6300 /
Fax 208-634-2967
Riverside Motel & Condominiums, P.O. Box 746, 400 East Lake / 208-634-5610 or
800-326-5610
The Woodsman Motel, P.O. Box 884 / Pets allowed / 208-634-7671
Shore Lodge, P.O. Box, 1006 501 West Lake / 208-634-2244 / Fax 208-634-7504
Village Inn Motel, P.O. Box 734 / 208-634-2344

CAMPGROUNDS
McCall Campground / 45 full hook-up sites, 16 pull-throughs, ice, grills, phone,
sewage disposal, laundry / Open May 1 through October 31 / 208-634-5165

RESTAURANTS

Clubhouse Restaurant, 1001 Reedy Lane / 208-634-4867

Harvest Moon Market & Delicatessen-Bakery, 1133 East Lake Street (just east on Lake from Jct of state route 55) / Open 8AM–5:30PM / Beer & wine for carry-out / 208-634-5578

Romano's Ristorante, 203 East Lake Street (state route 55 from jct of Lake Street) / Open 5:30–PM, closed in winter / Cocktails / 208-634-4396

SPORTING GOODS

Mays Hardware & Glass, P.O. Box 963, 309 Lake Street / 208-634-7665

Medley Sports, 809 3rd / 208-634-2216

HOSPITALS

McCall Memorial District Hospital, 1000 State Street / 208-634-2221

AIRPORT

McCall Memorial Airport / 208-634-3104

Boise Municipal Airport / Commercial airlines are United, Delta, Northwest, Southwest, Skywest, and Horizon / 208-383-3110

AUTO RENTAL

Aviauto Auto Rental / 208-634-3949

Pioneer Car Rental / 208-634-5445

AUTO SERVICE

Bruneau Tire & Auto Service, 617 North 3rd / 208-634-2252

Acheson Motors Inc., 219 North 3rd / 208-634-2196

FOR MORE INFORMATION

McCall Chamber of Commerce
P.O. Box D
McCall, ID 83638
208-634-7631

Washington County

County Population–8,550	County Area–948,000 acres
October Temperature–48°	Annual Precipitation–11.6"
Acres in CRP–20,759	

Washington County has some of the best all-around upland bird hunting in the state. It includes the tamed section of Hells Canyon along Brownlee Reservoir with good access from Weiser to Oxbow. Much of the private land is already tied up in bird hunting trespass rights, but there remains a lot of open public and private land.

UPLAND BIRDS
Pheasants, Gray (Hungarian) Partridge, Chukar, Sharp-tailed Grouse, Sage Grouse, Blue & Ruffed (Forest) Grouse, California Quail, Mountain Quail (Closed), Turkey

WATERFOWL
Ducks and Geese

Weiser
Population–4,607 • Elevation–2,123

ACCOMMODATIONS
Colonial Motel, 251 East Main / Pets allowed / 208-549-0150
Indianhead Motel & RV Park, 474 US Hwy 95 / Pets allowed / 208-549-0331
State Street Motel, 1279 State Street / Pets allowed / 208-549-1390

CAMPGROUNDS
Gateway RV Park / 20 full hook-up sites, laundry / 208-549-2539

RESTAURANTS
Pat's Cafe, 813 State Street / Open 7AM–10PM / 208-549-3962
Golden Horse, East Main / 208-549-2500
La Tejanita, 260 7th / 208-749-2768

SPORTING GOODS
Ace Hardware, East Main

VETERINARIANS
Weiser Vet Clinic, 815 West Idaho / 208-549-0944

HOSPITALS
Weiser Memorial, 645 East 5th / 208-549-0370

AIRPORTS
Boise Municipal Airport / 208-383-3110

AUTO RENTAL
Steve & Jim's Hometown Motors, 602 Hwy 95 / 208-549-3310

AUTO SERVICE
Service Parts, 55 West Main / 208-549-1661

FOR MORE INFORMATION
Weiser Chamber of Commerce
8 East Idaho Street
Weiser, ID 83672
208-549-0452

Cambridge
Population–328 • Elevation–2450

Cambridge is located on the edge of the Weiser River, just inside the Oregon/Idaho border in southwest Idaho. Cambridge offers easy access to prime pheasant grounds and it is a jumping off point for trips into Hell's Canyon for its excellent chukar hunting.

ACCOMMODATIONS
Frontier Motel and R.V. Park, P.O. Box 17 / Pets allowed / 208-257-3851
Hunters Inn, P.O. Box 313 / Pets allowed / 208-257-3325

RESTAURANTS
Bucky's Cafe, Highway 95 / 208-257-3330
Kay's Cafe, Highway 95 / 208-257-3561

HOSPITALS
Weiser Memorial, 645 East 5th / 208-549-0370

AIRPORTS
Boise Municipal Airport / 208-383-3110

AUTO RENTAL
Steve & Jim's Hometown Motors, 602 Hwy 95 / 208-549-3310

AUTO SERVICE
Cenex Service Station, Hwy 95

FOR MORE INFORMATION
City Market
P.O. Box 302
Cambridge, ID 83234
208-257-3252

Payette County

County Population–16,434	County Area–261,000 acres
October Temperature–49°	Annual Precipitation–10"
Acres in CRP–3,427	

Payette County is mostly private agricultural land with a mix of grain crops pasture land for livestock and orchards. The best upland bird and waterfowl hunting is along the Payette and Snake rivers.

UPLAND BIRDS
Pheasant, Gray (Hungarian) Partridge, Chukar, Sage Grouse, California Quail, Turkey

WATERFOWL
Ducks and Geese

Payette

Population–5,780 • Elevation–2,150

Payette rests on the extreme west edge of southwest Idaho, ideally suited for wingshooters chasing ducks, geese, forest grouse, quail, pheasants, Huns or turkeys. The town offers ample amenities.

ACCOMMODATIONS
Montclaire Motel, 625 South Main Payette / 208-642-2693
Other motels are located in Ontario, Oregon

VETERINARIAN
Ashton Clark Vet Clinic, 1844 NE 7th Avenue / 208-642-9391

SPORTING GOODS
Larry's Army Navy, 1531 Hwy 95 / 208-642-1000

RESTAURANTS
Sollie's Pasta and Steak, Corner of 6th Avenue and Main Street / 208-642-2433
Tips, 136 South Main / 208-642-4109

FOR MORE INFORMATION
Payette Chamber of Commerce
700 Center Avenue
Payette, ID 83661
208-642-2362

Gem County

County Population–11,844	County Area–359,000 acres
October Temperature–48°	Annual Precipitation–12"
Acres in CRP–27,981	

Gem County's mix of forested land to the northeast and grassy hill country and rich bottomlands along the Payette River make it a good bird hunting county only minutes from downtown Boise. Don't pass up the public land for gray partridge and chukar.

UPLAND BIRDS
Pheasants, Gray (Hungarian) Partridge, California Quail, Chukar, Blue & Ruffed (Forest) Grouse, Turkey

WATERFOWL
Ducks and Geese

Canyon County

County Population–90,076 October Temperature–49° Acres in CRP–928	County Area–383,000 acres Annual Precipitation–10"

Lake Lowell and the Snake and Boise rivers are waterfowl magnets that make this increasingly urban county one of the best duck and geese hunting areas of the state. Pheasant hunting also remains good, but nearly all the land is private. Fort Boise is one of the best Wildlife Management Areas in the state, but it gets a lot of pressure.

UPLAND BIRDS
Pheasants, California Quail, Gray (Hungarian) Partridge, Chukar, Turkey

WATERFOWL
Ducks and Geese

Nampa
Population–28,500 • Elevation–2492

Nampa is a small town that lies right off of Interstate 84 next to Lake Lowell. Besides providing excellent largemouth bass fishing, Lake Lowell is a huge draw for migratory waterfowl. The nearby Snake River offers pheasants and the surrounding desert areas harbor plenty of quail. Because of its proximity to the highway, Nampa is a good place to stop for a travelling hunter. It offers local hunters plenty of options, too.

ACCOMMODATIONS
Desert Inn, 115 9th Avenue / Allows pets / 208-467-1161
Five Crowns Inn, 908 3rd Street South / Allows pets / 208-466-3594
Shilo Inn, 617 Nampa Boulevard / Allows pets / 208-466-8993

CAMPGROUNDS
Mason Creek RV Park / 67 sites, phones, laundry, tent sites available / 208-465-7199

VETERINARIANS
Boulevard Veterinary Clinic, 807 2nd Street / 208-466-4358
Idaho Veterinary Hospital, 1420 North Midland Boulevard / 208-466-4613

SPORTING GOODS

Larry's Sporting Goods, 224 3rd Avenue / 208-467-9201
Nampa Army Navy Outdoor Outfitters, 3226 Garrity Boulevard / 208-467-5961
Gart Bros., 1031 Caldwell / 208-467-5711

RESTAURANTS

Noodles, 1802 Franklin Boulevard / 208-466-4400
Denny's, 607 Nampa Boulevard / 208-467-6579

AIRPORT

Boise Municipal Airport / Commercial airlines are United, Delta, Northwest, Southwest, Skywest, and Horizon / 208-383-3110

VISITOR INFO

Nampa Chamber
1305 3rd Street
Nampa, ID
208-466-4641 / Fax 208-467-1161

Owyhee County

County Population–8,392	County Area–4,904,000 acres
October Temperature–49°	Annual Precipitation–5"
Acres in CRP–15,900	

Owyhee County is big, wide open and a great place to hunt Chukars and quail. Its few roads and even fewer service centers make it a place only for the prepared. But its excellent hunting keeps bringing hunters back. The northern end near Canyon County gets most of the hunting since it has the best access.

UPLAND BIRDS
Chukar, California Quail, Sage Grouse, Pheasant, Gray (Hungarian) Partridge

WATERFOWL
Ducks and Geese

Bruneau
Population–100 • Elevation–2,501

Bruneau does not offer very much to the visiting hunter, except a place to sleep for the night. However, it rests in excellent bird country and there is some interesting geography nearby. Try hiking the Bruneau sand dunes between hunts for quail, chukar, sage grouse and doves. Closest air service is Boise

ACCOMMODATIONS
Pleasant Hill Country Inn, Box 179A / 208-845-2018
See Nampa for staying in Northwest side of county.

CAMPING
Bruneau Dunes State Park / 48 sites, 32 water and electric, tent sites available, sewage disposal, tables, grills / 208-366-7919

Ada and Boise Counties

Two County Population–209,775	County Area–1, 900,000 acres
October Temperature–48°	Annual Precipitation–14"
Acres in CRP–8772	

Idaho's capital and largest city lies on the Boise River nestled against the foothills of mountains that extend all the way across central Idaho. In Boise County, which covers the mountains and headwaters of the Boise and Payette rivers, forest grouse hunting is excellent. Urban sprawl is eating up much of the good farmland and formerly excellent pheasant hunting country. But there remains good gray partridge, chukar partridge and quail hunting in the public lands along the Snake River and on the outskirts of the urban area. The Boise River has excellent waterfowl hunting, but very limited access.

UPLAND BIRDS
Pheasants, Gray (Hungarian) Partridge, Chukar, Sharp-tailed Grouse, Blue & Ruffed (Forest) Grouse, California Quail, Turkey

WATERFOWL
Ducks and Geese

Boise
Population–130,000 • Elevation–2,726

Boise is Idaho's largest city and it offers all the amenities for a visiting wingshooter. And, it happens to rest in some of the best, most diversified bird country in the state, if not the entire West. Looking for sage grouse, chukar and quail? Head south to the Owyhee Desert. Prefer pheasants and Hungarian partridge? Try the Boise Foothills or walk one of the Snake River islands. If you want a forest grouse, head north out of town into the mountains where ruffed and blue grouse are abundant. Of course, waterfowl are plentiful along the Snake and Boise rivers.

ACCOMMODATIONS
Cabana Inn, 1600 Main Street / Pets allowed / 208-466-4641 / Fax 208-467-1161
Fairfield Inn by Marriott, 3300 South Shoshone / Pets allowed / 208-331-5656
Hampton Inn, 3270 South Shoshone / Pets allowed / 208-331-5600
Owyhee Plaza Hotel, 1109 Main Street / Pets allowed / 208-343-4611 /
Fax 208-336-3860

Comfort Inn, 2526 Airport Way (just south of I-84, exit 53 (Vista Avenue) / 60 rooms, whirlpool, small heated indoor pool / 208-336-0077

Boise Super 8 Lodge, 2773 Elder Street (just north of I-84, exit 53) / 110 rooms, small heated indoor pool / 208-344-8871

Best Western Vista Inn, 2645 Airport Way (just south of I-84, exit 53 (Vista Avenue) / 87 rooms, sauna, whirlpool / 208-336-8100

CAMPGROUNDS

Riverside RV Park / 42 sites, 32 full hook-ups, tables, grills / open May 1 through October 15 / 208-788-2020

Fiesta RV Park / 118 sites, 94 full hook-ups, tent sites available, sewage disposal, phone, laundry / 208-375-8207

KOA Boise / 72 full hook-up sites, tent sites available, laundry, sewage disposal, phone / 208-345-7673

RESTAURANTS

Denny's, 2580 Airport Way / 208-344-9090
　　　　2275 Main / 208-342-796
　　　　607 Nampa Boulevard / 208-467-6579 / Open 24 hours

The Tablerock Brew Pub, 705 Fulton / 208- 342-0944

El Cazador Mexican Grill, 5900 Fairview Avenue (north of I-84, Curtis Road exit and west on Fairview) / Open 11AM–10PM; Friday & Saturday to 11PM; Sunday 12 noon–10PM / / Beer & wine / 208-323-1801

Gamekeeper Restaurant, 1109 Main Street / Open 11:30AM–2PM and 5:30 10PM, Saturday from 5:30PM / Cocktails and lounge / 208-343-4611

Murphy's Seafood Chophouse, 1555 Broadway (2 miles north of I-84, exit 54) / Open 11AM–10PM; Friday & Saturday to 11PM; Sunday 10AM–10PM / Cocktails and lounge / 208-344-3691

Peg Leg Annie's, 3019 North Cole Road (3 miles north of I-84, exit 50) / Open 11:30AM –10PM; Friday & Saturday to 11PM; closed Sundays / Cocktails and lounge / 208-375-3050

The Sandpiper Restaurant, 1100 West Jefferson (downtown at 11th and Jefferson) / Open 11:30AM–2PM and 5:30–10PM; Friday & Saturday to 11PM; Sunday 5–9PM / Cocktails and lounge / 208-344-8911

SPORTING GOODS

Intermountain Outdoor Sports, 900 Vista Avenue / 208-345-3474

REI Recreational Equipment Inc, 8300 West Emerald / 208-322-1141

Sunset Sports, 5804 Fairview / 208-376-1100

Gart Bros., 1301 North Milwaukee / 208-378-9590
　　　　5050 Overland / 208-336-2255
　　　　670 East Boise / 208-344-2037

VETERINARIANS
Animal Emergency Clinic, 5238 Chinden Boulevard / 24-hour service /
208-376-4510
Ewing Animal Hospital, 2318 North 36th / 24-hour service / 208-342-5551
Westgate Veterinary Clinic, 7827 Fairview Avenue / Emergence service /
208-376-4407

HOSPITALS
St. Lukes Regional Medical Center, 190 East Bannock / Emergency: 208-386-2344
St. Alphonsus, 1055 North Cartes Road / 208-378-2121

AIRPORTS
Boise Municipal Airport / Commercial airlines are United, Delta, Northwest,
Southwest, Skywest, and Horizon / 208-383-3110

AUTO RENTAL
Dollar Rent A Car, Boise Air Terminal / 208-345-9727
National Car Rental, Boise Municipal Airport   / 208-383-3210
Budget Rent A Car, Boise Airport / 208-383-3090
1590 Vista Avenue / 208-343-2600

AUTO SERVICE
Dowdy's Automotive, 318 South Federal Way / 208-342-3651
Al's Car Care, 1645 Grove Street / 208-344-3800
A 2nd Opinion, 3817 West State / 208-644-4588

FOR MORE INFORMATION
Boise Convention & Visitor Bureau
P.O. Box 2106
168 North 9th, Suite 200
Boise, ID 83701
208-344-7777 / Fax / 208-344-6236

Elmore County

County Population–21,205	County Area–1,971,000 acres
October Temperature–49°	Annual Precipitation–7"
Acres in CRP–17,652	

Elmore County is one of the most diverse counties in the state with a mix of agricultural land, desert, mountains and river canyons. The best upland hunting is near Mountain Home with good waterfowl and forest grouse up in the mountains and canyons.

UPLAND BIRDS
Pheasant, Gray (Hungarian) Partridge, Chukar, Blue & Ruffed (Forest) Grouse, Sage Grouse, California Quail, Turkey

WATERFOWL
Ducks and Geese

Mountain Home

Population–8,900 • Elevation–3,180

Located west of Boise, just south of I-84, Mountain Home is a military town that offers ample amenities for the bird hunter. Sage grouse, quail, chukar, mountain grouse and ducks and geese can all be hunted nearby. Mountain Home's proximity to the interstate and Highway 20 north, makes it a good place to stop over or base a hunt. Just expect some noise from low-flying bomber planes. The Mountain Home Air Force Base and the Owyhee Bombing Range are not far away.

ACCOMMODATIONS
Best Western Foothills Motor Inn, P.O. Box 1106, 1080 Hwy 20 / Pets allowed / 208-587-8477 / Fax 208-587-5774
Motel Thunderbird, 910 Sunset Strip / Pets allowed / 208-587-7927
Sleep Inn, 1180 Hwy 20 / Pets allowed / 208-587-9743 / Fax 208-587-7382
Towne Center Motel, 410 North 2nd East / Pets allowed / 208-587-3373
Hi Lander Motel & Steak House, 615 3rd West, Hwy 30 East / 208-587-3311

CAMPGROUNDS
KOA Mountain Home / 43 full hook-ups, tent sites available, laundry, phone, tables, limited grocery / 208-587-5111

RESTAURANTS
J. B.'s, I-84 Exit 95 / 208-587-2264
High Lander Motel & Steak House, 615 South 3rd / 208-587-3311
Joe's Club & Basque Restaurant, 195 South 2nd East / 208-587-5055

SPORTING GOODS
Mountain Home Do It Center, 220 East 5 North / 208-587-4448
Red Barn Supply American, Legion Boulevard / 208-587-5711

VETERINARIANS
Knight Veterinary Clinic, 220 Elmhurst / 208-587-7941
Elmore Veterinary Hospital, 2360 East 15 North / 208-587-3116

HOSPITALS
Elmore Medical Center, 895 North 6 East / 208-587-5401

AIRPORTS
Mountain Home Aviation, 2610 Airbase Road / 208-587-3585
Boise Municipal Airport / Commercial airlines are United, Delta, Northwest,
   Southwest, Skywest, and Horizon / 208-383-3110

AUTO RENTAL
Far Less Auto Rental Inc, 690 North 2nd East / 800-427-7290
Practical Rent Car, 3740 Airbase Rd / 208-832-2277
U-Save Auto Rental , 1088 West 6 South / 208-587-4321

AUTO SERVICE
Foothills Chevron, Exit 95 I-84, 1060 Hwy 20 / 208-587-3753

VISITOR INFO
Desert Mountain Visitor Center, 2900 American Legion Boulevard /
   208-587-4334

Guides and Outfitters
Region 3–Southwest

CANYON CATS, INC.
P.O. Box 11, Riggins, ID 83549
Phone 208-628-3772 / Toll-free 1-888-628-3772
Contact–George Hauptman
Bird Hunting–Chukar
Accommodations–Backcountry lodge
Other Services–Steelhead fishing, rafting, drift boating

HUGHES RIVER EXPEDITIONS, INC.
P.O. Box 217, Cambridge, ID 83610
Phone 208-257-3477 / Fax 208-257-3476 / Toll-free 1-800-262-1882
Contact–Jerry Huges
E-mail–info@hughesriver.com
Web Site–http://www.hughesriver.com
Bird Hunting–Chukar, Forest Grouse
Accommodations–Cambridge, Payette, Weiser
Other Services–Steelhead fishing, rafting, drift boating
Special–Licensed to guide on Middle Fork of Salmon, Salmon River, and Hells
  Canyon of Snake River

SALMON RIVER CHALLENGE
P.O. Box 1299, Riggins, ID 83549
Phone 208-628-3264 / Fax 208-628-3264 / Toll-free 1-800-732-8574
Contact–Patrick Marek
E-mail–srcbbp@aol.com
Bird Hunting–Chukar, Forest Grouse
Accommodations–Rapid River Ranch, Riggins, Idaho
Other Services–Backcountry lake fishing, steelhead fishing, rafting, drift boating,
  charter boat fishing, horse pack trips, trail rides

SML OUTFITTERS
P.O. Box 72, Lakefork, ID 83635
Phone 208-325-8212
Bird Hunting–Forest Grouse
Accommodations–Backcountry lodge
Other Services–Big game hunting, backcountry lake fishing, river/stream fishing,
  horse pack trips, trail rides
Special–Working cattle ranch, dayrides to educate people

WAPITI MEADOW RANCH
HC 72, Cascade, ID 83611
Phone 208-633-3217 / Fax 208-633-3219
E-mail–WapitiMR@aol.com
Web Site–http://www.guestRanches.com/wapiti.htm
Bird Hunting–Forest Grouse
Accommodations–Exclusive Guest Ranch, limited to 12 guests per week.
Other Services–Big game hunting, backcountry lake fishing, river/stream fishing,
    horse pack trips, trail rides
Special–Charter air services

WHISKEY MOUNTAIN OUTFITTERS
HC 88, Box 1050, Murphy, ID 83650
Phon 208-495-2563
Contact–Jim Bass
Bird Hunting–Chukar, Forest Grouse
Accommodations–Guest Ranch in Owyhee County
Other Services–Big game hunting, fishing, cattle drives, trail rides

Region 4–Magic Valley

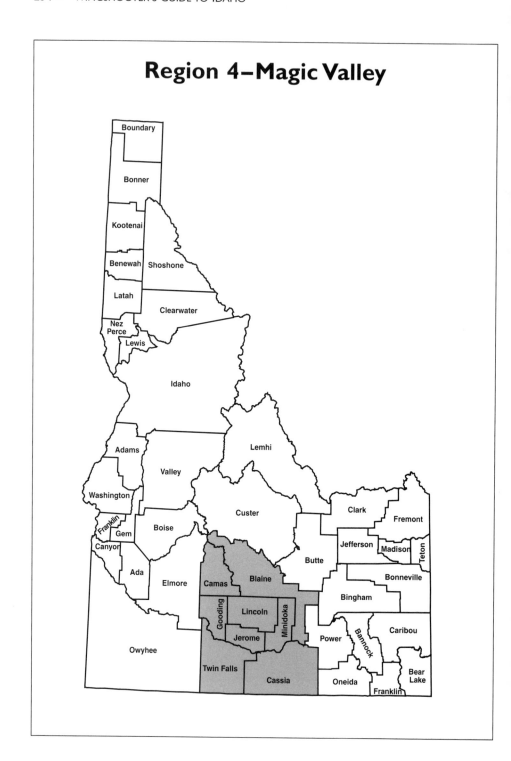

Region 4–Magic Valley

The Magic Valley Region is in the southernmost portion of the state and consists of Camas, Blaine, Gooding, Lincoln, Jerome, Minidoka, Twin Falls, and Cassia counties. Big game hunt units include 43, 44, 45, 46, 47, 48, 49, 52, 52a, 53, 54, 55, 56 and 57. Regional office is located in Jerome. Home to such natural marvels as Thousand Springs and Shoshone Falls, the Hagerman Valley provides some of state's best waterfowl habitat. Elevations range from 2,797 at the Snake River to 10,339 at Cache Peak.

Wildlife Management Areas
- Camas Prairie—3,046 acres, waterfowl, upland gamebirds; 3 miles southeast of Hill City via U.S. 20 (northeast of Mountain Home, southwest of Sun Valley).
- Billingsley Creek—275 acres, waterfowl, upland gamebirds; 2 miles northeast of Hagerman via U.S. 30 (north bank Snake River west of Twin Falls, south of Wendell).
- Hagerman—877 acres, upland gamebirds; 3 miles southeast of Hagerman via U.S. 30 (north bank Snake River west of Twin Falls).
- Niagara Springs—1,100 acres in two units, waterfowl, upland gamebirds; 7 miles south of Wendell on Interstate 84 (north bank Snake River).
- Bear Tracks Williams—600 acres in two units, waterfowl, upland gamebirds; 8.5 miles northeast of Richfield via U.S. 26/93 (approximately 10 miles south of Carey).
- Carey Lake—430 acres, waterfowl; 1 mile east of Carey via U.S. 20/26/93.

Blue & Ruffed Grouse Distribution
Region 4–Magic Valley

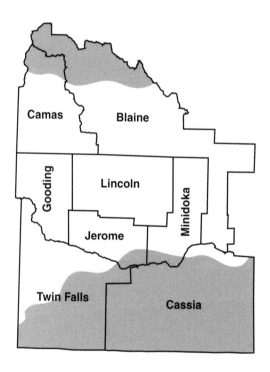

Chukar Distribution
Region 4–Magic Valley

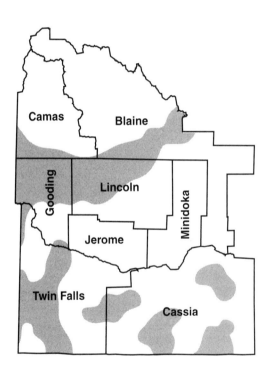

Gray (Hungarian) Partridge Distribution
Region 4–Magic Valley

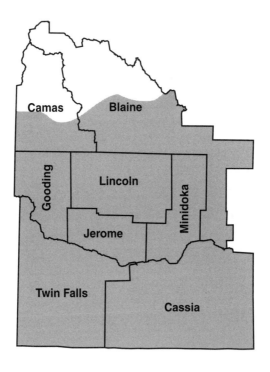

Pheasant Distribution
Region 4–Magic Valley

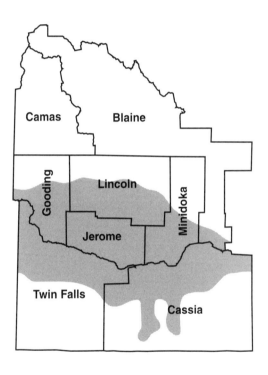

Quail Distribution
Region 4–Magic Valley

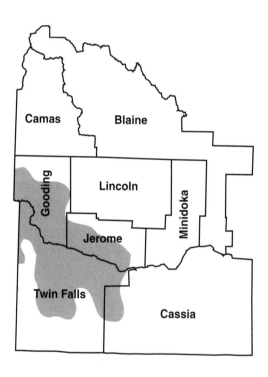

Sage Grouse Distribution
Region 4–Magic Valley

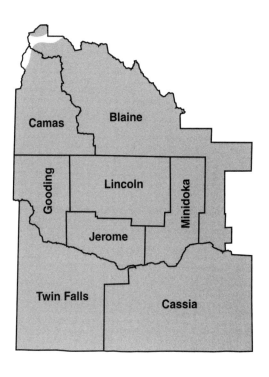

Sharp-tailed Grouse Distribution
Region 4–Magic Valley

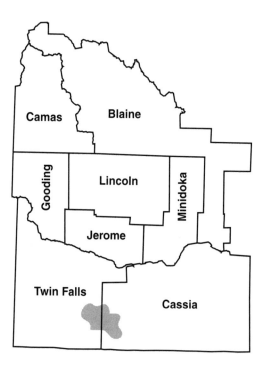

Spruce Grouse Distribution
Region 4–Magic Valley

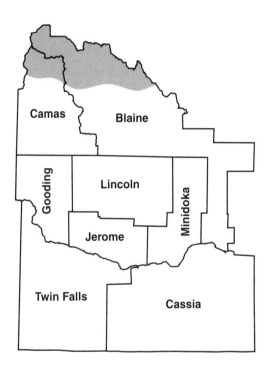

Camas

Blaine

Gooding

Lincoln

Minidoka

Jerome

Twin Falls

Cassia

Wild Turkey Distribution
Region 4–Magic Valley

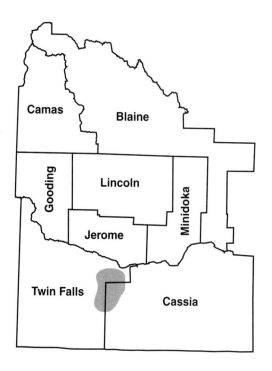

Blaine and Camas Counties

Two County Population–14,152	Two County Area–2,386,000 acres
October Temperature–48°	Annual Precipitation–11"
Acres in CRP–8,836	

Blaine and Camas Counties still have excellent pheasant habitat, but few birds, in the Big Wood River Valley. Further south, some excellent sage grouse country exists. There is top forest grouse country in the mountains surrounding Ketchum, Fairfield and north into the Sawtooths with some limited waterfowl habitat. The area is getting heavily developed and private access is difficult, although much of the best hunting is located on public lands.

UPLAND BIRDS
Pheasant, Gray (Hungarian) Partridge, Sage Grouse, Blue & Ruffed (Forest) Grouse

WATERFOWL
Ducks and Geese

Ketchum
Elevation–5,342 • Population–2,960

Ketchum is a quaint little town nestled between three awesome mountain ranges in the heart of central Idaho. Best known for its excellent skiing opportunities the town also offers other prime recreational action, like mountain biking, hiking, flyfishing and, of course, some excellent wingshooting. Ketchum offers comfortable, even plush, accommodations and some of the best restaurants this side of Seattle. The nightlife can prove, well, entertaining. Forest grouse, chukar and even a few sage grouse can be taken inside an hour drive from downtown. Talk to Scott Schnebly at Lost River Outfitters for tips on the area's wingshooting attractions.

ACCOMMODATIONS
Best Western Christiana Lodge, 651 Sun Valley Road / Pets allowed / 208-726-3351 or 800-535-3241
Heidelberg Inn, P.O. Box 5704 / Pets allowed / 208-726-5361 / Fax 208-726-2084
Sun Valley Resort, Sun Valley Road / 208-622-4111
Warm Springs Resort, P.O. Box 10009 / 208-726-8274
Bald Mountain Lodge, P.O. Box 426 / Pets allowed / 208-726-9963

CAMPGROUNDS
North Fork Campground, 8 miles north of Ketchum off Highway 75 / 39 sites, no hookups, tent sites available / 208-726-7672
Sun Valley RV Resort / 39 full hook-ups / Grocery, phone, swimming pool, sewage disposal / 208-726-3429

RESTAURANTS
The Pioneer, Box 986 / 208-726-3139
The Western Cafe, Box 4379 / Breakfast starts at 6AM / 208-726-3396
The Kneadery, 260 Leadville (east on Sun Valley from Hwy 75, south on Leadville) / Open 7:30AM–2PM / 208-726-9462
Michel's Christiania Restaurant Bar, 303 Walnut Avenue / Open 6:30–10PM / Cocktails and lounge / 208-726-3388

SPORTING GOODS
Silver Creek Outfitters, Box 418 Main Street North / 208-726-5282
Sun Valley Outfitters, Box 3400 Sun Valley 83353 / 208-622-3400
Lost River Outfitters, Box 3445 Main Street South / 208-726-1706

VETERINARIANS
Animal Center Sun Valley, 106 South Clear Creek Park, Hwy 75 South of Ketchum / 24-hour service / 208-726-7777
All Creatures Pets Clinic, 871 Warm Springs Road / 208-726-2229

HOSPITALS
Wood River Medical Center, Adjacent to the Sun Valley Mall / 208-622-3333

AIRPORT
Friedman Memorial Airport, 4 Airport Way / Delta, Skywest, Horizon / 208-788-4956

AUTO RENTAL
Avis Rent-A-Car, Hailey Airport / 208-788-9707

AUTO SERVICE
Mountain Motors Import Automotive Repair, 12726 Hwy 75 / 208-726-8505
Sun Valley Auto Center, 500 Bell Drive / 208-726-7242

FOR MORE INFORMATION
Ketchum Valley Chamber of Commerce
P.O. Box 2420, 411 Main Street
Ketchum, ID 83340
208-726-3423 / 800-634-3347
Fax 208-726-4533

Hailey

Population–2,800 • Elevation–5,342

Less noted than its glittery neighbor to the north (Ketchum), Hailey is a pleasant little town that offers excellent accommodations, including fine restaurants. Wing-shooting supplies can be purchased here and a full-service grocery will send you on your way with plenty of food. For those hunters seeking sage grouse or chukar in the Picabo Hills area, Hailey allows faster access than Ketchum.

ACCOMMODATIONS
Airport Inn, Fax, P.O. Box 984 / 208-788-3195 or 208-788-2477
The Hailey Hotel, P.O. Box 2051, 201 South Main Street / 208-788-3140
Hitchrack Hotel, 619 South Main / 208-788-2409

CAMPGROUNDS
North Fork Campground, 8 miles north of Ketchum off Highway 75 / 39 sites, no
  hookups, tent sites available / 208-726-7672
Sun Valley RV Resort, south of Ketchum off Highway 75 / 39 full hook-ups /
  Grocery, phone, swimming pool, sewage disposal / 208-726-3429

RESTAURANTS
The Hearthstone Inn, Main & Galena / 208-788-3002
Bullion St. Bistro, 17 West Bullion / 208-788-6401
Cafe at the Brewery, 202 West Main / 208-788-0805

SPORTING GOODS
Bob's Sports Pawn & Lock , 12 West Bullion / 208-788-3308

VETERINARIANS
Hailey Animal Clinic / 208-788-6225

HOSPITALS
Woodriver Hospital, South Main Street / 208-788-2222

AIRPORTS
Friedman Memorial Airport, 4 Airport Way / 208-788-4956

AUTO RENTAL
Avis Rent-A-Car, Hailey Airport / 208-788-9707

AUTO SERVICE
Gary's Automotive, 4171 Glenbrook Drive / 208-788-3676
Nelson's Auto Repair, 115 South River / 208-788-4171

FOR MORE INFORMATION
Hailey Chamber of Commerce
P.O. Box 100
Hailey, ID 83333
208-788-2700

Gooding County

County Population–11,633	County Area–464,000 acres
October Temperature–50°	Annual Precipitation–8.6"
Acres in CRP–240	

Gooding County has some of the best waterfowl hunting in the state along the Snake River near Hagerman. It also has excellent pheasant and gray partridge hunting on its private farms.

UPLAND BIRDS
Pheasant, Gray (Hungarian) Partridge, Chukar, Sage Grouse, California Quail

WATERFOWL
Ducks and Geese

Hagerman

Population–600 • Elevation–2,964

Some of the best goose hunting in North America is just outside your hotel door in Hagerman. The area also offers great duck shooting, plenty of pheasants and, seasonally, doves. Hagerman offers good food and comfortable accommodations.

ACCOMMODATIONS
Hagerman Valley Inn, P.O. Box 117, Hagerman / 208-837-6196
Sportsman's River Resort, 5 Gilhooley Lane / 208-837-6202

CAMPING
Hagerman RV Village, 18049 U.S. Highway 30 / 53 full hook-ups, laundry, phone, tent sites available / 208-837-4906

SPORTING GOODS
1,000 Springs Liquor, 361 South State / 208-837-6393
Hagerman Mini Mart, 531 South State Street / 208-837-4591

AIRPORTS
Twin Falls-Sun Valley Regional Airport / 208-733-5215

AUTO RENTAL

Avis Rent-A-Car, Twin Falls-Sun Valley Regional Airport / 208-733-5527
Budget Rent-A-Car, Twin Falls-Sun Valley Regional Airport / 208-734-4067
Hertz Rent-A-Car, 210 Shoshone West / 208-733-2668

FOR MORE INFORMATION

National Park Service
221 North State Street
Hagerman, ID 83332
208-837-4793

Twin Falls County

County Population–53,580	County Area–1,254,000 acres
October Temperature–49°	Annual Precipitation–9"
Acres in CRP–24,992	

Twin Falls County is among the best pheasant hunting counties in the state. It also includes some of the best waterfowl hunting along the Snake River.

UPLAND BIRDS
Pheasant, Gray (Hungarian) Partridge, Blue & Ruffed (Forest) Grouse, Sage Grouse, Sharp-tailed Grouse (closed), California Quail, Turkey

WATERFOWL
Ducks and Geese

Twin Falls

Population–27,750 • Elevation–3,747

Twin Falls is located in southern Idaho on the banks of the Snake River. Waterfowl hunting is especially good along the river while strong numbers of pheasants and sage grouse frequent the surrounding desert lands. Twin Falls offers plenty of amenities to the traveling hunter.

ACCOMMODATIONS
Best Western Inn, 906 Blue Lakes Boulevard / No pets allowed / 208-733-6095
Comfort Inn, 1893 Canyon Springs Road / Pets allowed / 208-734-7494
Motel 6, 1472 Blue Lakes Boulevard / No pets allowed / 208-734-3993
Motel 3, 248 2nd Avenue West / Pets allowed / 208-733-5630
Ameritel Inn, 1377 Blue Lakes Boulevard / 208-736-8000 or 800-822-TWIN / Fax 208-734-7777

CAMPGROUNDS
Anderson Best Holiday Trav-L-Park / 72 full hookups, tent sites available, laundry / 208-825-5336
KOA Twin / 14 full hookups, tent sites available, cabins for rent, laundry, ice, sewer disposal / 208-324-4169

RESTAURANTS
Elmer's Pancake & Steakhouse, 1824 Blue Lakes Boulevard / Open 6AM–11PM / 208-736-9073

Depot Grill, 545 Shoshone Street / Open 24 hours / 208-733-0710

The Sandpiper, 1309 Blue Lakes Boulevard (from I-84 exit 173, 3.5 miles south on US 93) / Open 11:30AM–2PM and 5–10PM; Sunday 5–9PM / Cocktails and lounge / 208-734-7000

La Casita, 111 South Park Avenue West / Beer and wine / 208-734-7974

Diamondfield Jack's, 1357 Blue Lakes Boulevard / Open 6AM–10PM, Friday and Saturday to 11PM / Cocktails and lounge / 208-734-5000

SPORTING GOODS
Blue Lakes Sporting Goods, 1236 Blue Lakes Boulevard / 208-733-6446

The Hatch, 1703 Addison Avenue East / 208-733-9111

Little Wood Troutfitters, 245 Main Avenue / 208-733-8453

VETERINARIANS
Addison Animal Clinic, 2285 Addison Avenue East / 208-733-0657

Green Cross Veterinary Hospital, 2118 Kimberly Road / 208-733-4653

HOSPITALS
Canyon View Hospital, 228 Shoup Avenue West / 208-733-4769

AIRPORTS
Twin Falls-Sun Valley Regional Airport / Delta, Horizon, Northwest / 208-733-5215

AUTO RENTAL
Avis Rent-A-Car, Twin Falls-Sun Valley Regional Airport / 208-733-5527

Budget Rent-A-Car, Twin Falls-Sun Valley Regional Airport / 208-734-4067

Hertz Rent-A-Car, 210 Shoshone West / 208-733-2668

AUTO SERVICE
B & G Automotive, 1275 Addison Avenue / 208-733-1645

Buck's Texaco Service, 303 Main Avenue East / 208-734-5599

FOR MORE INFORMATION
Twin Falls Chamber of Commerce
858 Blue Lakes Boulevard North
Twin Falls, ID 83301
208-733-3974 or 800-255-8946

Cassia County

County Population–19,532	County Area–1,638,000 acres
October Temperature–49°	Annual Rainfall–8.5"
Acres in CRP–61,641	

Cassia County is among the top bird hunting counties in the state. It has excellent pheasant and gray partridge hunting and good waterfowl hunting.

UPLAND BIRDS
Pheasants, Gray (Hungarian) Partridge, Sage Grouse, Blue & Ruffed (Forest) Grouse, Sharp-tailed Grouse (closed), California Quail, Turkey

WATERFOWL
Ducks and Geese

Jerome, Lincoln, and Minidoka Counties

County Populations–37,807	County Area–966,577 acres
October Temperature–49°	Annual Precipitation–8.6"
Acres in CRP–4,983	

Minidoka and Jerome County have lots of farms with grain crops and sugar beet that offer good pheasant and gray partridge hunting. Lincoln County is mostly desert with a few dense farm areas with a mix of grain crops and pasture land for livestock.

UPLAND BIRDS
Pheasant, Gray (Hungarian) Partridge, Chukar, Sage Grouse, California Quail

WATERFOWL
Ducks and Geese

Burley
Population–1,000 • Elevation–4,150

Burley is located just east of Twin Falls, off of I-84. Nearby Goose Creek Reservoir, Lake Walcott and the Snake River draw waterfowl to the area. Hunters can also find sage grouse and a few pheasants in the surrounding desert.

ACCOMMODATIONS
Best Western Burley Inn and Convention Center, 800 North Overland Avenue / 800-599-1849 / Allows pets
Budget Motel, 900 North Overland Avenue / 800-599-1849 / Allows pets
Greenwell Motel, 904 East Main / 208-678-5576 / Allows pets
Lampliter Motel, 304 East Main / 208-678-0031 / Allows pets
Starlite Motel, 510 Overland / 208-678-7766 / Allows pets

RESTAURANTS
Best Western Burley Inn and Convention Center, 800 North Overland Avenue / / Restaurant open 6AM–2AM / Cocktails and lounge / 800-599-1849
Cavazos Mexican Food, 1198 East Main Street / 208-678-9913
JBs Big Boy, 136 East 5th North / Open 5:30AM–11PM weekdays, 5:30AM–12AM weekends / 208-678-0803
Sodbuster Restaurant, 610 North Overland / Open 6:30AM–11PM daily / 208-677-2403
Pilots Lounge, 125 West Main Street / 208-678-7171

CAMPGROUNDS
Snake River RV Park / 130 sites, tent sites available, laundry, phone, grocery ice, grills / 208-654-2133

SPORTING GOODS
Donnelley's Sports, 1300 Overland Avenue / 208-677-4310
Pinetree Sports, 525 2165 Overland Avenue / 208-678-5869

VETERINARIANS
Ark Animal Hospital, 750 21st Street, Heyburn ID 83336 / 208-678-1177

AIRPORT
Twin Falls-Sun Valley Regional Airport / Delta, Horizon, Northwest / 208-733-5215

FOR MORE INFORMATION
Mini Cassia Chamber of Commerce
324 Scott Avenue
Rupert, ID 83350
800-333-3408

Guides and Outfitters
Region 4–Magic Valley

IDAHO GUIDE SERVICE
563 Trotter Drive, Twin Falls, ID 83301
Phone 208-734-4998 / Fax 208-735-1918
Contact–Olin Garner
E-mail–igs@magiclink.com
Web Site–http://www.magiclink.com/web/igs
Bird Hunting–Chukar·
Accommodations–Twin Falls
Other Services–River/stream fishing, steelhead fishing, jet boating, rafting, drift boating

PIONEER MOUNTAIN OUTFITTERS
3267 East 3225 North, Twin Falls, ID 83301
Phone 208-734-3679 / Fax 208-734-0711
Contact–Tom and Deb Proctor
Bird Hunting–Forest Grouse
Accommodations–Twin Falls
Other Services–Big game hunting, backcountry lake fishing, river/stream fishing, horse pack trips, trail rides

SILVER CREEK OUTFITTERS
Highway 75 Downtown, Box 418, Ketchum, ID 83340-0418
Phone 208-726-5282 / Toll Free 1-800-732-5687
Contact–Terry Ring
Bird Hunting–Forest Grouse, Sage Grouse
Accommodations–Ketchum, Sun Valley
Other Services–Flyfishing, fishing lessons

TRIANGLE C RANCH
Ron Gillett
P.O. Box 69, Stanley, ID 83278
Phone 208-774-2266 / Fax 208-774-2266 / Toll-free 1-800-303-6258
Contact–Ron Gillett
Bird Hunting–Chukar, Forest Grouse
Accommodations–Guest Ranch
Other Services–Big game hunting, backcountry lake fishing, river/stream fishing,
   rafting

WOOD RIVER OUTFITTERS
P.O. Box 10013, Ketchum, ID 83340
Phone 208-725-0666 / Fax 208-726-2922
Bird Hunting–Blue Grouse
Accommodations–Ketchum, Sun Valley
Other Services–Flyfishing, jet boating

Region 5–Southeast

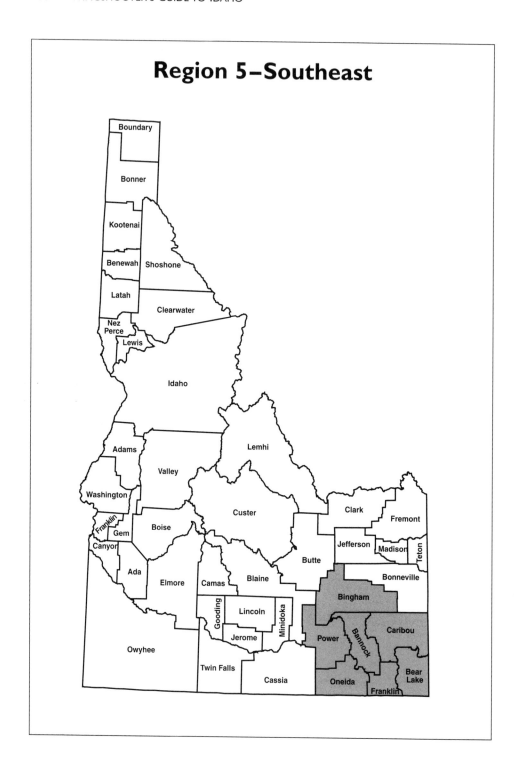

Region 5–Southeast

Located in the southeast corner of the state, this region consists of Bingham, Caribou, Bear Lake, Franklin, Bannock, Oneida, and Power counties. Big game hunt units include 66a, 68, 68a, 70, 71, 72, 73, 73a, 74, 75, 76, 77 and 78. The regional office is located in Pocatello. With Utah and Wyoming on the borders, this region has abundant wildlife and scenery. Its sharp-tailed grouse hunting ranks among the West's best. American Falls Reservoir draws thousands of waterfowl during migration periods. Elevations range from 4,354 at American Falls Reservoir to 9,957 at Meade Peak.

Wildlife Management Areas

- Sterling—3,304 acres, waterfowl, upland gamebirds; permit required for pheasant; 2 miles east of Aberdeen via State Highway 39 (north bank of American Falls Reservoir west of Blackfoot).
- Portneuf—3,104 acres, upland gamebirds; 12 miles south of Pocatello via County Road 450.
- Georgetown Summit—1,656 acres, upland gamebirds; 3 miles northeast of Georgetown (southeast of Soda Springs via U.S. 30).
- Montpelier—1,588 acres; upland gamebird hunting; 1 mile east of Montpelier via U.S. 30.
- Stocking Ranch—1,720 acres, including 7.5 miles of upper Blackfoot River above Blackfoot Reservoir; upland gamebirds, waterfowl; 20 miles north of Soda Springs via State Highway 34; 10 miles southwest of Gray's Lake via State Highway 34.

Blue & Ruffed (Forest) Grouse Distribution
Region 5–Southeast

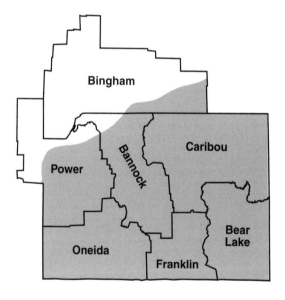

Chukar Distribution
Region 5–Southeast

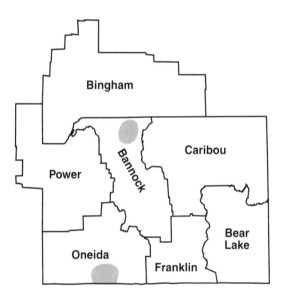

Gray (Hungarian) Partridge Distribution
Region 5–Southeast

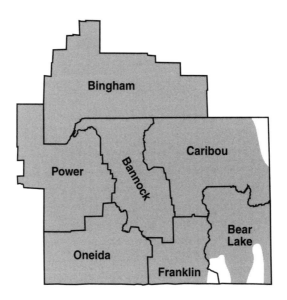

Pheasant Distribution
Region 5–Southeast

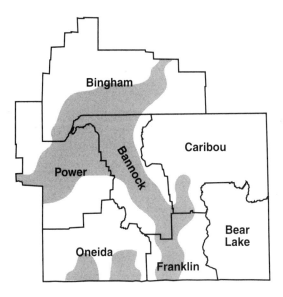

Sage Grouse Distribution
Region 5–Southeast

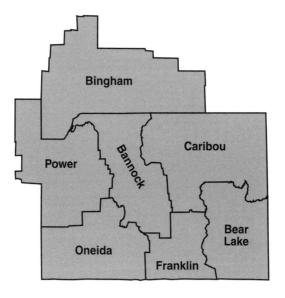

Sharp-tailed Grouse Distribution
Region 5–Southeast

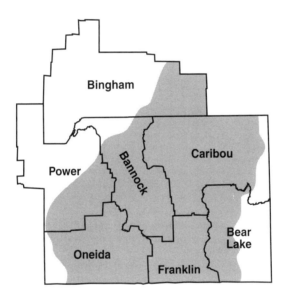

Wild Turkey Distribution
Region 5–Southeast

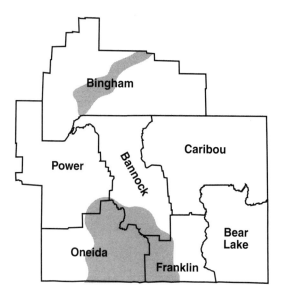

Bingham County

County Population–37,583
October Temperature–48°
Acres in CRP–42,545

County Area–1,341,440 acres
Annual Precipitation–9.5"

Bonneville and Bingham Counties should provide excellent bird hunting with so much land in the Conservation Reserve Program and hunting for gray partridge and sharp-tailed grouse has improved. However, pheasant numbers remain depressed. Forest Grouse hunting is excellent in the mountain forests and there remains pockets of good sage grouse hunting. The best hunting is east of Idaho Falls and Blackfoot.

UPLAND BIRDS
Pheasant, Gray (Hungarian) Partridge, Chukar, Sharp-tailed Grouse, Blue & Ruffed (Forest) Grouse, Sage Grouse, Turkey

WATERFOWL
Ducks and Geese

Power and Bannock Counties

Two-County Population–73,112	Two-County Area–1,609,000 acres
October Temperature–48°	Annual Precipitation–9.5"
Acres in CRP–98,145	

Power and Bannock Counties provide excellent bird hunting with a great deal of land in the Conservation Reserve Program and hunting for sage grouse, gray partridge and sharp-tailed grouse has improved. However, pheasant numbers remain depressed. Forest Grouse hunting is excellent in the mountain forests. The best hunting is west of Pocatello. Don't forget the Fort Hall Indian Reservation.

UPLAND BIRDS
Pheasant, Gray (Hungarian) Partridge, Chukar, Sharp-tailed Grouse, Blue & Ruffed (Forest) Grouse, Sage Grouse, Turkey

WATERFOWL
Ducks and Geese

Pocatello

Population–60,000 • Elevation–4,454

Pocatello lies in southeast Idaho, just west of the Caribou National Forest, where upland hunts for mountain grouse can be combined with treks afield for trophy mule deer. Pocatello offers all the amenities to a visiting sportsman, including fine lodging and dining.

ACCOMMODATIONS
Best Western Cottontree Inn, 1415 Bench Road / 208-237-7650 / Fax 208-238-1355 / Allows Pets
Comfort Inn, Bench Road / Allows pets / 208-237-8155
Howard Johnson, 1399 Bench Road / Allows pets / 208-237-1400 / Fax 208-238-0225
Motel 6, 291 West Burnside Avenue / Allows pets / 208-237-7880 / Fax 208-238-0225
Pocatello Park Quality Inn, Pocatello Creek Road / Allows pets / 208-234-4524 / Fax 208-234-4524

CAMPGROUNDS
Cowboy RV Park / 41 full hook-up sites, laundry, phone, tables, sewage disposal / 208-232-4587

RESTAURANTS
Denny's, 4310 Yellowstone Avenue, Chubbuck / 208-238-1223 / Open 24 hours
Buddy's, 626 East Lewis / 208-233-1172
Golden Wheel, 230 West Bonneville / 208-233-1613
The Sandpiper, 1400 Bench Road / Open 11AM–2PM and 5–10PM, Friday and Saturday to 10:30PM; Sunday 4:30–9PM / Cocktails and lounge / 208-233-1000
Frontier Pies Restaurant & Bakery, 1205 Yellowstone Avenue / Open 6AM–10PM, Friday and Saturday to 11PM / 208-237-7159
Porter House Grill, 1555 Pocatello Creek Road / Open 5:30–10PM / Cocktails and lounge / 208-233-2200

SPORTING GOODS
All Season Angler, 509 East Oak / 208-232-3042
Northwest Sports Center, 1509 Yellowstone Avenue / 208-238-0577
Gart Bros., 625 Yellowstone / 208-232-2981

VETERINARIANS
Alpine Animal Hospital, 4000 Yellowstone / Emergency service / 208-237-1111
Alta Animal Hospital, 1056 South Main Street / Emergency service / 208-233-0936
Community Animal Hospital, 833 North 12th Avenue / 208-233-6840

HOSPITALS
Bannock Regional Medical Center, 651 Memorial Drive / 208-239-1000

AIRPORTS
Pocatello Regional Airport / Skywest and Horizon / 208-234-6154

AUTO RENTAL
Budget Rent-A-Car, Pocatello Regional Airport / 208-233-0600
Avis Rent-A-Car, Pocatello Regional Airport / 208-232-3244
Hertz Rent-A-Car, Pocatello Regional Airport / 208-233-2970

AUTO SERVICE
Don Deckers , 429 North 5th / 208-233-5615
Mel Facer's Repair Service, 829 East Oak / 208-232-2305

FOR MORE INFORMATION
Pocatello Chamber of Commerce
2695 South 5th
Pocatello, ID 83201
208-234-7091

American Falls

Population–3,700 • Elevation–4,280

American Falls is a small town that rests on the banks of American Falls Reservoir, an important impoundment of the Snake River. Besides offering excellent angling for large trout, the reservoir attracts fall migrating ducks and geese in masses. Hunters can simply walk out their motel door, make a short drive and set out some decoys.

ACCOMMODATIONS
Hillview Motel, 279 Lakeview Road / Allows pets / 208-226-5151
Ronnez Motel, 411 Lincoln, P.O. Box 671 / 208-226-9658

RESTAURANTS
Lakeview Cafe, I-15 / 208-226-2194
Blue Moon Restaurant & Lounge, 180 Harrison / 208-226-7768
Rogelio's Mexican Restaurant, 616 Fort Hall Avenue / 208-226-7822

VETERINARIANS
American Falls Animal Clinic, 2773 Fairgrounds Road / 208-226-7181
Rudd Dell, 3016 Cedar Lane / 208-226-2786

HOSPITALS
Harms Memorial Hospital, 510 Roosevelt / 208-226-2327

AUTO SERVICE
Harris Garage, 149 Roosevelt / 208-226-2968
Jerry's Auto Clinic, 240 Roosevelt / 208-226-2320

AIRPORT
Pocatello Regional Airport / Skywest and Horizon / 208-234-6154

FOR MORE INFORMATION
American Falls Chamber
258 Idaho Street
American Falls, ID 83211
208-226-7214

Oneida and Franklin Counties

Two-County Population–12,724   Two-County Area–1,190,000 acres
October Temperature–48°   Annual Precipitation–9.1"
Acres in CRP–100,379

Oneida and Franklin counties are among the best bird hunting areas in the state. They have it all including excellent sharptail, sage grouse and pheasant. Forest grouse hunting is excellent in the mountain forests.

UPLAND BIRDS
Pheasant, Gray (Hungarian) Partridge, Chukar, Sharp-tailed Grouse, Blue & Ruffed (Forest) Grouse, Sage Grouse, Turkey

WATERFOWL
Ducks and Geese

Malad City
Population–2,015

Located just off of I-15 in extreme southeast Idaho, Malad City offers a stopping point for those hunters traveling out of Utah with a late start. Malad offers its own intriguing wingshooting options, too. Try ducks and geese in the agricultural lands or hit the grasslands for excellent sharp-tailed grouse and Hungarian partridge shooting. Mountain grouse frequent the Malad Range just east of town.

ACCOMMODATIONS
Village Inn Motel, 50 South 300 East / Allows pets / 208-766-4761

VETERINARIANS
Malad Valley Animal Clinic, Waas Avenue and 100 West / 208-766-2961

SPORTING GOODS
Jones Confectionary Lounge, 72 Bannock / 208-766-9914

RESTAURANTS
Quick Stop, 226 East 50 South / 208-766-4950
Dude Ranch Cafe, 65 North Main / 208-766-4327

AIRPORT
Pocatello Regional Airport / Skywest and Horizon / 208-234-6154

FOR MORE INFORMATION
Cherry Creek Visitor Center
Malad City, ID 83252
208-766-4788

Caribou and Bear Lake Counties

Two-County Population–13,047	Two-County Area–1,778,000 acres
October Temperature–49°	Annual Precipitation–11.3"
Acres in CRP–99,296	

Caribou and Bear Lake counties offer excellent upland bird and waterfowl hunting. Even though it's close to Utah, this area is often overlooked for birds despite excellent sharptail, forest and fair sage grouse habitat.

UPLAND BIRDS
Pheasant, Gray (Hungarian) Partridge, Sharp-tailed Grouse, Blue & Ruffed (Forest) Grouse, Sage Grouse, Turkey

WATERFOWL
Ducks and Geese

Soda Springs
Population–4,050 • Elevation 5,200

Maybe best known for its proximity to some huge mule deer in the Cache and Caribou national forests, Soda Springs also caters to the wingshooter. Ducks and geese frequent the mountain valleys and mountain grouse can be pursued in the aspen stands and mountain ridges in the forests.

ACCOMMODATIONS
Caribou Lodge & Motel, 110 West Second Street South / 208-547-3377
J-R Inn, 179 West 2nd Street South / 208-547-3366
Lakeview Motel, 341 West 2nd Street South / 208-547-4351
Trail Motel & Restaurant, 213 East 200 South / 208-547-3909

RESTAURANTS
Betty's Cafe, Highway 30 West / 208-547-4802
Ender's Cafe, 76 South Main / 208-547-4980
Cedar View Supper Club, Highway 30 West / 208-547-3301

FLY SHOPS AND SPORTING GOODS
Dave's Tackle and Sports, 190 South 2nd East / 208-547-3023

HOSPITAL
Caribou Memorial Hospital, 300 South 3rd West / 208-547-3341

AIRPORT
Allan Tigert Airport / 208-547-9927
Pocatello Regional Airport / Skywest and Horizon / 208-234-6154

AUTO REPAIR
Caribou Ford and Mercury, 355 East 2nd South / 208-547-4344
Hunzeker Chevrolet , 166 West 2nd South / 208-547-3324

FOR MORE INFORMATION
Soda Springs Chamber of Commerce
Soda Springs, ID 83276
208-547-2600

Guides and Outfitters

Region 5–Southeast

ANDERSON OUTFITTING
5646 Sorrell Drive, Pocatello, ID 83202
Phone 208-237-6544
Bird Hunting–Chukar, Forest Grouse
Accommodations–Pocatello, Soda Springs
Other Services–Big game hunting, backcountry lake fishing, river/stream fishing, jet boating, rafting, drift boating, horse pack trips

RUDEEN RANCH
612 Calder, American Falls, ID 83211
Phone–208-226-5591
Contact–Kent Rudeen
Bird Hunting–Forest Grouse
Accommodations–American Falls
Other Services–Big game hunting
Special–Ski trips into Bowen Canyon Bald Eagle Sanctuary

Region 6–Upper Snake

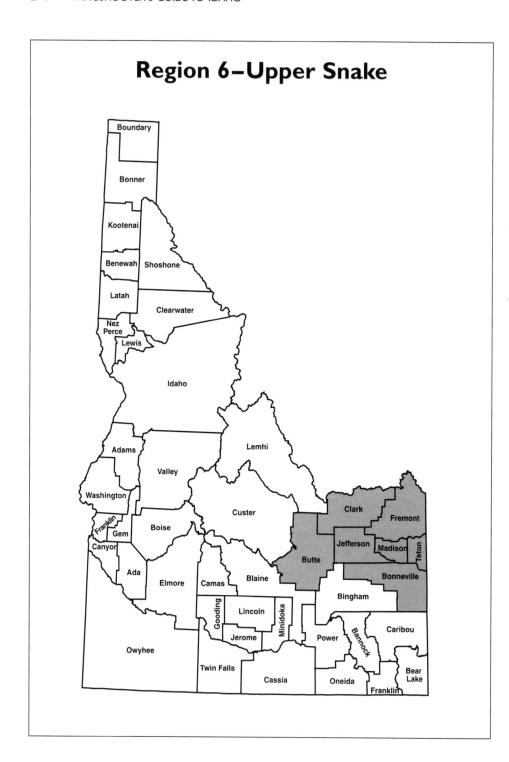

Region 6–Upper Snake

The Upper Snake Region is in the eastern part of state and consists of Clark, Butte, Jefferson, Madison, Teton, Fremont, and Bonneville counties. Big game hunt units include 50, 51, 58, 59, 59a, 60, 60a, 61, 62, 62a, 63, 63a, 64, 65, 66, 67 and 69. Regional office is located in Idaho Falls. Outdoor adventures, including sharptail, sage grouse, and waterfowl hunting, abound in the shadows of the Continental Divide and Grand Teton Mountains. Elevations range from 4,735 at Idaho Falls to 10,740 at Tyler Peak.

Wildlife Management Areas
- Tex Creek—18,000 acres, upland gamebirds; 20 miles southeast of Idaho Falls via U.S. 26 and Ririe Reservoir and Meadow Creek roads.
- Market Lake—5,000 acres, waterfowl, upland gamebirds; permit required for pheasant; 1 mile north of Roberts (15 miles north of Idaho Falls via Interstate 15).
- Cartier Slough—1,000 acres, waterfowl, upland gamebirds; 10 miles west of Rexburg via State Highway 33 (west bank of Henry's Fork River).
- Mud Lake—8,000 acres, waterfowl, upland gamebirds; permit required for pheasant; 2 miles north of Terreton via State Highway 33.
- Sand Creek—15,000 acres, waterfowl, upland gamebirds; 15 miles north of St. Anthony.

Blue & Ruffed (Forest) Grouse Distribution Region 5–Upper Snake

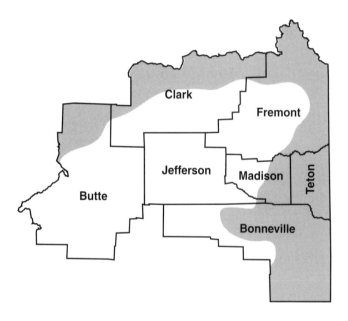

Chukar Distribution
Region 5–Upper Snake

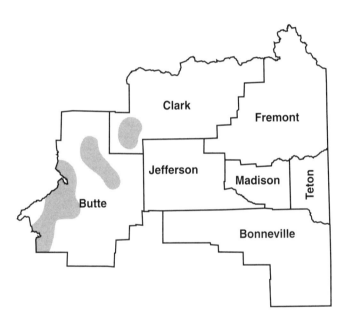

Gray (Hungarian) Partridge Distribution
Region 5–Upper Snake

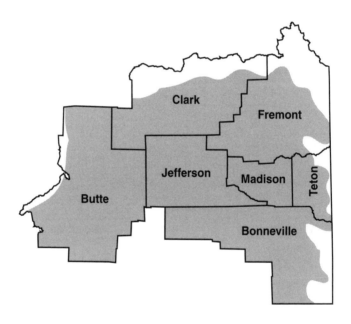

Pheasant Distribution
Region 5–Upper Snake

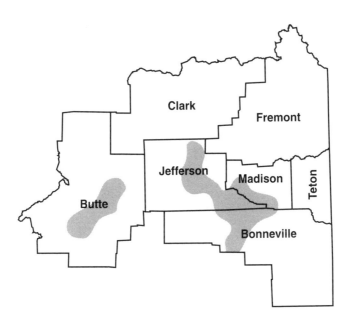

Sage Grouse Distribution
Region 5–Upper Snake

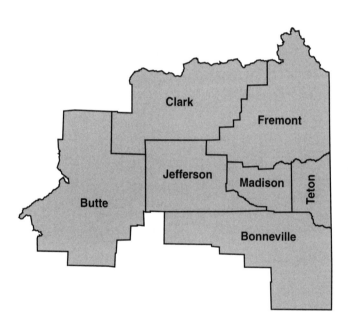

Sharp-tailed Grouse Distribution
Region 5–Upper Snake

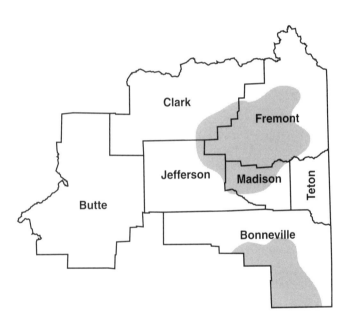

Spruce Grouse Distribution
Region 5–Upper Snake

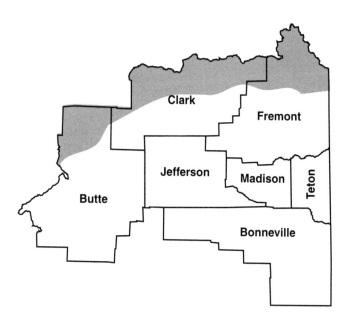

Wild Turkey Distribution
Region 5–Upper Snake

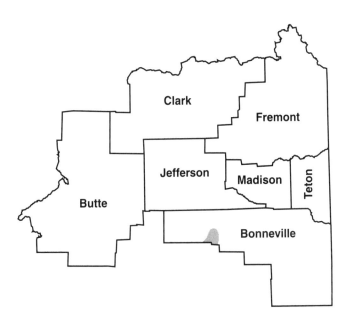

Butte and Clark Counties

Two-County Population–3,680	Two-County Area–2,555,000 acres
October Temperature–48°	Annual Precipitation–8"
Acres in CRP–10,881	

Butte and Clark Counties are among the least populated in the state. Mostly public land sagebrush desert, these two counties used to be prime sage grouse habitat. They have suffered from the reduction in habitat but still have pockets of good hunting.

UPLAND BIRDS
Pheasant, Gray (Hungarian) Partridge, Chukar, Sage Grouse, Sharp-tailed Grouse, Blue & Ruffed (Forest) Grouse

WATERFOWL
Ducks and Geese

Arco
Population–1230 • Elevation–5320

Not noted for its beauty, Arco is a small little town often used as a layover for hunters on their way from Boise to Idaho Falls or vice versa. However, Arco rests on the south end of the Big Lost Valley and the Big Lost Mountain Range, which includes Idaho's tallest peak, Mt. Bora. The valley is beautiful, so is Copper Basin, which rests northwest of town. The area offers sage grouse, waterfowl and mountain grouse in good numbers. Comfortable lodging and good food is available.

ACCOMMODATIONS
Arco Inn, 540 West Grand / 12 rooms, restaurant 1 block away / Allows pets / 208-527-3100

D.K. Motel, 316 South Front / 24 units, restaurant 1 block away / Allows pets / 208-527-8282

Lazy A Motel, P.O. Box 12 / Allows pets / 208-527 8262

Lost River Motel, P.O. Box 22 / Allows pets / 208-527-8914

CAMPGROUNDS
Craters of the Moon National Monument / 160 sites, 40 full hook-ups, water, shower, tent sites available / 208-532-1412

Mountain View RV Park / 34 RV sites, 32 water and electric hook-up sites, tent sites available / 800-845-1460

SPORTING GOODS
Dier's Home Improvement, 318 Sunset Drive / 208-527-3444

RESTAURANTS
Pickle's Place, 4440 South Front Street / 208-527-9944

AIRPORT
Idaho Falls Airport / Horizon, Skywest and Delta / 208-529-1221

FOR MORE INFORMATION
Lost River Valley Chamber of Commerce
P.O. Box 837
Arco, ID 83213

Fremont and Teton Counties

Two-County Population–14,376   Two-County Area–1,514,000 acres
October Temperature–46°   Annual Precipitation–18"
Acres in CRP–42,940

Fremont and Teton counties are a mix of low agricultural lands and desert and high mountain and forested plateau. Forest grouse hunting is excellent and there remain pockets of good sharptail and sage grouse hunting. Goose hunting is excellent on the Henry's Fork and Teton rivers.

UPLAND BIRDS
Pheasant, Gray (Hungarian) Partridge, Blue & Ruffed (Forest) Grouse, Sharp-tailed Grouse, Sage Grouse

WATERFOWL
Ducks and Geese

Island Park
Population–143 • Elevation–6,380

Best known for its proximity to the Henry's Fork River and excellent flyfishing for trout, Island Park is also a perfect location for the visiting waterfowl and upland bird hunter. Ducks and geese visit the area in masses and the surrounding forests are littered with forest grouse. Island Park is a resort area that offers camping, motel accommodations and good food.

ACCOMMODATIONS
A-Bar Motel, HC 66, Box 452 / 208-354-2778 / Allows pets,
Aspen Lodge, HC 66, Box 269 / Allows pets / 208-558-7407
Pond's Lodge, P.O. Box 258 / 208-558-7221 / Allows pets, $5 per day per pet /
26 cabins / Restaurant: breakfast (6:30AM), lunch & dinner
Best Western Teton West / Allows pets with $25 refundable deposit / 42 rooms
/ Restaurants and cocktails within walking distance / 208-354-2363 / Fax
208-354-2962
Pines Motel Guest Haus, P.O. Box 117, 105 South Main / Allows pets /
208-354-2778

CAMPGROUNDS
Sawtelle Mountain Resort / 72 full hook-ups, tent sites available, store /
800-574-0404
Redrock RV & Camping Park / 44 full hook-ups, tent sites available /
208-558-7442

RESTAURANTS
A-Bar Motel & Supper Club / 208- 558-7358
Ponds Lodge / 208-558-7221
Lucky Dog Retreat, Big Springs Road / 208-558-7455

SPORTING GOODS
Island Park Liquor & Sports, Elk Creek / 208-558-7448
Last Chance Outfitters / 800-428-8338
Henry's Fork Angler's, on Hwy 20 / Mike Lawson / 208-558-7525

VETERINARIANS
Closest is West Yellowstone or Rexburg

HOSPITALS
Closest in Rexburg or West Yellowstone

AIRPORT
Idaho Falls or Bozeman (140 miles)

AUTO RENTAL
Closest is Idaho Falls or West Yellowstone

FOR MORE INFORMATION
Island Park Chamber of Commerce
P.O. Box 83
Island Park, ID 83429
208-558-7755

Driggs
Population–2,900 • Elevation–6,200

Driggs is a fast-growing small town nestled in the hills just an hour away from Jackson, Wyoming. Sage grouse, Hungarian partridge, pheasants, mountain grouse and ducks and geese all call the area home. Driggs itself offers nice lodging and the best huckleberry milk shakes on Earth. Follow the signs when you get into town.

ACCOMMODATIONS
Teton Valley Lodge / No pets in rooms, 20 rooms, restaurant, hunting & fishing guided trips only / 208-354-2386
Teton Mountain View Inn, In Tetonia 7 miles north of Driggs on Hwy ll / 208-456-2741 or 800-625-2232

RESTAURANTS
Teton Bakery, North Main / 208-354-8116
Knight's British Rail, 63 Depot / 208-354-8365
Lost Horizon, Alta, Wyoming / 307-353-8226

SPORTING GOODS
Mountaineering Outfitters Inc., 62 North Main / 208-354-2222
Bill's Bait Tackle & Pawn Shop, 16 West Center Victor / 208-787-2600
Victor Emporium, 45 North Main Victor / 208-787-2221

HOSPITALS
Teton Valley Hospital, 283 North 1st, East Driggs / 208-354-2383

AIRPORTS
Teton Peaks Centennial Airport Grand Valley Aviation, Driggs / 208-354-8131 / Closest commercial air service in Jackson, WY, or Idaho Falls

AUTO RENTAL
Practical Rent-A-Car, 180 North Main / 208-354-8494

AUTO SERVICE
Driggs Garage, 106 North Main Driggs / 208-354-2326

FOR MORE INFORMATION
Teton Valley Chamber
P.O. Box 250
50 North Main Street
Driggs, ID 83422
208-354-2500

Madison and Jefferson Counties

Two-County Population–40,217   Two-County Area–1,106,000 acres
October Temperature–49°   Annual Precipitation–8.5"
Acres in CRP–24,450

Jefferson County used to be prime pheasant habitat, but today there is little more than the stocked hunting at Mud Lake and Market Lake Wildlife Management areas. Both areas and Camas Creek are good waterfowl areas. Madison County has some of the better sharptail hunting and good waterfowl along the Henry's Fork and Teton rivers.

UPLAND BIRDS
Pheasant, Gray (Hungarian) Partridge, Sharp-tailed Grouse, Blue & Ruffed (Forest) Grouse, Sage Grouse

WATERFOWL
Ducks and Geese

Rexburg
Population–12,800 • Elevation–4,850

Rexburg rests just off Interstate 15 north of Idaho Falls. Located out in the sprawling sagebrush lands of eastern Idaho, the town offers easy access to sage grouse hunting areas in the desert. Hunters can also access the north fork, south fork and main Snake rivers in minutes. Once on the water, they'll find abundant ducks and geese. Forest grouse frequent the forests just north of Rexburg. Nice restaurants and eateries are available.

ACCOMMODATIONS
Best Western Cottontree Inn, 450 West 4th South / Pets allowed for $5 / 100 rooms / Restaurant: breakfast (6AM), lunch, dinner / 208-356-4646
Callaway Motel, 361 South 2nd West / Allows pets / 208-356-5477
Rex's Motel, 357 West 4th South / Allows pets / 208-356-5477
Rexburg Days Inn, 271 South 2nd West / Allows pets / 43 rooms / Restaurant: 1 block, breakfast, lunch, dinner / 208-356-9222

CAMPGROUNDS
Rainbow Lake and Campground / 20 full hook-ups, sewage disposal, phone, ice, tables, tent sites available / 208-356-6036

RESTAURANTS
Me 'n Stan's,167 West Main Street / 208-356-7333
J.B.'s Big Boy, 150 West Main / 208-356-7722

VETERINARIANS
Kauer Veterinary Clinic, 4085 West 2000 South / 208-356-0489
Rexburg Veterinary Clinic, 588 North Hwy 33 / 208-356-4488

SPORTING GOODS
All American Sports, 226 North 2nd East Street / 208-356-0255
Pay Less Drug Store, 125 Valley River Drive / 208-356-8070

AIRPORT
Idaho Falls Airport / Horizon, Skywest and Delta / 208-529-1221

FOR MORE INFORMATION
Rexburg Chamber of Commerce
134 East Main Street, Suite 1
Rexburg, ID 83440
208-356-5700

Bonneville County

County Population–72,207	County Area–1,177,600 acres
October Temperature–48°	Annual Precipitation–9.5"
Acres in CRP–45,600	

Bonneville County should provide excellent bird hunting with so much land in the Conservation Reserve Program and hunting for gray partridge and sharp-tailed grouse has improved. However, pheasant numbers remain depressed. Forest Grouse hunting is excellent in the mountain forests and there remains pockets of good sage grouse hunting. The best hunting is east of Idaho Falls and Blackfoot.

UPLAND BIRDS
Pheasant, Gray (Hungarian) Partridge, Chukar, Sharp-tailed Grouse, Blue & Ruffed (Forest) Grouse, Sage Grouse, Turkey

WATERFOWL
Ducks and Geese

Idaho Falls
Population–50,000 • Elevation–3,900

Idaho Falls rests on the banks of the Snake River in eastern Idaho and offers all the amenities a wingshooter could need. Good restaurants, motels, and wingshooting opportunities are available. If you're looking for waterfowl, try ducks and geese along the Snake or at American Falls Reservoir. Pheasants can be hunted in the nearby agricultural lands. Hungarian partridge and sharp-tailed grouse are a short drive away.

ACCOMMODATIONS
Best Western Driftwood Motel, 575 River Parkway, Box 1037 / Allows pets, $10 / 74 rooms, coffee maker, refrigerators, microwaves / 2 restaurants 1 block away, breakfast (6AM), lunch, dinner / 208-523-2242

Idaho Falls Super 8 Motel, 705 Lindsay Boulevard / 208-522-0590 / Allows pets

Littletree Inn, 888 North Holmes / allows pets / 92 rooms / Restaurant & lounge: breakfast (6AM), lunch, dinner / 208-523-5993 / Fax 208-523-7104

Best Western Amerite, 900 Lindsay Boulevard / No pets / 126 rooms / Continental breakfast (5–10AM) / Restaurants & cocktails across street / 208-523-6000 or 800-600-6001 / Fax 208-523-0000

Motel West, 1540 West Broadway / Allows pets / 80 rooms / Restaurant: breakfast (6:30AM), lunch, dinner / 800-582-1063 / Fax 208-524-1144

CAMPGROUNDS
Indian Falls KOA, 1440 Lindsay Boulvard / 167 full hook-up sites, laundry, sewer disposal, tent sites available / 208-523-3362
Shady Rest Campground / 30 full hook-up sites, showers, sewage disposal, tent sites available / 208-524-0010

RESTAURANTS
JB's Big Boy, 1331 Broadway / Open 5:30AM–12AM weekdays, 5:30AM–1AM weekends / 208-522-4224
Sandpiper Restaurant, 750 Lindsay Boulevard / Open 11AM–2PM; Friday and Saturday 5–10:30PM; Sunday 4:30–9PM / Cocktails and lounge / 208-524-3344
O'Callahan's, 780 Lindsay Boulevard / Open 6AM–10pm, Sunday to 9PM / Cocktails and lounge / 208-523-1818
Melina's Mexican Restaurant, 187 East First Street / Open 11AM–9PM, Friday and Saturday to 10PM; Sunday 12–8PM / Beer and wine / 208-524-5430

SPORTING GOODS
Jimmy's All Season Angler, 275 A Street / 208-524-7160
Gun's & Gear, 2627 West Broadway / 208-525-6446
Gart Sports, 2090 North Yellowstone Hwy / 208-524-2525

VETERINARIANS
Countryside Veterinary Hospital, 3120 South Woodruff Avenue / Emergency service / 208-522-8010
Eastside Pet Clinic, 285 South Woodruff / 208-529-2217
Skyline Animal Clinic, 1378 South Grizzly / Emergency service / 208-529-3244

HOSPITALS
Eastern Idaho Regional Medical Center, 3100 Channing Way / 208-529-6111

AIRPORTS
Idaho Falls Airport / Horizon, Skywest and Delta / 208-529-1221

AUTO RENTAL
Avis Rent-A-Car, Idaho Falls Airport / 208-522-4225
Budget Rent-A-Car, Idaho Falls Airport / 208-522-8800
Hertz Rent-A-Car, Idaho Falls Airport / 208-529-3101

AUTO SERVICE
Gary's Truck U Auto Repair, 1435 Lindsay Boulevard / 208-522-7834
Vern & Larry's Service, 1130 East 17th Street / 208-522-1516

VISITOR INFO
Eastern Idaho Visitor Information Center
505 Lindsay Boulevard
Idaho Falls, ID 83401
208-523-1010 or 800-634-3246

Swan Valley

Population–138 • Elevation–5,020

One of the more scenic locales in Idaho, Swan Valley sits next to the South Fork Snake River east of Idaho Falls. Besides killer fishing opportunities in the river, Swan Valley offers quick access to prime forest grouse grounds and it attracts waterfowl in droves. Not large, Swan Valley is a pretty place to stay and there are some basic accommodations.

ACCOMMODATIONS

Granite Creek Guest Ranch, P.O. Box 340, Ririe, 35 miles east of Idaho Falls on Hwy 26 / 208-538-7140 / Fax 208-538-7876

South Fork Lodge, P.O. Box 22, 4 miles west of Swan Valley on Hwy 26 / No pets / 11 rooms / Restaurant: breakfast (7AM), lunch, dinner, cocktails / 208-483-2112

Swan Valley Bed & Breakfast, P.O. Box 115, 535 Swan Lane, 45 miles northeast of Idaho Falls / 208-483-4663 or 800-241-SWAN

RESTAURANTS

Twigs, Highway 26 / 208-483-2400

Sandy Mite Fly Shop & Cafe / 208-483-2609

The Lodge at Palisades Creek / 208-483-2222

South Fork Lodge / 208-483-2112

FLY SHOPS AND SPORTING GOODS

Berg's Fly Shop & Cafe / 208-483-2609

The Lodge at Palisades Creek / 208-483-2222

South Fork Fly Shop, Highway 26 / 208-483-2722

RESTAURANTS

Sandy Mite Fly Shop & Cafe / 208-483-2609

FOR MORE INFORMATION

South Fork Lodge
P.O. Box 22
Swan Valley, ID 83449
208-483-2112

Guides and Outfitters
Region 6–Upper Snake

DALE ROBSON
1111 North Hwy 32, Felt, ID 83424
Phone 208-456-2861 / Fax 208-456-2805 / Toll-free 1-800-717-2513
Bird Hunting–Forest Grouse
Accommodations–Tetonia, Driggs, Ashton
Other Services–Big game hunting, river/stream fishing, horse pack trips, trail rides

HEART MOUNTAIN OUTFITTER
Box 147, Dubois, ID 83423
Phone 208-374-5370
Bird Hunting–Forest Grouse
Accommodations–Dubois
Other Services–Big game hunting

TETON RIDGE RANCH
200 Valley View Road, Tetonia, ID 83452
Phone 208-456-2650 / Fax 208-456-2218
Contact–Albert Tilt
Bird Hunting–Forest Grouse
Accommodations–Guest Ranch
Other Services–Big game hunting, river/stream fishing, horse pack trips
Special–Sporting clays

TETON VALLEY LODGE
379 Adams Road, Driggs, ID 83422
Phone–208-354-2386 (summer) / Fax 208-354-8125
Contact–Randy Berry
Bird Hunting–Forest Grouse
Accommodations–Riverside lodge, cabins
Other Services–Flyfishing, horse pack trips
Special–Duck hunting

WILD HORSE CREEK RANCH
P.O. Box 398, Mackay, ID 83251
Phone 208-588-2575 / Fax 208-588-2575
Contact–Bill Shields
Off Season Address–5004 Homesite Drive, Yakima, WA 98908 /
Phone 509-966-5419
Bird Hunting–Forest Grouse
Accommodations–Guest Ranch
Other Services–Big game hunting, backcountry lake fishing, river/stream fishing,
horse pack trips, trail rides

Region 7–Salmon

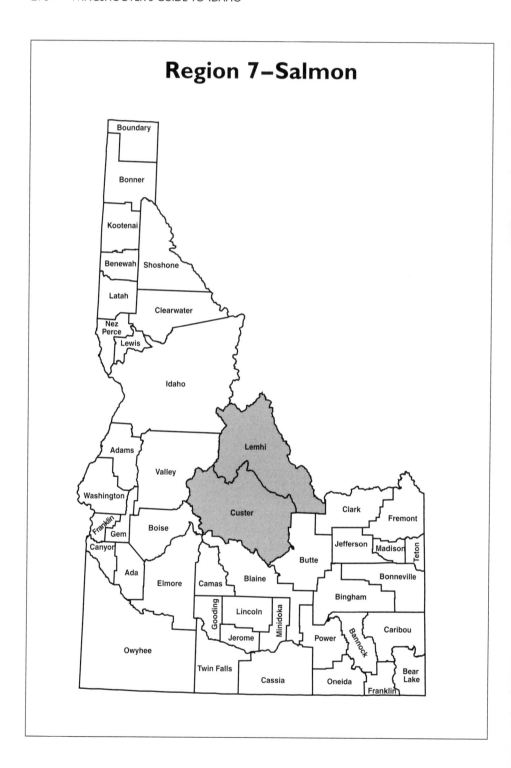

Region 7–Salmon

Located in the state's east-central area, the region consists of Lemhi and Custer counties. Big game hunt units include 21, 21a, 27, 28, 29, 30, 30a, 36, 36a, 36b, 37 and 37a. The regional office is located in Salmon. Famous for the "River of No Return," the Salmon is one of the few undammed waterways left in America. It embraces the largest single wilderness in the lower 48 states. Hunters find excellent forest grouse hunting and the chance for sage grouse. The Lemhi River Valley harbors good pheasant populations. Elevations reach up to 12,662 at Borah Peak, the highest mountain in Idaho.

Blue & Ruffed (Forest) Grouse Distribution
Region 7–Salmon

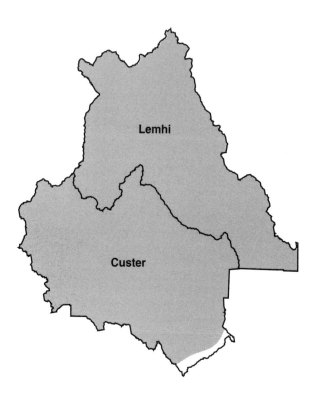

Chukar Distribution
Region 7–Salmon

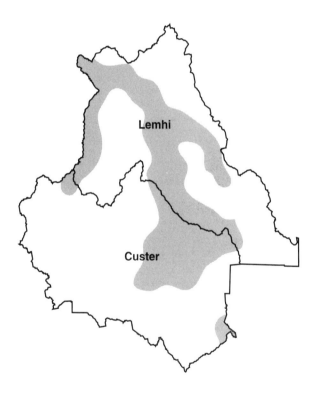

Gray (Hungarian) Partridge Distribution
Region 7–Salmon

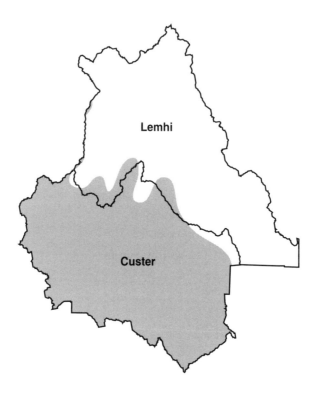

Pheasant Distribution
Region 7–Salmon

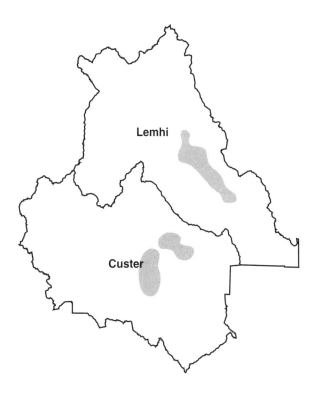

Sage Grouse Distribution
Region 7–Salmon

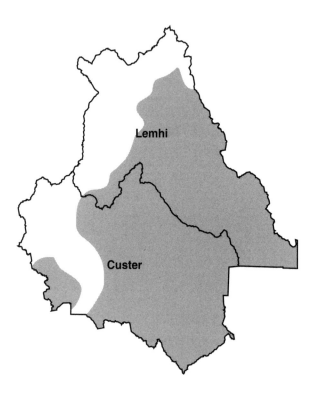

Spruce Grouse Distribution
Region 7–Salmon

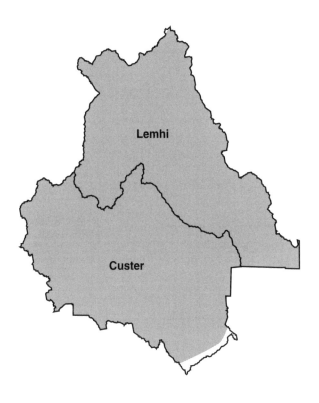

Custer County

County Population–4,133	County Area–3,162,000 acres
October Temperature–48°	Annual Precipitation–12"
Acres in CRP–812	

Custer County is one of the most beautiful in Idaho with both the Sawtooth and White Cloud Mountains, big wilderness country and the Salmon River. It also has some vast range land in the valleys.

UPLAND BIRDS
Gray (Hungarian) Partridge, Chukar, Blue & Ruffed (Forest) Grouse, Sage Grouse, Pheasant

WATERFOWL
Ducks and Geese

Challis
Population–1,200 • Elevation–5,280

Often called "Gateway to the Frank Church River of No Return Wilderness," Challis, a quaint little town, offers ample opportunity for bird hunters just passing through on their way to various hunting grounds, or local options, like waterfowl on the Salmon River, sage grouse in nearby flatlands and forest grouse in the surrounding mountains.

ACCOMMODATIONS
Challis Motor Lodge & Lounge, P.O. Box 6 / Pets allowed / 208-879-2251
Holiday Lodge Motel, HC 63, Box 1667 / 208-879-2259
Northgate Inn, HC 63, Box 1665 / Pets allowed / 208-879-2490
The Village Inn, P.O. Box 6, on Hwy 93 / Pets allowed / 208-879-2239

RESTAURANTS
Antonio's, 9th & Main Street / 208-879-2210
Y-Inn, 1200 North Main Street / 208-879-4426
The Village Inn, Hwy 93 / 208-879-2239

SPORTING GOODS
Twin Peaks Sports / 208-879-2317

VETERINARIANS
Rodney Evans / 208-879-4439

HOSPITALS
Western Montana Clinic, Clinic Road / 208-879-4351
Closest hospital is in Salmon

AIRPORT
Idaho Falls Airport / Horizon, Skywest and Delta / 208-529-1221
Boise Municipal Airport / Commercial airlines are United, Delta, Northwest,
Southwest, Skywest, and Horizon / 208-383-3110

AUTO RENTAL
Closest is Idaho Falls or Boise

AUTO SERVICE
Four Knocks, Hwy 93 / 208-879-2369
Doug's Chevron, 9th & Main / 208- 879-4404

FOR MORE INFORMATION
Challis Chamber of Commerce
P.O. Box 1130
Challis, ID 83226
208-879-2771

Stanley

Population–99 • Elevation–6,260

A more scenic town in the West you likely will not find. Nestled under the watchful eye of the Sawtooth Mountains, Stanley offers wingshooters excellent opportunities on forest grouse and waterfowl, with lesser chances for sage grouse. And, of course, there is scenery galore. Stanley also offers excellent meals and comfortable accommodations.

ACCOMMODATIONS

Creek Side Lodge, P.O. Box 110, on banks of Valley Creek / Allows pets / 208-774-2213

Sawtooth Hotel, P.O. Box 52 / Allows pets / 208-774-9947

Idaho Rocky Mountain Ranch, HC 64, Box 9934 / 208-774-3544

Sessions Lodge, HC 64, Box 9696, 12 miles south of Stanley and 50 miles north of Ketchum / Allows pets / 208-774-3366

Redwood Motel, P.O. Box 55 / 208-774-3531

CAMPGROUNDS

Elk Mountain RV Resort, 4 miles west of Stanley / 25 full hook-ups, laundry, phone, tent sites available / 800-428-9203

RESTAURANTS

Mountain Village, 208-774-3317

Sawtooth Motel & Cafe, 208-774-9947

SPORTING GOODS

Jerry's Country Store & Motel / 208-774-3566

VETERINARIANS

Closest Vet is in Ketchum

HOSPITALS

Closest hospital is in Ketchum

AIRPORT

Boise Municipal Airport / Commercial airlines are United, Delta, Northwest, Southwest, Skywest, and Horizon / 208-383-3110

AUTO RENTAL

National Car Rental at Mountain Village, Stanley Hwy 21 / Available Memorial Day to Labor Day / 208-774-3661

AUTO SERVICE

Stanley Stop, Hwy 21 / 208-774-3482

FOR MORE INFORMATION

Stanley Sawtooth Chamber
P.O. Box 8
Stanley, ID 83278
208-774-3411

Lemhi County

County Population–6,899

October Temperature–49

Acres in CRP–225

County Area–2,936,000 acres

Annual Precipitation–10"

Lemhi County is a diverse county with some surprisingly good bird hunting. Pheasant numbers are good. Sage grouse roam the Birch Creek and Pasimeroi valleys and forest grouse flourish in the mountains. Good chukar hunting is found in the Salmon River canyons.

UPLAND BIRDS
Pheasant, Gray (Hungarian) Partridge, Chukar, Sage Grouse, Gambel's Quail (closed)

WATERFOWL
Ducks and Geese

Salmon

Population–3,200 • Elevation–4,000

The former haunt of Elmer Keith, Salmon is a growing little tourist town, complete with its fair share of trendy espresso bars. On the other hand, Salmon retains its old West heritage. Lemhi County is cowboy country and Salmon is the social hub for those hard-working men. Private ranches offer excellent hunting for sage grouse and pheasants. Chukar, Hungarian partridge and forest grouse can be found, often in high numbers, in the surrounding public land tracts.

ACCOMMODATIONS
Motel Deluxe, P.O. Box 863 / Allows pets / 208-756-2231
Suncrest Motel, 705 South Challis Street / Allows pets / 208-756-2294
Stagecoach Inn Motel, 201 Hwy 93 North / 208-756-4251
Williams Lake Resort / P.O. Box 1150 / 208-756-2007

CAMPGROUNDS
Salmon River RV Park / 9 full hook-ups, sewage disposal, grocery store, ice, tent sites available / 208-756-4521
Salmon Meadows Campground / 44 full hook-ups, ice, grocery, ice, phone, tent sites available / 208-756-2640

RESTAURANTS
Salmon River Coffee Shop, 606 Main / 208-756-3521
Shady Nook, Hwy 95 North / 208-756-4182
Union Avenue Depot, 720 Union Avenue / 208-756-2095

SPORTING GOODS
Silver Spur Sports, 403 Main / 208-756-2833
All Season Sports, 109 South Center / 208-756-4904

VETERINARIANS
Blue Cross Veterinary Clinic, 1610 Main Street / 208-756-3331
Salmon River Veterinary Clinic, Hwy 28 / 208-756-3587
Horizon Veterinary Services, 710 Lemhi Avenue / 208-756-4164

AIRPORT
Closest commercial service in Idaho Falls (170 miles) or Missoula (140 miles)

AUTO RENTAL
Closest auto rental is Idaho Falls or Missoula

FOR MORE INFORMATION
Salmon Chamber of Commerce
200 Main Street, Suite 1
Salmon, ID 83467
208-756-2100

Guide and Outfitters
Region 7–Salmon

AGGIPAH RIVER TRIPS
P.O. Box 425, Salmon, ID 83467
Phone 208-756-4167
Bird Hunting–Chukar
Accommodations–Salmon
Other Services–Steelhead fishing, rafting, drift boating

CASTLE CREEK OUTFITTERS/RANCH
P.O. Box 2008, Salmon, ID 83467
Phone 208-756-2548
Contact–Shane McAfee
Bird Hunting–Forest Grouse
Accommodations–Guest Ranch
Other Services–Big game hunting, backcountry lake fishing, river/stream fishing, horse pack trips, trail rides

HAPPY HOLLOW VACATIONS
HC 61, Box 14, Salmon, ID 83467
Phone 208-756-3954
Contact–Martin Capps
Bird Hunting–Forest Grouse
Accommodations–Guest Ranch
Other Services–Big game hunting, backcountry lake fishing, river/stream fishing, steelhead fishing, rafting, drift boating, horse pack trips, trail rides, cattle drives/roundups

TWIN PEAKS RANCH
P.O. Box 774, Salmon, ID 83467
Phone 208-894-2290 / Fax 208-894-2429 or 208-756-4049 /
    Toll-free 1-800-659-4899 or 1-800-396-2628
Contact–Melvin Reingold
Bird Hunting–Chukar, Forest Grouse
Accommodations–Guest Ranch
Other Services–Big game hunting, backcountry lake fishing, river/stream fishing, steelhead fishing, jet boating, rafting, horse pack trips, trail rides, cattle drives/roundups

310 — WINGSHOOTER'S GUIDE TO IDAHO

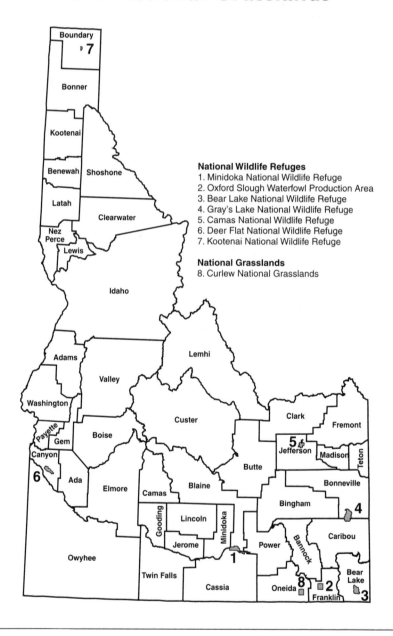

National Wildlife Refuges and National Grasslands

National Wildlife Refuges
1. Minidoka National Wildlife Refuge
2. Oxford Slough Waterfowl Production Area
3. Bear Lake National Wildlife Refuge
4. Gray's Lake National Wildlife Refuge
5. Camas National Wildlife Refuge
6. Deer Flat National Wildlife Refuge
7. Kootenai National Wildlife Refuge

National Grasslands
8. Curlew National Grasslands

National Wildlife Refuges and Grasslands

Idaho's six national wildlife refuges and one waterfowl production area are administered by the U.S. Fish and Wildlife Service for waterfowl production and migration staging areas. Several also harbor essential upland gamebird habitat. Southeastern Idaho's bonus for upland birds is the Curlew National Grasslands administered by the Caribou National Forest.

Four of Idaho's NWRs and a USFWS waterfowl production areas are located in eastern Idaho and administered by its Pocatello office. The state's two other national wildlife refuges are west of Boise and north of Sandpoint, almost on the Canadian border.

Southeast Idaho NWR Complex

The Southeast Idaho NWR Complex office in Pocatello administers Bear Lake NWR, Camas NWR, Gray's Lake NWR, Minidoka NWR, and the Oxford Slough Waterfowl Production Area. For more information, call or write:

U.S. Fish and Wildlife Service
1246 Yellowstone Avenue, A-4
Pocatello, ID 83201-4372
1-208-237-6616

Minidoka National Wildlife Refuge

Minidoka National Wildlife Refuge
Rt 4, Box 290
Rupert, ID 83350
1-208-436-3589

Directions: From Rupert, which is 75 miles west of Pocatello on Interstate 84, drive 6 miles northeast on State Highway 24 via Acequia, then 6 miles east on County Road 400 North.

Waterfowl: Up to 100,000 ducks and geese are present during spring and fall migrations. Hunters should be aware that tundra swans frequent shallow bays and shores of the lake, and are not a legal hunting species in Idaho.

Upland birds: Mourning doves, some sharp-tailed grouse and pheasant.

Hunting: Parts of refuge annually closed to hunting to provide sanctuary for waterfowl. Some roads also closed during hunting season. Obtain map from headquarters before going into marsh.

Habitat: 20,721 acres, including 11,000 surface acres of Lake Walcott on the Snake River. Surrounding uplands are typical high desert sagebrush and grassland.

Oxford Slough Waterfowl Production Area

For information, contact Southeast Idaho NWR Complex office in Pocatello.

Directions: Located 10 miles northwest of Preston, which is 70 miles southwest of Pocatello on U.S. Highway 91. From Pocatello go south on Interstate 15 to Virginia, then south on U.S. 91; 3 miles south of Swanlake, turn west onto road to Oxford and continue 1 mile to Oxford Slough.

Waterfowl: Key production area for redhead ducks; look for other resident ducks and migrants.

Upland birds: Limited upland bird hunting.

Hunting: Parts of refuge may be closed to hunting to provide sanctuary for waterfowl. Some roads may be closed during hunting season. Obtain map from headquarters in Pocatello or at gate before going into marsh.

Habitat: 1,890 acres of marshes, meadows and uplands.

Gray's Lake National Wildlife Refuge

Gray's Lake National Wildlife Refuge
HC 70, Box 4090/74 Gray's Lake Road
Wayan, ID 83285
1-208-574-2755

Directions: Drive south from Pocatello on Interstate 15 and take U.S. Highway 30 to Soda Springs (about 60 miles). From Soda Springs, go north on State Highway 34 about 35 miles, turn at refuge sign 2 miles west of Wayan. (Alternate Route: From Idaho Falls drive 65 miles east on U.S. Highway 26 to Alpine, Wyo., turn south on U.S. 89 and drive 10 miles to Freedom. From Freedom, drive 20 miles west to Wayan and turn north to refuge.)

Waterfowl: Nesting area for Canada geese and variety of diving and dabbling ducks; look for migrants in fall.

Cranes: Gray's Lake is nesting area for largest concentration of greater sandhill cranes in West and primary migration staging area. Also site of attempt to establish second wild flock of endangered whooping cranes. Idaho initiated its federal option in 1995 for a sandhill crane hunting season in designated areas. Check current regulations; apply for hunting permit if required. Hunting will be on nearby private land; landowner permission necessary if no permit required. Know how to identify whooping cranes to avoid mistakes.

Upland birds: Limited upland bird hunting; forest grouse in nearby Caribou National Forest.

Hunting: Parts of refuge annually closed to hunting to provide sanctuary for waterfowl and cranes. Few roads open during hunting season. Obtain map from headquarters before going into marsh.

Habitat: 18,330 acres of high mountain marsh in basin below Caribou Mountains; water levels often depleted by irrigation diversions.

Bear Lake National Wildlife Refuge

Bear Lake National Wildlife Refuge
Box 9, 370 Webster Street
Montpelier, ID 83254
1-208-847-1757

Directions: Drive south from Pocatello on I-15 to turn off on U.S. 30. From Soda Springs, drive 30 miles south on U.S. 30 to Montpelier. Refuge located 7 miles southwest of Montpelier. From town, drive 3 miles southwest on U.S. 89, turn east onto Bear Lake County Airport Road and drive 5 miles to north entrance of refuge.

Waterfowl: Key nesting area for Canada geese and redhead ducks; also nesting and staging area for other waterfowl and sandhill cranes.

Upland birds: Limited upland bird hunting.

Hunting: Parts of refuge closed to hunting to provide sanctuary for waterfowl. Some roads closed during hunting season. Obtain map from headquarters or at gate before going into marsh.

Habitat: 17,600 acres of marsh, open water, and grasslands at elevation of 5,900 feet in Bear Lake/Bear River valley. Marsh often severely depleted of water due to irrigation diversions in late summer.

Camas National Wildlife Refuge

Camas National Wildlife Refuge
2150 East 2350 North
Hamer, ID 83425
1-208-662-5423

Directions: Located 35 miles north of Idaho Falls. Drive north on Interstate 15 and turn east at Hamer; go north on frontage road 3 miles and turn west over I-15 overpass at sign, continue west 1.5 miles to refuge.

Waterfowl: Nesting area for Canada geese and diving ducks and key staging area for migrating waterfowl. Look for spill over from nearby Idaho Fish and Game wildlife management areas: Market Lake WMA, north of Roberts, and Mud Lake WMA, north of Terreton and Mud Lake.

Upland birds: Limited upland bird hunting; a few sage grouse, sharp-tailed grouse, mourning doves. Attempts to maintain pheasant population discontinued. (Idaho Fish and Game releases pen-raised pheasants at nearby Mud Lake and Market Lake wildlife management areas.)

Hunting: Parts of refuge closed to hunting to provide sanctuary for waterfowl. Many roads closed during hunting season. Obtain map from headquarters before going into marsh.

Habitat: 10,578 acres of marshes, ponds, meadows and sagebrush uplands.

Curlew National Grasslands

For more information, contact the following U.S. national forest offices:
Caribou National Forest
Federal Building, Suite 294
250 South Fourth Avenue
Pocatello, Idaho 83201
1-208-236-7500

Also:

Malad Ranger District
75 South 140 East, P.O. Box 142
Malad, Idaho 83252
1-208-766-4743

Directions: Four miles south of Malad City on Interstate 15 turn west on State Highway 38 and drive 20 miles west to tiny community of Hollbrook. Follow sign directions to separate units of Curlew National Grasslands north and south of Hollbrook along State Highway 37. Alternate route is to take Interstate 86 west from Pocatello or American Falls to Rockland exit and turn south on State Highway 37. Hollbrook is 32 miles south of I-86.

Upland birds: Sage grouse, sharp-tailed grouse, gray partridge, ring-necked pheasant, mourning dove.

Waterfowl: Stone Reservoir on Deep Creek attracts variety of dabbling and diving ducks as well as Canada and snow geese.

Hunting: Grasslands and Stone Reservoir are open to hunting. Respect signs for closed roads and areas not open to off-road driving. Check with Malad Ranger District for other restrictions.

Habitat: Totals 47,700 acres in three units of high plains short-grass prairie and rocky rolling hills, interspersed with brushy windbreaks and shelterbelts, sagebrush thickets, and brushy creek draws and coulees. Stone Reservoir on Deep Creek may be depleted in fall by summer irrigation drawdowns.

Curlew is the only national grasslands in Idaho that represents the Great Basin Ecosystem. Like other national refuges, much of its acreage was purchased in the drought years of the 1930s from failed homesteaders who could not make a living on the West's arid high plains.

Deer Flat National Wildlife Refuge

Deer Flat National Wildlife Refuge
13751 Upper Embankment Road
Nampa, ID 83686
1-208-467-9278 / 1-208-888-5582

Directions: Located 5 miles southwest of Nampa, which is 12 miles west of Boise on Interstate 84. From Nampa, turn off 12th Street and drive west on Lake Lowell Road to Upper Embankment Road; refuge headquarters are 1 mile west of upper embankment.

Waterfowl: Lake Lowell is a wintering area for 60,000 to more than 110,000 ducks, mostly mallards, and more than 10,000 Canada geese. A 110-mile string of 107 Snake River islands managed by refuge also provides ideal habitat for Canada geese, ducks and upland gamebirds.

Upland birds: California quail and some bobwhite quail, pheasants, mourning doves.

Hunting: Lake Lowell is closed to goose hunting. Lake and marsh areas open to duck and upland gamebird hunting are located along south shore and northeast corner. Snake River islands are open to goose and duck hunting as well as upland gamebird hunting. Obtain maps before hunting.

Habitat: The Lake Lowell sector—10,587 acres—includes a Bureau of Reclamation reservoir. Annual irrigation drawdown exposes mud flats where extensive stands of smartweed attract large numbers of birds. Sagebrush flats and riparian woodlands also present.

Snake River Islands: This sector of the refuge complex includes 107 islands on the Snake River, extending for 113 miles from Ada-Canyon county line to Brownlee Reservoir. Island cover is varied, with grass, brush, and trees providing wildlife habitat.

In addition to waterfowl hunting, islands provide opportunities for upland gamebirds—pheasant, quail and forest grouse. Hunters without boats can hunt either bank of Snake River at numerous Idaho Fish and Game public access sites. For location information, obtain a copy of IDFG's Idaho's Sportsman's Access Guide.

Kootenai National Wildlife Refuge

Kootenai National Wildlife Refuge
HCR 60, Box 283
Bonners Ferry, ID 83805
1-208-267-3888

Directions: Located west of Bonners Ferry, 18 miles south of Canadian border in the Kootenai River Valley. Bonners Ferry is 35 miles north of Sandpoint on U.S. Highway 95. From Bonners Ferry go west on dike road along south bank of Kootenai River for 5 miles to the refuge; refuge headquarters another 1.5 miles. Watch for logging trucks.

Waterfowl: Canada geese may number 2,500 in fall; also key nesting and migration staging area for numerous species of ducks. Mallards are the main nesting species; migrants mostly mallards, wigeon, and pintails. Tundra swans also present but not a legal hunting species in Idaho.

Upland birds: Wild turkey, mourning doves, forest grouse.

Hunting: Parts of refuge closed to hunting to provide sanctuary for waterfowl. Some roads may be closed during hunting season. Obtain map from headquarters or at gate before going into marsh.

Habitat: 2,775 acres of ponds, grasslands, cultivated croplands, shrubs and timbered western edge on foothills of Selkirk Mountains.

Idaho Indian Reservations

Fort Hall Indian Reservation

The Shoshone-Bannock Tribes of the Fort Hall Indian Reservation issue permits to hunt and fish on their lands, south of the Snake River, west of Blackfoot, and north of Pocatello. Hunting permits issued by the Shoshone-Bannock Tribes include waterfowl and ring-necked pheasant. The tribes also require a refundable deposit against possible damages.

The Michaud Flats area of the Fort Hall Indian Reservation, south of American Falls Reservoir, is considered one of the premier geese hunting sites in eastern Idaho.

The Fort Hall Bottoms on the south bank of the Snake River above the mouth of the reservoir also attract numerous ducks and geese. The same area ranks among the best spots in eastern Idaho for ring-necked pheasant hunting.

For the record, the Fort Hall Bottoms hold some of the best spring creek fisheries for Yellowstone cutthroat, brown, and rainbow trout in the West.

Tribal hunting and fishing permits include information on where nonresidents are permitted on the reservation. Study it carefully to avoid trespass.

Fees and regulations change annually. For more information, call the Fort Hall Hunting and Fishing Department at **1-208-238-3808**.

For general Fort Hall Indian Reservation information, call **1-208-238-3700**.

Note: Idaho Department of Fish and Game's Region 1 in its waterfowl hunting regulations surrounds the Fort Hall Indian Reservation. Opening and closing dates correspond with dates set by the tribes to avoid confusion for hunters on lands and waters adjacent to the reservation.

All state and federal lands in Waterfowl Region 1 outside the reservation in Bannock and Bingham counties and the western half of Power County are open to hunting with a state hunting license and state and federal waterfowl stamps. Hunters should be familiar with Fort Hall's boundaries to avoid trespass. Landowner permission also is required to hunt on private farmlands in the area.

Other Tribes in Idaho

The Shoshone-Bannock Tribes are one of five Indian tribes in Idaho.

The Nez Perce Tribe issues a permit to fish for sea-running steelhead trout in the Clearwater River, which is the northern border of the Nez Perce Indian Reservation, east of Lewiston. Anglers may fish for steelhead in the Clearwater with either a tribal permit, which is available at local fishing tackle shops, or an IDFG permit. The Nez Perce Tribe has yet to exercise its right to issue hunting permits.

Idaho Indian Reservations

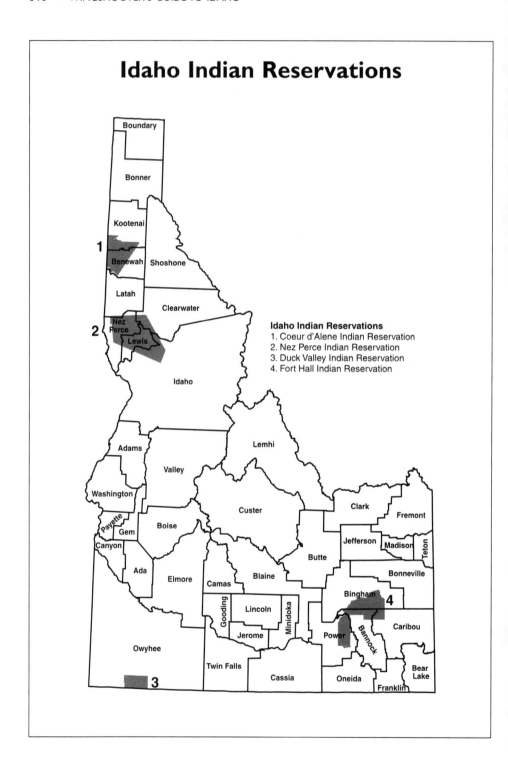

Idaho Indian Reservations
1. Coeur d'Alene Indian Reservation
2. Nez Perce Indian Reservation
3. Duck Valley Indian Reservation
4. Fort Hall Indian Reservation

The Coeur d'Alene Tribe of northern Idaho does not permit hunting or fishing on its lands.

The Kootenai Tribe of northern Idaho does not permit hunting or fishing on its lands.

The Northwest Band of the Shoshoni Nation permits fishing on a few ponds, but no hunting on the Duck Creek Indian Reservation, which straddles the Idaho-Nevada border south of Boise.

Idaho National Forests

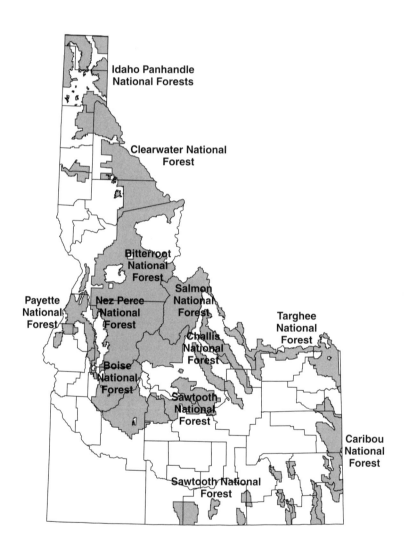

Idaho Panhandle
National Forests

Clearwater National
Forest

Bitterroot
National
Forest

Salmon
National
Forest

Payette
National
Forest

Nez Perce
National
Forest

Targhee
National
Forest

Challis
National
Forest

Boise
National
Forest

Sawtooth
National
Forest

Caribou
National
Forest

Sawtooth National
Forest

Federal Public Land in Idaho

Approximately 30 million acres of Idaho are administered as national forests and federal range lands open to the public for hunting, fishing and other recreational pursuits.

The U.S. Forest Service administers more than 17.2 million acres of mountainous forest lands. They include five wilderness areas and a national recreation area. The forest service also manages a national grasslands. Idaho's 3.4 million acres of wilderness and 9 million acres of roadless areas make up the largest combined tract of roadless forests in the Lower 48 States.

The U.S. Bureau of Land Management administers more than 12 million acres of public range lands in the high desert plains of eastern, southcentral and southwest Idaho. It also administers small pockets of land in north Idaho.

Two additional large expanses of federal lands in eastern Idaho are closed to hunting; Craters of the Moon National Monument, south of Arco, is a major tourism attraction and worth a side trip. However, the Idaho National Engineering and Environmental Laboratory, west of Idaho Falls, is a U.S. Department of Energy research facility entirely closed to public access, except during guided tours.

U.S. Forest Service and National Forests

There are 10 national forests in Idaho, including the Panhandle National Forest that is composed of the Coeur d'Alene, Kaniksu and St. Joe national forests. All are open to hunting under the rules and regulations of the Idaho Department of Fish and Game.

Vehicles are not permitted in wilderness areas, although landing strips are maintained for fly-ins by outfitters and owners of private land in-holdings. Also, many national forest roads are closed in fall to reduce hunting pressure on big game animals. Study travel maps for individual forests before hunting.

Travel maps and forest information, including wilderness areas, are available from each forest's supervisor office and their respective district ranger offices.

Panhandle National Forest

More than 2.5 million acres north and south of Sandpoint, and east and south of Coeur d'Alene. Includes part of the Mallard-Larkin Pioneer Area. District ranger offices are located at Wallace, Avery, Fernan, St. Maries, Sandpoint, Bonners Ferry, and Priest Lake.

Supervisor
Idaho Panhandle National Forest
1201 Ironwood Drive
Coeur d'Alene, ID 83814
208-765-7223

Clearwater National Forest

Nearly 1 million acres north and east of Orofino. Includes part of the Selway-Bitterroot Wilderness and the Mallard-Larkin Pioneer Area. District ranger offices are located at Orofino, Kamiah, Kooskia and Potlatch, Idaho. An office is also located in Lolo, Montana.

> Supervisor
> Clearwater National Forest
> 12730 Highway 12
> Orofino, ID 83544
> 208-476-4541

Nez Perce National Forest

More than 2.2. million acres east and south of Grangeville. Includes portions of five wilderness areas: Selway-Bitterroot, Frank Church-River of No Return, Gospel Hump, and Hells Canyon. District ranger offices are located at Grangeville, Elk City, Red River, White Bird and Kooskia.

> Supervisor
> Nez Perce National Forest
> East U.S. Highway 13
> Route 2, P.O. Box 475
> Grangeville, ID 83530
> 208-983-1950

Payette National Forest

More than 2.5 million acres north and east of McCall and northwest and southeast of Council. Includes portions of Frank Church-River of No Return and Hells Canyon wilderness areas. District ranger offices are located at McCall, Council, Weiser and New Meadows.

> Supervisor
> Payette National Forest
> 106 West Park Street
> P.O. Box 1026
> McCall, ID 83638
> 208-634-8151

Boise National Forest

More than 2.6 million acres north and east of Boise and east of Cascade. Includes portions of Frank Church-River of No Return Wilderness. District ranger offices are located at Boise, Emmett, Cascade, Lowman, Idaho City and Mountain Home.

> Supervisor
> Boise National Forest
> 1750 Front Street
> Boise, ID 83702
> 208-364-4100

Sawtooth National Forest

More than 2.1 million acres; majority of the forest is north of Ketchum-Sun Valley, scattered portions are located southeast of Twin Falls. Includes the Sawtooth National Recreation Area and Sawtooth Wilderness. District offices are located at Fairfield, Ketchum, Stanley, and Burley.

> Supervisor
> Sawtooth National Forest
> 2647 Kimberly Road East
> Twin Falls, ID 83301
> 208-737-3200
>
> also:
>
> Supervisor
> Sawtooth National Recreation Area
> Star Route
> Ketchum, ID 83340
> 1-208-726-7672

Challis National Forest

More than 2.5 million acres west and south of Challis; under joint supervision of Salmon National Forest. Includes one-third of Frank Church-River of No Return Wilderness. District ranger offices located at Challis, Clayton, and Mackay.

> Supervisor
> Challis National Forest
> U.S. Highway 93 North
> H/C 63 Box 1671
> Challis, ID 83226
> 208-879-2285
>
> also:
>
> Supervisor
> Salmon National Forest
> U.S. Highway 93 North
> P.O. Box 729
> Salmon, ID 83467
> 208-756-2215

Salmon National Forest
More than 1.8 million acres east and southeast of Salmon; also administers Challis National Forest. Includes portion of Frank Church-River of No Return Wilderness. District ranger offices located at Salmon, North Fork, Cobalt, and Leadore.

Supervisor
Salmon National Forest
U.S. Highway 93 North
P.O. Box 729
Salmon, ID 83467
208-756-2215

Targhee National Forest
More than 1.8 million acres north, east and south of St. Anthony; it also administers northern portion of Caribou National Forest. Large parts of Targhee in Wyoming include the Jedidiah Smith Wilderness and Winegar Hole Wilderness. District ranger offices located at Ashton, Island Park, Driggs, Dubois, and Idaho Falls.

Supervisor
Targhee National Forest
420 North Bridge Street
P.O. Box 208
St. Anthony, ID 83445
208-624-3151

Caribou National Forest
About 1 million acres east, south and southeast of Pocatello; also administers Curlew National Grasslands. District ranger offices located at Pocatello, Soda Springs, Malad, and Montpelier.

Supervisor
Caribou National Forest
Federal Building, Suite 294
250 South Fourth Avenue
Pocatello, ID 83201
208-236-7500

U.S. Bureau of Land Management Public Rangelands

There are approximately 12 million acres of public rangelands administered by the Bureau of Land Management and they include many key waterways that lace southern Idaho's high plains deserts, sagebrush plateaus and lava flows. These riparian zones are critical gamebird and wildlife habitat in the semi-arid region. Also of importance to upland gamebird and big game hunters are Idaho BLM lands in dry mountain foothills adjacent to the state's 10 forests.

Idaho's BLM headquarters are located in Boise. District administrative offices are located at Boise, Idaho Falls, Burley, Shoshone, Salmon and Coeur d' Alene. The BLM maintains a system of remote public campgrounds. Recreation and travel maps are available from Idaho BLM headquarters and each of the district offices:

Idaho BLM State Office
1387 South Vinnell Way
Boise, ID 83709-1657
208-373-4000

Boise BLM District

Areas of interest include the Boise Front mountain foothills and remote Owyhee desert and mountains, and lower Snake River, Owyhee River and Jarbridge River drainages. District also administers the Snake River Birds of Prey National Conservation Area and the Owyhee Scenic Byway:

Boise BLM District Office
3948 Development Avenue
Boise, ID 83705-5389
208-384-3300

Burley BLM District

Areas of interest include middle Snake River, and the Bruneau River, Bruneau sand dunes, Salmon Falls Creek, Raft River and Lower Goose Creek drainages:

Burley BLM District Office
200 S. Oakley Highway
Route 3, Box 1
Burley, ID 83318-9501
208-678-5514

Idaho BLM Index Maps

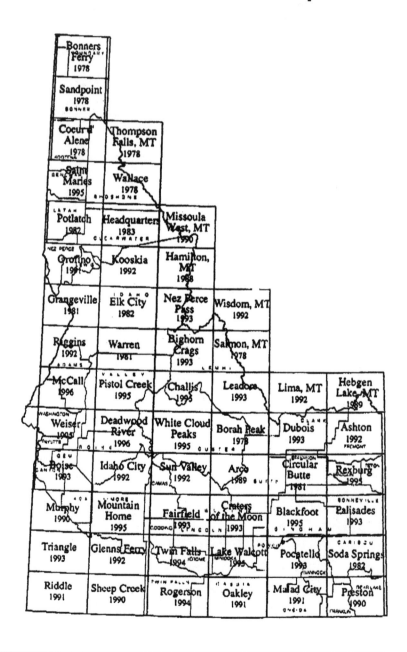

Shoshone BLM District

Areas of interest include the Great Rift Desert, Middle Snake River, and the Little Wood and Big Wood river drainages:

Shoshone BLM District Office
400 West F Street
P.O. Box 2-B
Shoshone, ID 83352-1522
208-886-2206

Idaho Falls BLM District

Areas of interest include the Big Butte Desert, St. Anthony Sand Dunes, Centennial and Bitterroot mountain foothills, and Big Lost River, Little Lost River, Birch Creek, Camas Creek, Blackfoot River and Bear Lake drainages. District also cooperatively manages South Fork of Snake River and the St. Anthony Sand Dunes - Sand Creek wildlife wintering area:

Idaho Falls BLM District Office
1405 Hollipark
Idaho Falls, ID 83401-2196
208-524-7500

also:

Idaho Falls Visitor Center
(USFS, BLM, Idaho Falls Chamber of Commerce)
208-523-3278

Salmon BLM District

Areas of interest are upper Salmon River and Bitterroot mountain foothills, and East Fork of Salmon, Lemhi River and Pahsimeroi River drainages. District also administers the Lewis and Clark Scenic Byway.

Salmon BLM District
Highway 93 South
P.O. Box 430
Salmon, ID 83467-0430
208-756-5400

Coeur d' Alene BLM District

District has scattered pockets of federal land in north-central Idaho. It cooperatively manages lower Salmon River:

Coeur d' Alene BLM District Office
1808 North Third Street
Coeur d'Alene, ID 83814-3407
208-769-5000

APPENDIX I
Guided Hunts

Learn All You Can About Your Outfitter First

by Idaho Outfitters and Guides Association

Idaho's outfitters are friendly, helpful, knowledgeable people. They also are as varied as the state's landscapes. One may be a master storyteller, another a person of action and few words. One may specialize in high-adventure, physically challenging trips. Another may concentrate on relaxing excursions for all ages. One may provide a luxury, everything-included trip. Another may supply you with equipment and instructions to do your own trip. So take the time to browse the list provided and to talk to individual outfitters on the phone. Find the one who best matches your interests and needs.

Early Planning Questions

Before you book a trip, take a few minutes with yourself, family, friends or group to talk over what each member wants from the trip. Ask yourselves:

- What are your priorities for this trip? Do you want to relax, get away from it all, spend time with your family, have an adventure, take risks, test your limits?
- How long do you want to be away? A day, a weekend, a week, two weeks, or longer?
- When do you want to go? How flexible are the dates and times?
- Where do you want to go? What kind of terrain/scenery are you looking for? Mountains, meadows, lakes, canyonlands?
- How much can you spend? Be sure to include travel, meals, and the trip itself.
- Where do you want to stay? Tent camp, wilderness lodge, remote log cabin, motel at the edge of town, deluxe guest ranch?
- How many people? Do you want to travel only with your private group? Or would you enjoy meeting others?

For Families/Mixed Groups

Idaho outfitters can recommend trips and activities suited to many different ages and abilities. Some trips are specially designed for families or youth groups with or without experience in the outdoors. Others are designed for older, skilled groups looking for challenge and adventure.

Food

Idaho outfitters take pride in their cuisine. Ask about their cooking styles and specialties. Let your outfitter know in advance if you have any special dietary requirements.

Special Needs

Idaho outfitters often can meet the special needs of guests. Ask about accessibility and special accommodations ahead of time. Inquire about adaptive trips. If you have a medical condition, be sure to notify the outfitter when inquiring about the trip.

What's Included (What's Not)

Make sure you understand what the price includes and what it doesn't. How much gear will the outfitter provide? How much will you need to bring? What meals are included? Does the outfitter provide transportation from the airport or is that additional? Be specific about which supplies and services you want to have included.

Reservations/Cancellations

Find out how much lead time you need to reserve a trip. Some Idaho trips and guest ranches are in such demand that it is best to reserve a year in advance. Others may require a three- to nine-month lead time. Very short trips, such as an afternoon rafting trip or family horseback outing, can wait until the day or week before. Remember to ask about deposits and cancellation policies. Many outfitters recommend trip cancellation insurance in case of an emergency.

Risks/Releases

Although Idaho outfitters emphasize safety first, risks can never be totally eliminated. You may be asked to sign an acknowledgment of risk or to agree to accept the inherent risk of an activity.

Stay in Touch

Stay in touch with your outfitter. He or she will provide you with complete trip information. It may include travel arrangements, packing lists, reading lists, pre-trip fitness suggestions, and where to stay before and after your trip. If you have questions, call your outfitter and ask. With an Idaho Outfitters and Guides Association member, you can expect ready answers — and a great trip!!

Editor's Note: Ask your chosen outfitter or guest ranch for references and call them before signing a contract.

Outfitters and Guest Ranches in Idaho

The majority of outfitters and guest ranches who list forest grouse (FG) as part of their services are big game outfitters. Many western and central Idaho outfitters who list chukar (CH) provide float boat or jetboat services. Other gamebirds listed include Hungarian partridge (HP), blue grouse (BG), and upland gamebirds (UG).

A partial list of in-state outfitting services available include:

Aggipah River Trips, 208-756-4167, Salmon, ID; Bill Brent; CH.

Anderson Outfitting, 208-237-6544, Pocatello, ID; Robert Anderson; FG.

Barker River Trips, 208-743-7459 or 1-800-353-7459, Lewiston, ID; John Barker; CH, FG.

Beamer's Hells Canyon Tours and Excursions, 509-758-4800 or 1-800-522-6966, Lewiston, ID; James and Jill Koch; CH.

Bighorn Outfitters, 208-756-3992, Carmen, ID; George Butcher; CH, FG.

Boulder Creek Outfitters, 208-486-6232, Peck, ID; Tim Craig; FG.

Castle Creek Outfitters and Guest Ranch, 208-756-2548, Salmon, ID; Shane McAfee; FG.

Canyon Cats, 208-934-8326 or 628-3772, Gooding, ID; George Hauptman; CH.

Clearwater Outfitters, 208-476-5971, Orofino, ID; Thomas Rucker; FG.

Discovery River Expeditions, 208-628-3319, Riggins, ID;Lester Lowe; CH.

Eakin Ridge Outfitters, 208-264-5274, Salmon, ID; Lamont Anderson; CH, FG.

Epley's Whitewater Adventures, 208-634-5173 or 1-800-233-1813, McCall, ID; Ted Epley; CH.

Exodus, 208-628-3484; 1-800-992-3484, Riggins, ID; Richard Bradbury; CH.

Far & Away Adventures/Middle Fork River Co., 208-726-8888 or 1-800-232-8588, Sun Valley, ID; Steve Lentz; CH.

Flying B Ranch, 208-935-0755, Kamiah, ID; Robert Burlingame; CH, FG.

Gospel Mountain Outfitters, 208-628-3553, Lucile, ID; Jim Dande; CH, FG, HP.

Happy Hollow Vacations, 208-756-3954, Salmon, ID; Martin Capps; FG.

Hells Canyon Fishing Charters, 208-983-2803 or 1-800-626-3714, Council, ID; Richard Cook; CH.

Hells Canyon Lodge, 208-743-0030 or 1-800-727-6190, Lewiston, ID; Jason Schultz; CH.

Hidden Creek Ranch, 208-689-3209 or 1-800-446-3833, Harrison, ID; John Muir, Iris Behr; FG.

High Adventure River Tours, 208-733-0123, Twin Falls, ID; Randy McBride; CH.

High Roller Excursions, 208-743-5243, Lewiston, ID; Lee Eddins; CH.

High Desert Enterprises, 208-852-1416, Preston, ID; Chris Maisel; CH, FG, HP.

High Desert Ranch, 208-549-2200, Weiser, ID; Lynn Whitaker; UG; FG.

Horse Creek Outfitters, 208-879-5400, Challis, ID; Jim Thomas; FG.

Hughes River Expeditions, 208-257-3477, Cambridge, ID; Jerry Hughes; CH, FG, HP.

Idaho Guide Service, 208-734-4998, Twin Falls, ID; Olin Garner; CH.

Indian Creek Guest Ranch, 208-394-2126, North Fork, ID; Jack Briggs; FG.

Intermountain Excursions, 208-746-0249, Lewiston, ID; Darrell Bentz; CH.

Kingfisher Expeditions, 208-756-4688, Salmon, ID; Steve Settles; CH.

Lochsa River Outfitters, 208-926-4149, Kooskia, ID; Jacey Nygaard; FG.

Lost River Outfitters, 208-726-1706, Ketchum, ID; Scott Schnebly; CH, UG.

Mackay Bar Corp., 208-344-9904 Boise, ID; Vince Ivanoff; CH, FG.

Mackay Wilderness River Trips, 208-344-1881, Boise, ID; Brent Estep; CH, FG.

Middle Fork Lodge, 208-362-9621, Boise, ID; Marry Ossenkop, Scott Farr; CH, FG.

Middle Fork Rapid Transit, 208-734-7890 or 1-800-342-9728, Twin Falls, ID; Greg Edson; CH.

Middle Fork River Expeditions, 206-324-0364 Stanley, ID; Patrick Ridle; CH.

Middle Fork Wilderness Outfitters, 208-726-5999, Ketchum, ID; Gary Shelton, CH.

Mile High Outfitters, 208-879-4403, Challis, ID; Travis Bullock; CH, FG.

Moose Creek Outfitters, 208-476-5227, Orofino, ID; Richard Norris; FG.

Moser's Idaho Adventure River Trips, 208-756-2986, Salmon, ID; Gary Moser; CH.

Moyie River Outfitters, 208-267-2108, Bonners Ferry, ID; Stanley Sweet; FG.

Mystic Saddle Ranch, 208-774-3591, Stanley, ID; Jeffrey Bitton; FG.

Northwest Voyageurs, 208-628-3021 or 1-800-727-9977, Lucile, ID; Jeff Peavy; CH.

Pioneer Mountain Outfitters, 208-734-3679, Twin Falls, ID; Tom Proctor; FG.

R & R Outdoors, 208-628-3033 or 1-800-574-1224, Pollock, ID; Robert Black; CH.

Rapid River Outfitters, 208-628-3862, Riggins, ID; Kerry Brennan; CH.

Rawhide Outfitters, 208-756-4276, Salmon, ID; John Cranney; CH.

Red River Corrals, 208-842-2228, Elk City, ID; Archie George; FG.

Red Woods Outfitters, 208-628-3673, Pollock, ID; Noland Woods; CH.

Renshaw Outfitting, 208-926-4520 or 1-800-452-2567, Kamiah, ID; Jim Renshaw; FG.

Ridge Runner Outfitters, 208-935-0757, Kamiah, ID; Ray Chirstopherson; CH.

River Adventures Limited, 208-628-3952, Riggins, ID; Sam Whitten; CH.

River Odysseys West, 208-765-0841, Coeur dÕAlene, ID; Peter Grubb; CH.

Rocky Mountain River Tours, 208-345-2400, Boise, ID; David Mills; CH.

Rudeen Ranch, 208-226-5591, American Falls, ID; Kent Rudeen; FG.

Salmon River Challenge, 208-628-3264, Riggins, ID; Patrick Marek; CH, FG.

Salmon River Experience, 208-882-2385 or 1-800-892-9223, Moscow, ID; Charles Boyd; CH.

Salmon River Lodge, 208-756-3817 or 1-800-635-4717, Salmon, ID; Jim Dartt; CH, FG.

Salmon River Tours Co., 208-865-2375, North Fork, ID; Michael Mclain; CH, FG.

Sevy Guide Service, 208-774-2200, Stanley, ID; Robert Sevy; CH, FG.

Shattuck Creek Ranch & Outfitters, 208-826-3405, Elk River, ID; Andre Molsee, FG.

Shepp Ranch, 208-343-7729, Boise, ID; Virginia Hopfenbeck; CH.

Silver Cloud Outfitters, 208-756-6215, Slamon, ID; Jerry Meyers; CH.

Silver Creek Outfitters, 208-726-5282 or 1-800-732-5687, Ketchum, ID; Terry Ring; UG.

Snake River Outfitters, 208-743-6276, Lewiston, ID; Norman Riddle; CH.

Snug Outfitters, 208-622-9302, Sun Valley, ID; Bill Mason; CH, UG.

St. Joe Hunting & Fishing Camp, 208-245-4002, St. Maries, ID; Willard Judge; FG.

Stanley Potts Outfitters, 208-394-2135, Shoup, ID; FG.

Stub Creek, 208-865-2474, North Fork, ID; Dale Stansberry; CH, FG.

Sun Valley River Co., 208-726-7404, Sun Valley, ID; Jon McGregor; CH.

The River Company, 208-726-8890 or 1-800-398-0346 or 1-800-765-1407, Sun Valley, ID; CH.

Triangle C Ranch, 208-774-2266, Stanley, ID; Ron Gillett; CH, FG.

Triple O Outfitters, 208-464-2349, Pierce, ID; Harlan Opdahl; FG.

Twin Peaks Ranch, 208-894-2990 or 1-800-659-4899 or 1-800-396-2628, Salmon, ID; Melvin Reingold; FG.

Wally York and Son, 208-842-2367, Elk City, ID; FG.

Wapiti River Guides, 208-628-3523 or 1-800-488-9872, Riggins, ID; Gary Lane; CH.

Warren River Expeditions, 208-756-6387 or 1-800-765-0421, Salmon, ID; David Warren; CH.

Whitewater Outfitters, 208-926-4231, Kamiah, ID; Lester "Zeke" West; CH, FG.

Wild Horse Creek Ranch, 208-588-2575, Mackay, ID; Bill Shields; FG.

Wood River Outfitters, 208-726-3030, Ketchum, IF; Gary Harper; BG.

Yellow Wolf Ranch, 208-983-9208, Whitebird, ID; Edd Wolsum; CH.

Waterfowl Outfitters

Four outfitters offer waterfowl (WF) guiding services are in eastern Idaho.

Henry's Fork Anglers, 208-624-3590 or 1-800-788-4479, St. Anthony, ID; Mike Lawson; WF, FG.

South Fork Expeditions, 208-521-1613, Swan Valley, ID; John Hill Jr.; WF.

Teton Valley Lodge, 208-354-2386, Driggs, ID; Randy Berry; WF, FG.

Three Rivers Ranch, 208-652-3750, Ashton, ID; Lonnie Allen; WF, FG.

For a complete directory of all persons and businesses licensed as outfitters and guides, or their representatives, contact the state licensing board:

State of Idaho Outfitters & Guides Licensing Board
1365 N. Orchard, Room 172
Boise, ID; 83706
Phone: 1-208-327-7380
FAX: 1-208-327-7167

For additional information, contact:

Idaho Outfitters and Guides Association
P.O. Box 95
Boise, ID 83701
Phone: 1-208-342-1438
Fax: 1-208-338-7830

APPENDIX 2
Shooting Preserves in Idaho

The number of private shooting preserves for upland gamebirds doubled from seven to 14 between 1990 and 1996. "In general, interest in this activity seems to be increasing," said Tom Hemker, IDFG's upland gamebird manager.

More than half of Idaho's shooting preserves are located in west-central and southwestern Idaho. However, Hemker noted that High Desert Ranch, a 4,800-acre preserve near Weiser, closed in 1996 and was offered for sale. For updates on shooting preserves, Hemker can be contacted at IDFG's Boise office.

Fees And Regulations

Fees for annual use of Idaho shooting preserves vary but usually include a membership fee of a few hundred dollars, plus an additional charge of $10 to $15 per bird. Daily nonmember shooting fees also are available.

By law, shooting preserves in Idaho must be open to anyone willing to pay the fees. Also, each shooter must have a valid Idaho hunting license or a $5 shooting preserve license.

Idaho's shooting preserve season runs from August 15 to April 15. Shooting hours are the same as for regular hunting seasons.

Released game farm birds must be toe-clipped or banded. Any wild bird taken incidentally out of season on a shooting preserve must be banded with a $3 IDFG band.

Licensed Shooting Preserves

The following businesses are considered shooting preserves and have been issued IDFG vendor licenses:

Region 2—Clearwater
Flying B Ranch—1,307 acres; pheasant, chukar and gray partridge, and quail; Bob Burlingame, Flying B Ranch, Kamiah, ID 83536; 208-935-0775.

Yellow Wolf Ranch—200 acres; pheasant; Ed Woslum, Yellow Wolf Ranch, Whitebird, ID 83554; 208-983-9208.

Region 3—Southwest
The Ranch (Big Willow Creek)—1,084 acres; pheasant, quail, chukar; Tom Pence, 5433 Big Willow Road, Payette, ID 83661; 208-278-5472.

Skyline Ranch—240 acres; pheasant, quail, chukar; George Hyer, RT 2 Box 14A, Homedale, ID 83628; 208-337-4443

Idaho Game Bird—180 acres; pheasant; James Davenport, RT 1 Box1212, Homedale, ID 83628; 208-337-4826

Lucky Brands Ranch—320 acres; pheasant, chukar; Rex Lanham, HC 33 Box 1450, Boise, ID 83706; 208-344-1971.

Region 4—Magic Valley

Tews Ranch—690 acres; pheasant, chukar, quail; Rusty Tews, 745 North 550 West, RT 1, Shoshone, ID 83352; 208-886-2100.

Cedar Canyon—333 acres; pheasant; Steve Torix, RT 2 Box 2356, Paul, ID 83347; 208-438-5203.

Sage Basin Preserve—640 acres; pheasant, quail, chukar, grouse; C. Jeff Bragg, 550 North 800 East, Jerome, ID 83338; 208-324-1282.

Sun Country Shooting—200 acres; pheasant, quail; Alan Johnson, 550 North 250 East, Shoshone, ID 83352; 208-886-2985.

Region 5—Southeast

Malad Valley Hunts—320 acres; pheasant, quail, chukar, grouse; Brett Rose, 330 Upper Saint John Road, Malad, ID 83252; 208-766-4208.

Caribou Bird Preserve—1,371 acres; pheasant. The reserve is located near Thatcher, ID; license holder is Kimball Evans, 850 Whipple Drive, Lehi, Utah; booking agent is Charles Willingham, 149 East Main Street, St. Anthony, ID 83445; 208-624-3717.

Region 6—Upper Snake

Fullmer Ranch—620 acres; pheasant, chukar; Albert Fullmer, RT 1 Box 44, Darlington, ID 83231; 208-588-3383.

APPENDIX 3
Hunter's Checklist

Clothing (One-day Hunt)

____ High-topped hunting boots (never hunt in tennis shoes)

____ Chaps or iron-cloth pants

____ Gaiters

____ Gloves

____ Balaclava or stocking cap

____ Rain gear

____ Wool sweater and wind breaker

____ Change of clothes

____ Extra socks

____ Canteen or water bottle

____ Camera and film

____ Notebook and pencil

____ Day pack / fanny pack

Hunting Gear

____ Hunting license, tags or stamps

____ Shotgun(s) and shells

____ Knife(s)

____ Binoculars

____ Waterfowl or turkey calls

____ Decoys

____ Camo face paint (turkey hunts)

____ Dog supplies: food, water, dishes, collar, lead, whistle, foot booties

____ Cooler and plastic bags for gamebirds

Survival kit

____ First aid kit

____ Signal mirror

____ Whistle

____ Matches (water proof) or lighter

____ Fire starter

____ Hexamine or Trioxane

____ Flagging tape

____ Water purification Tabs

____ Rope

____ Dental floss (world's strongest string)

____ Fish hooks

____ Snake kit

____ Space blanket

____ 5' Surgical tube (straw / solar still)

____ 5 × 5 plastic sheet

____ Pin flash light / extra batteries, candle(s)

Utensils

____ Mess kit

____ Spoon, fork, butter knife

____ Cup

____ Canteen

____ Sterno stove / small hiking stove

____ Sterno fuel / hiking stove fuel

____ Water filter

____ P38 GI can opener

Camping

____ Backpack

____ Light-weight tent

____ Sleeping bag

____ Sleeping pad

____ Flash light / extra batteries

____ Tarp (6 x 8) or space blanket

____ Hand ax or folded buck saw

____ Knife sharpener

____ Maps

____ Compass

____ Garbage bags

____ Entrenching tool

____ Toilet paper

Backroad vehicle checklist

____ Spare tire(s), heavy duty bumper jack, lug wrench, air compressor

____ Tire chains, ditch shovel, ax, buck saw

____ Tow rope, come-a-long, jumper cables

____ Spare fan belt, hoses

____ Vehicle repair tools

____ Gasoline can (filled)

____ Extra engine oil, transmission fluid

____ Five-gallon water can (filled)

____ County maps, Bureau of Land Management or U.S. Forest Service maps

____ Extra keys (one for hunting partner; second attached to vehicle under-carriage)

____ Check everything—battery, tires, air filters, fuel filter, hoses, radiator and coolant, thermostat, oil, transmission fluid etc.—before leaving home

APPENDIX 4
Map Sources

Idaho Department of Fish and Game
- For a map order form, call 1-800-635-7820
  or IDFG Headquarters at 208-334-3700
- 1:100,000 topographical maps by the Idaho Department of Transportation

Bureau of Land Management
- State Office: 208-373-4000 or see District Office listings starting on page 321
- BLM Index Maps

U.S. Geological Survey
- Box 25046, MS 504, Denver Federal Center, Denver, CO 80225
- U.S. Geological Survey quad maps showing relief of terrain

U.S. Forest Service
- See Forest Supervisor listings starting on page 317
- Travel plan maps of each forest, including all drainages, roads, and road closures

Idaho Department of Transportation
- P.O. Box 7129, Boise, ID 83707 / 208-334-8000
- Statewide road and river drainage system maps

Index

NOTES

NOTES

WILDERNESS ADVENTURES
GUIDEBOOK SERIES

If you would like to order additional copies of this book or our other Wilderness Adventures Press guidebooks, please fill out the order form below or call **1-800-925-3339** or **fax 406-763-4911.**

Mail to:
Wilderness Adventures Press, P.O. Box 627, Gallatin Gateway, MT 59730

Ship to:
Name _____

Address _____

City _____ State_____ Zip_____

Home Phone_____ Work Phone_____

Payment: ☐ Check ☐ Visa ☐ Mastercard ☐ Discover ☐ American Express

Card Number _____ Expiration Date_____

Qty	Title of Book and Author	Price	Total
	Wingshooter's Guide to Montana	$26.00	
	Wingshooter's Guide to South Dakota	$26.95	
	Wingshooter's Guide to North Dakota	$26.95	
	Wingshooter's Guide to Arizona	$26.95	
	Wingshooter's Guide to Idaho	$26.95	
	Wingshooter's Guide to Iowa (7/98)	$26.95	
	Wingshooter's Guide to Kansas (7/98)	$26.95	
	Flyfisher's Guide to Montana	$26.95	
	Flyfisher's Guide to Idaho	$26.95	
	Total Order + shipping & handling		

Shipping and handling: $4.00 for first book, $2.50 per additional book, up to $14.00 maximum